The Quran With Tafsir Ibn Kathir Part 4 of 30: Ale Imran 093 To An Nisaa 023

The Quran With Tafsir Ibn Kathir
Part 4 of 30:
Ale Imran 093 To An Nisaa 023

With
Arabic Script, Transliteration of Arabic, Meaning in English
and Ibn Kathir's Abridged Tafsir (Explanation)

Muhammad Saed Abdul-Rahman
BSc, DipHE

© Muhammad Saed Abdul-Rahman,2012
ISBN 978-1-86179-837-4

All Rights reserved

British Library Cataloguing in Publication Data. A Catalogue record for this book is available from the British Library

Designed, Typeset and produced by:
MSA Publication Limited, 4 Bello Close, Herne Hill,
London SE24 9BW
United Kingdom

Cover design: Houriyah Abdul-Rahman

TABLE OF CONTENTS

TABLE OF CONTENTS V

PRELUDE XI
   OPENING SERMAN XI
   OUR MISSION XII
   BIOGRAPHY OF HAFIZ IBN KATHIR (701 H - 774 H) XII
      Ibn Kathir's Teachers xii
      Ibn Kathir's Students xiii
      Ibn Kathir's Books xiii
      Ibn Kathir's Death xiv

PREFACE XV
   ABOUT THIS BOOK XV
   PERFORMING PROSTRATION WHILE READING THE QUR'AN XV

PART 4 FULL ARABIC TEXT 1

INTRODUCTION TO CHAPTER (SURAH) 3: AL-I-'IMRAN (THE FAMILY OF IMRAN) 12
   IBN KATHIR'S INTRODUCTION 12

CHAPTER (SURAH) 3: AL-I-'IMRAN (THE FAMILY OF 'IMRAN), VERSES 093-200 12
   Surah: 3 Ayah: 93, Ayah: 94 & Ayah: 95 12
      Tafsir Ibn Kathir 13
         The Questions that the Jews Asked Our Prophet 13
   Surah: 3 Ayah: 96 & Ayah: 97 15
      Tafsir Ibn Kathir 16
         The Ka`bah is the First House of Worship 16
         The Names of Makkah, Such As `Bakkah 16
         The Station of Ibrahim 16
         Al-Haram, the Sacred Area, is a Safe Area 17
         The Necessity of Performing Hajj 19
         Meaning of `Afford' in the Ayah 20
         The One who Denies the Necessity of Hajj Becomes a Disbeliever 21
   Surah: 3 Ayah: 98 & Ayah: 99 21
      Tafsir Ibn Kathir 21
         Chastising the People of the Book for Their Disbelief and Blocking the Path of Allah 21
   Surah: 3 Ayah: 100 & Ayah: 101 22
      Tafsir Ibn Kathir 22
         Warning Muslims Against Imitating People of the Scriptures 22
   Surah: 3 Ayah: 102 & Ayah: 103 24
      Tafsir Ibn Kathir 24
         Meaning of Taqwa of Allah 24
         The Necessity of Holding to the Path of Allah and the Community of the Believers 25

Surah: 3 Ayah: 104, Ayah: 105, Ayah: 106, Ayah: 107, Ayah: 108 & Ayah: 109 27
    Tafsir Ibn Kathir 28
        The Command to Establish the Invitation to Allah 28
        The Prohibition of Division 29
        The Benefits of Brotherly Ties and Unity and the Consequence of Division on the Day of the Gathering 30

Surah: 3 Ayah: 110, Ayah: 111 & Ayah: 112 31
    Tafsir Ibn Kathir 32
        Virtues of the Ummah of Muhammad (peace and blessings of Allah be upon him) - the Best Nation Ever 32
        Another Hadith that Establishes the Virtues of the Ummah of Muhammad in this Life and the Hereafter 34
        The Good News that Muslims will Dominate the People of the Book 36

Surah: 3 Ayah: 113, Ayah: 114, Ayah: 115, Ayah: 116 & Ayah: 117 37
    Tafsir Ibn Kathir 38
        Virtues of the People of the Scriptures Who Embrace Islam 38
        The Parable of What the Disbelievers Spend in This Life 39

Surah: 3 Ayah: 118, Ayah: 119 & Ayah: 120 40
    Tafsir Ibn Kathir 41
        The Prohibition of Taking Advisors From Among the Disbelievers 41

Surah: 3 Ayah: 121, Ayah: 122 & Ayah: 123 43
    Tafsir Ibn Kathir 44
        The Battle of Uhud 44
        The Reason Behind the Battle of Uhud 44
        Reminding the Believers of Their Victory at Badr 46

Surah: 3 Ayah: 124, Ayah: 125, Ayah: 126, Ayah: 127, Ayah: 128 & Ayah: 129 46
    Tafsir Ibn Kathir 48
        The Support of the Angels 48

Surah: 3 Ayah: 130, Ayah: 131, Ayah: 132, Ayah: 133, Ayah: 134, Ayah: 135 & Ayah: 136 52
    Tafsir Ibn Kathir 54
        Interest (Riba) is Prohibited 54
        The Encouragment to Do Good for which Paradise is the Result 54

Surah: 3 Ayah: 137, Ayah: 138, Ayah: 139, Ayah: 140, Ayah: 141, Ayah: 142 & Ayah: 143 59
    Tafsir Ibn Kathir 60
        The Wisdom Behind the Losses Muslims Suffered During Uhud 60

Surah: 3 Ayah: 144, Ayah: 145, Ayah: 146, Ayah: 147 & Ayah: 148 62
    Tafsir Ibn Kathir 63
        The Rumor that the Prophet was Killed at Uhud 63

Surah: 3 Ayah: 149, Ayah: 150, Ayah: 151, Ayah: 152 & Ayah: 153 67
    Tafsir Ibn Kathir 68
        The Prohibition of Obeying the Disbelievers; the Cause of Defeat at Uhud 68
        The Defeat that the Muslims Suffered During the Battle of Uhud 71
        The Ansar and Muhajirin Defended the Messenger 71

Table of Contents

Surah: 3 Ayah: 154 & Ayah: 155 73
   Tafsir Ibn Kathir 74
      Slumber Overcame the Believers; the Fear that the Hypocrites Suffered 74
      Some of the Believers Give Flight on the Day of Uhud 75
Surah: 3 Ayah: 156, Ayah: 157 & Ayah: 158 76
   Tafsir Ibn Kathir 77
      Prohibiting the Ideas of the Disbeleivers about Death and Predestination 77
Surah: 3 Ayah: 159, Ayah: 160, Ayah: 161, Ayah: 162, Ayah: 163 & Ayah: 164 77
   Tafsir Ibn Kathir 79
      Among the Qualities of Our Prophet Muhammad are Mercy and Kindness 79
      The Order for Consultation and to Abide by it 80
      Trust in Allah After Taking the Dec 81
      Treachery with the Spoils of War was not a Trait of the Prophet 81
      The Honest and Dishonest are Not Similar 84
      The Magnificent Blessing in the Advent of Our Prophet Muhammad 85
Surah: 3 Ayah: 165, Ayah: 166, Ayah: 167 & Ayah: 168 86
   Tafsir Ibn Kathir 87
      The Reason and Wisdom Behind the Defeat at Uhud 87
Surah: 3 Ayah: 169, Ayah: 170, Ayah: 171, Ayah: 172, Ayah: 173, Ayah: 174 & Ayah: 175 89
   Tafsir Ibn Kathir 90
      Virtues of the Martyrs 90
      The Battle of Hamra' Al-Asad 94
Surah: 3 Ayah: 176, Ayah: 177, Ayah: 178, Ayah: 179 & Ayah: 180 96
   Tafsir Ibn Kathir 97
      Comforting the Messenger of Allah 97
      The Censure of Selfishness, and Warning Against it 99
Surah: 3 Ayah: 181, Ayah: 182, Ayah: 183 & Ayah: 184 101
   Tafsir Ibn Kathir 102
      Allah Warns the Idolators 102
Surah: 3 Ayah: 185 & Ayah: 186 103
   Tafsir Ibn Kathir 104
      Every Soul Shall Taste Death 104
      Who Shall Gain Ultimate Victory 104
      The Believer is Tested and Hears Grieving Statements from the Enemy 105
Surah: 3 Ayah: 187, Ayah: 188 & Ayah: 189 107
   Tafsir Ibn Kathir 107
      Chastising the People of the Scriptures for Breaking the Covenant and Hiding the Truth 107
      Chastising Those Who Love to be Praised for What They Have not Done 108
Surah: 3 Ayah: 190, Ayah: 191, Ayah: 192, Ayah: 193 & Ayah: 194 109
   Tafsir Ibn Kathir 110
      The Proofs of Tawhid for People of Understanding, their Characteristics, Speech, and Supplications 110
Surah: 3 Ayah: 195 113

Tafsir Ibn Kathir 114
   Allah Accepts the Supplication of Men of Understanding 114
Surah: 3 Ayah: 196, Ayah: 197 & Ayah: 198... 115
  Tafsir Ibn Kathir 116
   Warning Against Being Deceived by This Life; the Rewards of the Righteous Believers . 116
Surah: 3 Ayah: 199 & Ayah: 200... 117
  Tafsir Ibn Kathir 118
   The Condition of Some of the People of the Scriptures and their Rewards 118
   The Command for Patience and Ribat 120

INTRODUCTION TO CHAPTER (SURAH) 4: AN-NISAA (THE WOMEN) 123

IBN KATHIR'S INTRODUCTION 123
   Virtues of Surat An-Nisa, A Madinan Surah 123

CHAPTER (SURAH) 4: AN-NISAA (THE WOMEN), VERSES 001-023 124

Surah: 4 Ayah: 1 124
  Tafsir Ibn Kathir 125
   The Command to have Taqwa, a Reminder about Creation, and Being Kind to Relatives
   125
Surah: 4 Ayah: 2, Ayah: 3 & Ayah: 4.. 126
  Tafsir Ibn Kathir 127
   Protecting the Property of the Orphans 127
   The Prohibition of Marrying Female Orphans Without Giving a Dowry 127
   The Permission to Marry Four Women 128
   Marrying Only One Wife When One Fears He Might not Do Justice to His Wives 129
   Giving the Dowry is Obligatory 129
Surah: 4 Ayah: 5 & Ayah: 6... 130
  Tafsir Ibn Kathir 131
   Holding the Property of the Unwise in Escrow 131
   Spending on the Unwise with Fairness 131
   Giving Back the Property of the Orphans When They Reach Adulthood 131
   Poor Caretakers are Allowed to Wisely Spend from the Money of the Orphan Under Their
   Care, to Compensate for Their Work 132
Surah: 4 Ayah: 7, Ayah: 8, Ayah: 9 & Ayah: 10.. 133
  Tafsir Ibn Kathir 134
   The Necessity of Surrendering the Inheritance According to the Portions that Allah
   Ordained 134
   Observing Fairness in the Will 135
   A Stern Warning Against Those Who Use Up the Orphan's Wealth 136
Surah: 4 Ayah: 11 136
  Tafsir Ibn Kathir 137
   Learning the Various Shares of the Inheritance is Encouraged 137
   The Reason Behind Revealing Ayah 4:11 137
   Males Get Two Times the Share of Females for Inheritance 138
   The Share of the Females When They Are the Only Eligible Heirs 139

- Share of the Parents in the Inheritance 139
- First the Debts are Paid Off, then the Will, then the Fixed Inheritance 140

Surah: 4 Ayah: 12 .... *140*
- Tafsir Ibn Kathir 141
  - Share of the Spouses in the Inheritance 141
  - The Meaning of Kalalah 142
  - The Ruling Concerning Children of the Mother From Other Than the Deceased's Father 142

Surah: 4 Ayah: 13 & Ayah: 14 .... *143*
- Tafsir Ibn Kathir 143
  - Warning Against Transgressing the Limits for Inheritance 143

Surah: 4 Ayah: 15 & Ayah: 16 .... *144*
- Tafsir Ibn Kathir 145
  - The Adulteress is Confined in her House; A Command Later Abrogated 145

Surah: 4 Ayah: 17 & Ayah: 18 .... *147*
- Tafsir Ibn Kathir 147
  - Repentance is Accepted Until one Faces death 147

Surah: 4 Ayah: 19, Ayah: 20, Ayah: 21 & Ayah: 22 .... *149*
- Tafsir Ibn Kathir 150
  - Meaning of 'Inheriting Women Against Their Will 150
  - Women Should not Be Treated with Harshness 150
  - Live With Women Honorably 151
  - The Prohibition of Taking Back the Dowry 152
  - Marrying the Wife of the Father is Prohibited 153

Surah: 4 Ayah: 23 .... *154*
- Tafsir Ibn Kathir 154
  - Degrees of Women Never Eligible for One to Marry 154
  - 'Suckling' that Establishes Prohibition for Marriage 155
  - The Stepdaughter is Prohibited in Marriage Even if She Was Not Under the Guardianship of Her Stepfather 156
  - Meaning of 'gone in unto them 157
  - Prohibiting the Daughter-in-Law for Marriage 157
  - A Doubt and Rebuttal 157
  - The Prohibition of Taking Two Sisters as Rival Wives 158

PRELUDE

Opening Serman

Indeed, all praise is due to Allah. We praise Him and seek His help and forgiveness. We seek refuge with Allah from our soul's evil and our wrong doings. He whom Allah guides, no one can misguide; and he whom He misguides, no one can guide

I bear witness that there is no (true) god except Allah – alone without a partner, and I bear witness that Muhammad (peace and blessings of Allah be upon him) is His 'abd (servant) and messenger.

يَـٰٓأَيُّهَا ٱلَّذِينَ ءَامَنُوا۟ ٱتَّقُوا۟ ٱللَّهَ حَقَّ تُقَاتِهِۦ وَلَا تَمُوتُنَّ إِلَّا وَأَنتُم مُّسْلِمُونَ ۝

O you who believe! Fear Allâh (by doing all that He has ordered and by abstaining from all that He has forbidden) as He should be feared. (Obey Him, be thankful to Him, and remember Him always), and die not except in a state of Islâm (as Muslims (with complete submission to Allâh)).

يَـٰٓأَيُّهَا ٱلنَّاسُ ٱتَّقُوا۟ رَبَّكُمُ ٱلَّذِى خَلَقَكُم مِّن نَّفْسٍ وَٰحِدَةٍ وَخَلَقَ مِنْهَا زَوْجَهَا وَبَثَّ مِنْهُمَا رِجَالًا كَثِيرًا وَنِسَآءً ۚ وَٱتَّقُوا۟ ٱللَّهَ ٱلَّذِى تَسَآءَلُونَ بِهِۦ وَٱلْأَرْحَامَ ۚ إِنَّ ٱللَّهَ كَانَ عَلَيْكُمْ رَقِيبًا ۝

O mankind! Be dutiful to your Lord, Who created you from a single person (Adam), and from him (Adam) He created his wife (Hawwâ (Eve)) and from them both He created many men and women; and fear Allâh through Whom you demand (your mutual rights), and (do not cut the relations of) the wombs (kinship). Surely, Allâh is Ever an All-Watcher over you.

يُصْلِحْ لَكُمْ أَعْمَـٰلَكُمْ وَيَغْفِرْ لَكُمْ ذُنُوبَكُمْ ۗ وَمَن يُطِعِ ٱللَّهَ وَرَسُولَهُۥ فَقَدْ فَازَ فَوْزًا عَظِيمًا ۝

He will direct you to do righteous good deeds and will forgive you your sins. And whosoever obeys Allâh and His Messenger (peace be upon him), he has indeed achieved a great achievement (i.e. he will be saved from the Hell-fire and will be admitted to Paradise).

Indeed, the best speech is Allah's Book and the best guidance is Muhammad's () guidance. The worst affairs (of religion) are those innovated (by people), for every such innovation is an act of misguidance leading to the Fire

Our Mission

Our mission is to gather in one place, for the English-speaking public, all relevant information needed to make the Qur'an more understandable and easier to study. This book tries to do this by providing the following:

1. The Arabic Text for those who are able to read Arabic
2. Transliteration of the Arabic text for those who are unable to read the Arabic script. This will give them a sample of the sound of the Qur'an, which they could not otherwise comprehend from reading the English meaning.
3. The meaning of the qur'an (translated by Dr. Muhammad Taqi-ud-Din Al-Hilali, Ph.D. and Dr. Muhammad Muhsin Khan)
4. Explanation (abridged Tafsir) by Ibn Kathir (translated by Safi-ur-Rahman al-Mubarakpuri)

We hope that by doing this an ordinary English-speaker will be able to pick up a copy of this book and study and comprehend The Glorious Qur'an in a way that is acceptable to the understanding of the Rightly-guided Muslim Ummah (Community).

Biography of Hafiz Ibn Kathir (701 H - 774 H)

By the Honored Shaykh `Abdul-Qadir Al-Arna'ut, may Allah protect him.

He is the respected Imam, Abu Al-Fida', `Imad Ad-Din Isma il bin 'Umar bin Kathir Al-Qurashi Al-Busrawi - Busraian in origin; Dimashqi in training, learning and residence.

Ibn Kathir was born in the city of Busra in 701 H. His father was the Friday speaker of the village, but he died while Ibn Kathir was only four years old. Ibn Kathir's brother, Shaykh Abdul-Wahhab, reared him and taught him until he moved to Damascus in 706 H., when he was five years old.

Ibn Kathir's Teachers

Ibn Kathir studied Fiqh - Islamic jurisprudence - with Burhan Ad-Din, Ibrahim bin `Abdur-Rahman Al-Fizari, known as Ibn Al-Firkah (who died in 729 H). Ibn Kathir heard Hadiths from `Isa bin Al-Mutim, Ahmad bin Abi Talib, (Ibn Ash-Shahnah) (who died in 730 H), Ibn Al-Hajjar, (who died in 730 H), and the Hadith narrator of Ash-Sham (modern day Syria and surrounding areas); Baha Ad-Din Al-Qasim bin Muzaffar bin `Asakir (who died in 723 H), and Ibn Ash-Shirdzi, Ishaq bin Yahya Al-Ammuddi, also known as `Afif Ad-Din, the Zahiriyyah Shaykh who died in 725 H, and Muhammad bin Zarrad. He remained with Jamal Ad-Din, Yusuf bin Az-Zaki AlMizzi who died in 724 H, he benefited from his knowledge and also married his daughter. He also read with Shaykh Al-Islam, Taqi Ad-Din Ahmad bin `Abdul-Halim bin `Abdus-Salam bin Taymiyyah who died in 728 H. He also read with the Imam Hafiz and historian Shams Ad-Din, Muhammad bin Ahmad bin Uthman bin Qaymaz Adh-Dhahabi, who died in 748 H. Also, Abu Musa Al-Qarafai, Abu Al-Fath Ad-Dabbusi and

'Ali bin `Umar As-Suwani and others who gave him permission to transmit the knowledge he learned with them in Egypt.

In his book, Al-Mu jam Al-Mukhtas, Al-Hafiz Adh-Dhaliabi wrote that Ibn Kathir was, "The Imam, scholar of jurisprudence, skillful scholar of Hadith, renowned Faqih and scholar of Tafsir who wrote several beneficial books."

Further, in Ad-Durar Al-Kdminah, Al-Hafiz Ibn Hajar AlAsqalani said, "Ibn Kathir worked on the subject of the Hadith in the areas of texts and chains of narrators. He had a good memory, his books became popular during his lifetime, and people benefited from them after his death."

Also, the renowned historian Abu Al-Mahasin, Jamal Ad-Din Yusuf bin Sayf Ad-Din (Ibn Taghri Bardi), said in his book, AlManhal As-Safi, "He is the Shaykh, the Imam, the great scholar `Imad Ad-Din Abu Al-Fida'. He learned extensively and was very active in collecting knowledge and writing. He was excellent in the areas of Fiqh, Tafsfr and Hadith. He collected knowledge, authored (books), taught, narrated Hadith and wrote. He had immense knowledge in the fields of Hadith, Tafsir, Fiqh, the Arabic language, and so forth. He gave Fatawa (religious verdicts) and taught until he died, may Allah grant him mercy. He was known for his precision and vast knowledge, and as a scholar of history, Hadith and Tafsir."

Ibn Kathir's Students

Ibn Hajji was one of Ibn Kathir's students, and he described Ibn Kathir: "He had the best memory of the Hadith texts. He also had the most knowledge concerning the narrators and authenticity, his contemporaries and teachers admitted to these qualities. Every time I met him I gained some benefit from him."

Also, Ibn Al-`Imad Al-Hanbali said in his book, Shadhardt Adh-Dhahab, "He is the renowned Hafiz `Imad Ad-Din, whose memory was excellent, whose forgetfulness was miniscule, whose understanding was adequate, and who had good knowledge in the Arabic language." Also, Ibn Habib said about Ibn Kathir, "He heard knowledge and collected it and wrote various books. He brought comfort to the ears with his Fatwas and narrated Hadith and brought benefit to other people. The papers that contained his Fatwas were transmitted to the various (Islamic) provinces. Further, he was known for his precision and encompassing knowledge."

Ibn Kathir's Books

1 - One of the greatest books that Ibn Kathir wrote was his Tafsir of the Noble Qur'an, which is one of the best Tafsir that rely on narrations [of Ahadith, the Tafsir of the Companions, etc.]. The Tafsir by Ibn Kathir was printed many times and several scholars have summarized it.

2- The History Collection known as Al-Biddyah, which was printed in 14 volumes under the name Al-Bidayah wanNihdyah, and contained the stories of the Prophets and previous nations, the Prophet's Seerah (life story) and Islamic history until his time. He also added a book Al-Fitan, about the Signs of the Last Hour.

3- At-Takmil ft Ma`rifat Ath-Thiqat wa Ad-Du'afa wal Majdhil which Ibn Kathir collected from the books of his two Shaykhs Al-Mizzi and Adh-Dhahabi; Al-Kdmal and Mizan Al-Ftiddl. He added several benefits regarding the subject of Al-Jarh and AtT'adil.

4- Al-Hadi was-Sunan ft Ahadith Al-Masdnfd was-Sunan which is also known by, Jami` Al-Masdnfd. In this book, Ibn Kathir collected the narrations of Imams Ahmad bin Hanbal, Al-Bazzar, Abu Ya`la Al-Mawsili, Ibn Abi Shaybah and from the six collections of Hadith: the Two Sahihs [Al-Bukhari and Muslim] and the Four Sunan [Abu Dawud, At-Tirmidhi, AnNasa and Ibn Majah]. Ibn Kathir divided this book according to areas of Fiqh.

5-Tabaqat Ash-Shaf iyah which also contains the virtues of Imam Ash-Shafi.

6- Ibn Kathir wrote references for the Ahadith of Adillat AtTanbfh, from the Shafi school of Fiqh.

7- Ibn Kathir began an explanation of Sahih Al-Bukhari, but he did not finish it.

8- He started writing a large volume on the Ahkam (Laws), but finished only up to the Hajj rituals.

9- He summarized Al-Bayhaqi's 'Al-Madkhal. Many of these books were not printed.

10- He summarized `Ulum Al-Hadith, by Abu `Amr bin AsSalah and called it Mukhtasar `Ulum Al-Hadith. Shaykh Ahmad Shakir, the Egyptian Muhaddith, printed this book along with his commentary on it and called it Al-Ba'th Al-Hathfth fi Sharh Mukhtasar `Ulum Al-Hadith.

11- As-Sfrah An-Nabawiyyah, which is contained in his book Al-Biddyah, and both of these books are in print.

12- A research on Jihad called Al-Ijtihad ft Talabi Al-Jihad, which was printed several times.

Ibn Kathir's Death

Al-Hafiz Ibn Hajar Al-Asqalani said, "Ibn Kathir lost his sight just before his life ended. He died in Damascus in 774 H." May Allah grant mercy upon Ibn Kathir and make him among the residents of His Paradise.

PREFACE

In the name of Allah, Most Gracious, Most Merciful.

About this book

The previous publication of this book included some background information to the chapters of the Qur'an by an Islamic scholar known as Abul Ala Maududi. This information was used to shed more light on the chapters by giving a summery of why each chapter was given its name, It's period of revelation and the circumstances surrounding its revelatiom. However, some Muslims objected to the inclusion of the contributions of Maududi.

In this new publication of Tafsir Ibn Kathir, we have removed all traces of the contribution of Abul Ala Maududi. Personally, I do not know the reasons for the objections to Maududi, but this work concerns only the tafsir of Ibn Kathir, so we have not included anything from Maududi in it. We have also corrected all the typing and formatting errors found in the previous publication. We have not alter the structure of the book. The reader is still able to read the full Arabic Text of the thirty Parts of the Qur'an and follow its meanings in the English language. The transliteration of the Arabic text should also give the reader a taste of the sound of the original Arabic.

May Almighty Allah accept this effort from us, and make it a source of blessings for us in this world and in the next. I bear witness that there is none worthy of worship but Allah and I bear witness that Muhammad (may the peace and blessings of Allah be upon him) is the slave and messenger of Allah.

Performing Prostration While Reading the Qur'an

Question:

Could you please give a list of the Qur'anic verses when a prostration is recommended? What happens if we read these verses and not perform a prostration?

A. Jalil

Answer:

There are 15 verses in the Qur'an that mention prostration before God Almighty as a good action by God-fearing believers. Therefore, it is strongly recommended to perform such a prostration when we read or listen to any of these verses, whether during prayer or in any situation.

Some scholars are of the view that even if one has not performed ablution, one should prostrate oneself. These verses are given here, starting with the Arabic title of the surah which is followed by two numbers, the first indicating the surah, and the second indicating the verse,: Al-Araf 7: 206; Al-Raad 13: 15; Al-Nahl 16: 50; Al-Isra 17: 109; Maryam 19: 58; Al-Hajj 22: 18 & 22: 77; Al-Furqan 25: 60; Al-Naml 27: 26;

Al-Sajdah 32: 15; Saad 38: 25; Fussilat 41: 38; Al-Najm 53: 62; Al-Inshiqaq 84: 21 and Al-Alaq 96: 19.

If you do not perform a prostration when you read or listen to any of these verses, you have done badly because you miss out on the reward of performing a prostration for God. You incur no sin and violate no divine order.

Reference:
http://archive.arabnews.com/?page=5&section=0&article=97811&d=1&m=7&y=2007

The Glorious Qur'an Juz' 4 (Part 4): Chapter (Surah) 3: Al-I-'Imran (The Family of Imran) 093 To Chapter (Surah) 4: An-Nisaa (The Women) 023

PART 4 FULL ARABIC TEXT

Chapter (Surah) 3: Al-i-'Imran 093-200

۞ كُلُّ ٱلطَّعَامِ كَانَ حِلًّا لِّبَنِىٓ إِسْرَٰٓءِيلَ إِلَّا مَا حَرَّمَ إِسْرَٰٓءِيلُ عَلَىٰ نَفْسِهِۦ مِن قَبْلِ أَن تُنَزَّلَ ٱلتَّوْرَىٰةُ ۗ قُلْ فَأْتُوا۟ بِٱلتَّوْرَىٰةِ فَٱتْلُوهَآ إِن كُنتُمْ صَٰدِقِينَ ۝ فَمَنِ ٱفْتَرَىٰ عَلَى ٱللَّهِ ٱلْكَذِبَ مِنۢ بَعْدِ ذَٰلِكَ فَأُو۟لَٰٓئِكَ هُمُ ٱلظَّٰلِمُونَ ۝ قُلْ صَدَقَ ٱللَّهُ ۗ فَٱتَّبِعُوا۟ مِلَّةَ إِبْرَٰهِيمَ حَنِيفًا وَمَا كَانَ مِنَ ٱلْمُشْرِكِينَ ۝ إِنَّ أَوَّلَ بَيْتٍ وُضِعَ لِلنَّاسِ لَلَّذِى بِبَكَّةَ مُبَارَكًا وَهُدًى لِّلْعَٰلَمِينَ ۝ فِيهِ ءَايَٰتٌۢ بَيِّنَٰتٌ مَّقَامُ إِبْرَٰهِيمَ ۖ وَمَن دَخَلَهُۥ كَانَ ءَامِنًا ۗ وَلِلَّهِ عَلَى ٱلنَّاسِ حِجُّ ٱلْبَيْتِ مَنِ ٱسْتَطَاعَ إِلَيْهِ سَبِيلًا ۚ وَمَن كَفَرَ فَإِنَّ ٱللَّهَ غَنِىٌّ عَنِ ٱلْعَٰلَمِينَ ۝ قُلْ يَٰٓأَهْلَ ٱلْكِتَٰبِ لِمَ تَكْفُرُونَ بِـَٔايَٰتِ ٱللَّهِ وَٱللَّهُ شَهِيدٌ عَلَىٰ مَا تَعْمَلُونَ ۝ قُلْ يَٰٓأَهْلَ ٱلْكِتَٰبِ لِمَ تَصُدُّونَ عَن سَبِيلِ ٱللَّهِ مَنْ ءَامَنَ تَبْغُونَهَا عِوَجًا وَأَنتُمْ شُهَدَآءُ ۗ وَمَا ٱللَّهُ بِغَٰفِلٍ عَمَّا تَعْمَلُونَ ۝ يَٰٓأَيُّهَا ٱلَّذِينَ ءَامَنُوٓا۟ إِن تُطِيعُوا۟ فَرِيقًا مِّنَ ٱلَّذِينَ أُوتُوا۟ ٱلْكِتَٰبَ يَرُدُّوكُم بَعْدَ إِيمَٰنِكُمْ كَٰفِرِينَ ۝ وَكَيْفَ تَكْفُرُونَ وَأَنتُمْ تُتْلَىٰ عَلَيْكُمْ ءَايَٰتُ ٱللَّهِ وَفِيكُمْ رَسُولُهُۥ ۗ وَمَن يَعْتَصِم بِٱللَّهِ فَقَدْ هُدِىَ إِلَىٰ صِرَٰطٍ مُّسْتَقِيمٍ ۝ يَٰٓأَيُّهَا ٱلَّذِينَ ءَامَنُوا۟ ٱتَّقُوا۟ ٱللَّهَ حَقَّ تُقَاتِهِۦ وَلَا تَمُوتُنَّ إِلَّا وَأَنتُم مُّسْلِمُونَ ۝ وَٱعْتَصِمُوا۟ بِحَبْلِ ٱللَّهِ جَمِيعًا وَلَا تَفَرَّقُوا۟ ۚ وَٱذْكُرُوا۟ نِعْمَتَ ٱللَّهِ عَلَيْكُمْ إِذْ كُنتُمْ أَعْدَآءً فَأَلَّفَ بَيْنَ قُلُوبِكُمْ فَأَصْبَحْتُم بِنِعْمَتِهِۦٓ إِخْوَٰنًا وَكُنتُمْ عَلَىٰ شَفَا حُفْرَةٍ مِّنَ ٱلنَّارِ فَأَنقَذَكُم مِّنْهَا

كَذَٰلِكَ يُبَيِّنُ ٱللَّهُ لَكُمْ ءَايَٰتِهِۦ لَعَلَّكُمْ تَهْتَدُونَ ۝ وَلْتَكُن مِّنكُمْ أُمَّةٌ يَدْعُونَ إِلَى ٱلْخَيْرِ وَيَأْمُرُونَ بِٱلْمَعْرُوفِ وَيَنْهَوْنَ عَنِ ٱلْمُنكَرِ ۚ وَأُو۟لَٰٓئِكَ هُمُ ٱلْمُفْلِحُونَ ۝ وَلَا تَكُونُوا۟ كَٱلَّذِينَ تَفَرَّقُوا۟ وَٱخْتَلَفُوا۟ مِنۢ بَعْدِ مَا جَآءَهُمُ ٱلْبَيِّنَٰتُ ۚ وَأُو۟لَٰٓئِكَ لَهُمْ عَذَابٌ عَظِيمٌ ۝ يَوْمَ تَبْيَضُّ وُجُوهٌ وَتَسْوَدُّ وُجُوهٌ ۚ فَأَمَّا ٱلَّذِينَ ٱسْوَدَّتْ وُجُوهُهُمْ أَكَفَرْتُم بَعْدَ إِيمَٰنِكُمْ فَذُوقُوا۟ ٱلْعَذَابَ بِمَا كُنتُمْ تَكْفُرُونَ ۝ وَأَمَّا ٱلَّذِينَ ٱبْيَضَّتْ وُجُوهُهُمْ فَفِى رَحْمَةِ ٱللَّهِ هُمْ فِيهَا خَٰلِدُونَ ۝ تِلْكَ ءَايَٰتُ ٱللَّهِ نَتْلُوهَا عَلَيْكَ بِٱلْحَقِّ ۗ وَمَا ٱللَّهُ يُرِيدُ ظُلْمًا لِّلْعَٰلَمِينَ ۝ وَلِلَّهِ مَا فِى ٱلسَّمَٰوَٰتِ وَمَا فِى ٱلْأَرْضِ ۚ وَإِلَى ٱللَّهِ تُرْجَعُ ٱلْأُمُورُ ۝ كُنتُمْ خَيْرَ أُمَّةٍ أُخْرِجَتْ لِلنَّاسِ تَأْمُرُونَ بِٱلْمَعْرُوفِ وَتَنْهَوْنَ عَنِ ٱلْمُنكَرِ وَتُؤْمِنُونَ بِٱللَّهِ ۗ وَلَوْ ءَامَنَ أَهْلُ ٱلْكِتَٰبِ لَكَانَ خَيْرًا لَّهُم ۚ مِّنْهُمُ ٱلْمُؤْمِنُونَ وَأَكْثَرُهُمُ ٱلْفَٰسِقُونَ ۝ لَن يَضُرُّوكُمْ إِلَّآ أَذًى ۖ وَإِن يُقَٰتِلُوكُمْ يُوَلُّوكُمُ ٱلْأَدْبَارَ ثُمَّ لَا يُنصَرُونَ ۝ ضُرِبَتْ عَلَيْهِمُ ٱلذِّلَّةُ أَيْنَ مَا ثُقِفُوٓا۟ إِلَّا بِحَبْلٍ مِّنَ ٱللَّهِ وَحَبْلٍ مِّنَ ٱلنَّاسِ وَبَآءُو بِغَضَبٍ مِّنَ ٱللَّهِ وَضُرِبَتْ عَلَيْهِمُ ٱلْمَسْكَنَةُ ۚ ذَٰلِكَ بِأَنَّهُمْ كَانُوا۟ يَكْفُرُونَ بِـَٔايَٰتِ ٱللَّهِ وَيَقْتُلُونَ ٱلْأَنۢبِيَآءَ بِغَيْرِ حَقٍّ ۚ ذَٰلِكَ بِمَا عَصَوا۟ وَّكَانُوا۟ يَعْتَدُونَ ۞ ۝ لَيْسُوا۟ سَوَآءً ۗ مِّنْ أَهْلِ ٱلْكِتَٰبِ أُمَّةٌ قَآئِمَةٌ يَتْلُونَ ءَايَٰتِ ٱللَّهِ ءَانَآءَ ٱلَّيْلِ وَهُمْ يَسْجُدُونَ ۝ يُؤْمِنُونَ بِٱللَّهِ وَٱلْيَوْمِ ٱلْءَاخِرِ وَيَأْمُرُونَ بِٱلْمَعْرُوفِ وَيَنْهَوْنَ عَنِ ٱلْمُنكَرِ وَيُسَٰرِعُونَ فِى ٱلْخَيْرَٰتِ وَأُو۟لَٰٓئِكَ مِنَ ٱلصَّٰلِحِينَ ۝ وَمَا يَفْعَلُوا۟ مِنْ خَيْرٍ فَلَن يُكْفَرُوهُ ۗ وَٱللَّهُ عَلِيمٌۢ بِٱلْمُتَّقِينَ ۝ إِنَّ ٱلَّذِينَ كَفَرُوا۟ لَن تُغْنِىَ عَنْهُمْ أَمْوَٰلُهُمْ وَلَآ أَوْلَٰدُهُم مِّنَ ٱللَّهِ شَيْـًٔا ۖ وَأُو۟لَٰٓئِكَ أَصْحَٰبُ ٱلنَّارِ ۚ هُمْ فِيهَا خَٰلِدُونَ ۝ مَثَلُ مَا يُنفِقُونَ فِى هَٰذِهِ ٱلْحَيَوٰةِ ٱلدُّنْيَا كَمَثَلِ رِيحٍ فِيهَا صِرٌّ أَصَابَتْ حَرْثَ قَوْمٍ ظَلَمُوٓا۟

أَنفُسَهُمْ فَأَهْلَكَتْهُ ۚ وَمَا ظَلَمَهُمُ ٱللَّهُ وَلَٰكِنْ أَنفُسَهُمْ يَظْلِمُونَ ۝ يَٰٓأَيُّهَا ٱلَّذِينَ ءَامَنُوا۟ لَا تَتَّخِذُوا۟ بِطَانَةً مِّن دُونِكُمْ لَا يَأْلُونَكُمْ خَبَالًا وَدُّوا۟ مَا عَنِتُّمْ قَدْ بَدَتِ ٱلْبَغْضَآءُ مِنْ أَفْوَٰهِهِمْ وَمَا تُخْفِى صُدُورُهُمْ أَكْبَرُ ۚ قَدْ بَيَّنَّا لَكُمُ ٱلْءَايَٰتِ ۖ إِن كُنتُمْ تَعْقِلُونَ ۝ هَٰٓأَنتُمْ أُو۟لَآءِ تُحِبُّونَهُمْ وَلَا يُحِبُّونَكُمْ وَتُؤْمِنُونَ بِٱلْكِتَٰبِ كُلِّهِۦ وَإِذَا لَقُوكُمْ قَالُوٓا۟ ءَامَنَّا وَإِذَا خَلَوْا۟ عَضُّوا۟ عَلَيْكُمُ ٱلْأَنَامِلَ مِنَ ٱلْغَيْظِ ۚ قُلْ مُوتُوا۟ بِغَيْظِكُمْ ۗ إِنَّ ٱللَّهَ عَلِيمٌۢ بِذَاتِ ٱلصُّدُورِ ۝ إِن تَمْسَسْكُمْ حَسَنَةٌ تَسُؤْهُمْ وَإِن تُصِبْكُمْ سَيِّئَةٌ يَفْرَحُوا۟ بِهَا ۖ وَإِن تَصْبِرُوا۟ وَتَتَّقُوا۟ لَا يَضُرُّكُمْ كَيْدُهُمْ شَيْـًٔا ۗ إِنَّ ٱللَّهَ بِمَا يَعْمَلُونَ مُحِيطٌ ۝ وَإِذْ غَدَوْتَ مِنْ أَهْلِكَ تُبَوِّئُ ٱلْمُؤْمِنِينَ مَقَٰعِدَ لِلْقِتَالِ ۗ وَٱللَّهُ سَمِيعٌ عَلِيمٌ ۝ إِذْ هَمَّت طَّآئِفَتَانِ مِنكُمْ أَن تَفْشَلَا وَٱللَّهُ وَلِيُّهُمَا ۗ وَعَلَى ٱللَّهِ فَلْيَتَوَكَّلِ ٱلْمُؤْمِنُونَ ۝ وَلَقَدْ نَصَرَكُمُ ٱللَّهُ بِبَدْرٍ وَأَنتُمْ أَذِلَّةٌ ۖ فَٱتَّقُوا۟ ٱللَّهَ لَعَلَّكُمْ تَشْكُرُونَ ۝ إِذْ تَقُولُ لِلْمُؤْمِنِينَ أَلَن يَكْفِيَكُمْ أَن يُمِدَّكُمْ رَبُّكُم بِثَلَٰثَةِ ءَالَٰفٍ مِّنَ ٱلْمَلَٰٓئِكَةِ مُنزَلِينَ ۝ بَلَىٰٓ ۚ إِن تَصْبِرُوا۟ وَتَتَّقُوا۟ وَيَأْتُوكُم مِّن فَوْرِهِمْ هَٰذَا يُمْدِدْكُمْ رَبُّكُم بِخَمْسَةِ ءَالَٰفٍ مِّنَ ٱلْمَلَٰٓئِكَةِ مُسَوِّمِينَ ۝ وَمَا جَعَلَهُ ٱللَّهُ إِلَّا بُشْرَىٰ لَكُمْ وَلِتَطْمَئِنَّ قُلُوبُكُم بِهِۦ ۗ وَمَا ٱلنَّصْرُ إِلَّا مِنْ عِندِ ٱللَّهِ ٱلْعَزِيزِ ٱلْحَكِيمِ ۝ لِيَقْطَعَ طَرَفًا مِّنَ ٱلَّذِينَ كَفَرُوٓا۟ أَوْ يَكْبِتَهُمْ فَيَنقَلِبُوا۟ خَآئِبِينَ ۝ لَيْسَ لَكَ مِنَ ٱلْأَمْرِ شَىْءٌ أَوْ يَتُوبَ عَلَيْهِمْ أَوْ يُعَذِّبَهُمْ فَإِنَّهُمْ ظَٰلِمُونَ ۝ وَلِلَّهِ مَا فِى ٱلسَّمَٰوَٰتِ وَمَا فِى ٱلْأَرْضِ ۚ يَغْفِرُ لِمَن يَشَآءُ وَيُعَذِّبُ مَن يَشَآءُ ۚ وَٱللَّهُ غَفُورٌ رَّحِيمٌ ۝ يَٰٓأَيُّهَا ٱلَّذِينَ ءَامَنُوا۟ لَا تَأْكُلُوا۟ ٱلرِّبَوٰٓا۟ أَضْعَٰفًا مُّضَٰعَفَةً ۖ وَٱتَّقُوا۟ ٱللَّهَ لَعَلَّكُمْ تُفْلِحُونَ ۝ وَٱتَّقُوا۟ ٱلنَّارَ ٱلَّتِىٓ أُعِدَّتْ لِلْكَٰفِرِينَ ۝ وَأَطِيعُوا۟ ٱللَّهَ وَٱلرَّسُولَ لَعَلَّكُمْ تُرْحَمُونَ ۝ ۞ وَسَارِعُوٓا۟ إِلَىٰ مَغْفِرَةٍ مِّن

رَبِّكُمْ وَجَنَّةٍ عَرْضُهَا ٱلسَّمَوَٰتُ وَٱلْأَرْضُ أُعِدَّتْ لِلْمُتَّقِينَ ۝ ٱلَّذِينَ يُنفِقُونَ فِى ٱلسَّرَّآءِ وَٱلضَّرَّآءِ وَٱلْكَٰظِمِينَ ٱلْغَيْظَ وَٱلْعَافِينَ عَنِ ٱلنَّاسِ ۗ وَٱللَّهُ يُحِبُّ ٱلْمُحْسِنِينَ ۝ وَٱلَّذِينَ إِذَا فَعَلُواْ فَٰحِشَةً أَوْ ظَلَمُوٓاْ أَنفُسَهُمْ ذَكَرُواْ ٱللَّهَ فَٱسْتَغْفَرُواْ لِذُنُوبِهِمْ وَمَن يَغْفِرُ ٱلذُّنُوبَ إِلَّا ٱللَّهُ وَلَمْ يُصِرُّواْ عَلَىٰ مَا فَعَلُواْ وَهُمْ يَعْلَمُونَ ۝ أُوْلَٰٓئِكَ جَزَآؤُهُم مَّغْفِرَةٌ مِّن رَّبِّهِمْ وَجَنَّٰتٌ تَجْرِى مِن تَحْتِهَا ٱلْأَنْهَٰرُ خَٰلِدِينَ فِيهَا ۚ وَنِعْمَ أَجْرُ ٱلْعَٰمِلِينَ ۝ قَدْ خَلَتْ مِن قَبْلِكُمْ سُنَنٌ فَسِيرُواْ فِى ٱلْأَرْضِ فَٱنظُرُواْ كَيْفَ كَانَ عَٰقِبَةُ ٱلْمُكَذِّبِينَ ۝ هَٰذَا بَيَانٌ لِّلنَّاسِ وَهُدًى وَمَوْعِظَةٌ لِّلْمُتَّقِينَ ۝ وَلَا تَهِنُواْ وَلَا تَحْزَنُواْ وَأَنتُمُ ٱلْأَعْلَوْنَ إِن كُنتُم مُّؤْمِنِينَ ۝ إِن يَمْسَسْكُمْ قَرْحٌ فَقَدْ مَسَّ ٱلْقَوْمَ قَرْحٌ مِّثْلُهُۥ ۚ وَتِلْكَ ٱلْأَيَّامُ نُدَاوِلُهَا بَيْنَ ٱلنَّاسِ وَلِيَعْلَمَ ٱللَّهُ ٱلَّذِينَ ءَامَنُواْ وَيَتَّخِذَ مِنكُمْ شُهَدَآءَ ۗ وَٱللَّهُ لَا يُحِبُّ ٱلظَّٰلِمِينَ ۝ وَلِيُمَحِّصَ ٱللَّهُ ٱلَّذِينَ ءَامَنُواْ وَيَمْحَقَ ٱلْكَٰفِرِينَ ۝ أَمْ حَسِبْتُمْ أَن تَدْخُلُواْ ٱلْجَنَّةَ وَلَمَّا يَعْلَمِ ٱللَّهُ ٱلَّذِينَ جَٰهَدُواْ مِنكُمْ وَيَعْلَمَ ٱلصَّٰبِرِينَ ۝ وَلَقَدْ كُنتُمْ تَمَنَّوْنَ ٱلْمَوْتَ مِن قَبْلِ أَن تَلْقَوْهُ فَقَدْ رَأَيْتُمُوهُ وَأَنتُمْ تَنظُرُونَ ۝ وَمَا مُحَمَّدٌ إِلَّا رَسُولٌ قَدْ خَلَتْ مِن قَبْلِهِ ٱلرُّسُلُ ۚ أَفَإِيْن مَّاتَ أَوْ قُتِلَ ٱنقَلَبْتُمْ عَلَىٰٓ أَعْقَٰبِكُمْ ۚ وَمَن يَنقَلِبْ عَلَىٰ عَقِبَيْهِ فَلَن يَضُرَّ ٱللَّهَ شَيْئًا ۗ وَسَيَجْزِى ٱللَّهُ ٱلشَّٰكِرِينَ ۝ وَمَا كَانَ لِنَفْسٍ أَن تَمُوتَ إِلَّا بِإِذْنِ ٱللَّهِ كِتَٰبًا مُّؤَجَّلًا ۗ وَمَن يُرِدْ ثَوَابَ ٱلدُّنْيَا نُؤْتِهِۦ مِنْهَا وَمَن يُرِدْ ثَوَابَ ٱلْءَاخِرَةِ نُؤْتِهِۦ مِنْهَا ۚ وَسَنَجْزِى ٱلشَّٰكِرِينَ ۝ وَكَأَيِّن مِّن نَّبِىٍّ قَٰتَلَ مَعَهُۥ رِبِّيُّونَ كَثِيرٌ فَمَا وَهَنُواْ لِمَآ أَصَابَهُمْ فِى سَبِيلِ ٱللَّهِ وَمَا ضَعُفُواْ وَمَا ٱسْتَكَانُواْ ۗ وَٱللَّهُ يُحِبُّ ٱلصَّٰبِرِينَ ۝ وَمَا كَانَ قَوْلَهُمْ إِلَّآ أَن قَالُواْ رَبَّنَا ٱغْفِرْ لَنَا ذُنُوبَنَا وَإِسْرَافَنَا فِىٓ أَمْرِنَا وَثَبِّتْ أَقْدَامَنَا وَٱنصُرْنَا عَلَى

ٱلْقَوْمَ ٱلْكَٰفِرِينَ ۝ فَـَٔاتَىٰهُمُ ٱللَّهُ ثَوَابَ ٱلدُّنْيَا وَحُسْنَ ثَوَابِ ٱلْءَاخِرَةِ ۗ وَٱللَّهُ يُحِبُّ ٱلْمُحْسِنِينَ ۝ يَٰٓأَيُّهَا ٱلَّذِينَ ءَامَنُوٓا۟ إِن تُطِيعُوا۟ ٱلَّذِينَ كَفَرُوا۟ يَرُدُّوكُمْ عَلَىٰٓ أَعْقَٰبِكُمْ فَتَنقَلِبُوا۟ خَٰسِرِينَ ۝ بَلِ ٱللَّهُ مَوْلَىٰكُمْ ۖ وَهُوَ خَيْرُ ٱلنَّٰصِرِينَ ۝ سَنُلْقِى فِى قُلُوبِ ٱلَّذِينَ كَفَرُوا۟ ٱلرُّعْبَ بِمَآ أَشْرَكُوا۟ بِٱللَّهِ مَا لَمْ يُنَزِّلْ بِهِۦ سُلْطَٰنًا ۖ وَمَأْوَىٰهُمُ ٱلنَّارُ ۚ وَبِئْسَ مَثْوَى ٱلظَّٰلِمِينَ ۝ وَلَقَدْ صَدَقَكُمُ ٱللَّهُ وَعْدَهُۥٓ إِذْ تَحُسُّونَهُم بِإِذْنِهِۦ ۖ حَتَّىٰٓ إِذَا فَشِلْتُمْ وَتَنَٰزَعْتُمْ فِى ٱلْأَمْرِ وَعَصَيْتُم مِّنۢ بَعْدِ مَآ أَرَىٰكُم مَّا تُحِبُّونَ ۚ مِنكُم مَّن يُرِيدُ ٱلدُّنْيَا وَمِنكُم مَّن يُرِيدُ ٱلْءَاخِرَةَ ۚ ثُمَّ صَرَفَكُمْ عَنْهُمْ لِيَبْتَلِيَكُمْ ۖ وَلَقَدْ عَفَا عَنكُمْ ۗ وَٱللَّهُ ذُو فَضْلٍ عَلَى ٱلْمُؤْمِنِينَ ۝ ۞ إِذْ تُصْعِدُونَ وَلَا تَلْوُۥنَ عَلَىٰٓ أَحَدٍ وَٱلرَّسُولُ يَدْعُوكُمْ فِىٓ أُخْرَىٰكُمْ فَأَثَٰبَكُمْ غَمًّۢا بِغَمٍّ لِّكَيْلَا تَحْزَنُوا۟ عَلَىٰ مَا فَاتَكُمْ وَلَا مَآ أَصَٰبَكُمْ ۗ وَٱللَّهُ خَبِيرٌۢ بِمَا تَعْمَلُونَ ۝ ثُمَّ أَنزَلَ عَلَيْكُم مِّنۢ بَعْدِ ٱلْغَمِّ أَمَنَةً نُّعَاسًا يَغْشَىٰ طَآئِفَةً مِّنكُمْ ۖ وَطَآئِفَةٌ قَدْ أَهَمَّتْهُمْ أَنفُسُهُمْ يَظُنُّونَ بِٱللَّهِ غَيْرَ ٱلْحَقِّ ظَنَّ ٱلْجَٰهِلِيَّةِ ۖ يَقُولُونَ هَل لَّنَا مِنَ ٱلْأَمْرِ مِن شَىْءٍ ۗ قُلْ إِنَّ ٱلْأَمْرَ كُلَّهُۥ لِلَّهِ ۗ يُخْفُونَ فِىٓ أَنفُسِهِم مَّا لَا يُبْدُونَ لَكَ ۖ يَقُولُونَ لَوْ كَانَ لَنَا مِنَ ٱلْأَمْرِ شَىْءٌ مَّا قُتِلْنَا هَٰهُنَا ۗ قُل لَّوْ كُنتُمْ فِى بُيُوتِكُمْ لَبَرَزَ ٱلَّذِينَ كُتِبَ عَلَيْهِمُ ٱلْقَتْلُ إِلَىٰ مَضَاجِعِهِمْ ۖ وَلِيَبْتَلِىَ ٱللَّهُ مَا فِى صُدُورِكُمْ وَلِيُمَحِّصَ مَا فِى قُلُوبِكُمْ ۗ وَٱللَّهُ عَلِيمٌۢ بِذَاتِ ٱلصُّدُورِ ۝ إِنَّ ٱلَّذِينَ تَوَلَّوْا۟ مِنكُمْ يَوْمَ ٱلْتَقَى ٱلْجَمْعَانِ إِنَّمَا ٱسْتَزَلَّهُمُ ٱلشَّيْطَٰنُ بِبَعْضِ مَا كَسَبُوا۟ ۖ وَلَقَدْ عَفَا ٱللَّهُ عَنْهُمْ ۗ إِنَّ ٱللَّهَ غَفُورٌ حَلِيمٌ ۝ يَٰٓأَيُّهَا ٱلَّذِينَ ءَامَنُوا۟ لَا تَكُونُوا۟ كَٱلَّذِينَ كَفَرُوا۟ وَقَالُوا۟ لِإِخْوَٰنِهِمْ إِذَا ضَرَبُوا۟ فِى ٱلْأَرْضِ أَوْ كَانُوا۟ غُزًّى لَّوْ كَانُوا۟ عِندَنَا مَا مَاتُوا۟ وَمَا قُتِلُوا۟ لِيَجْعَلَ ٱللَّهُ ذَٰلِكَ حَسْرَةً فِى قُلُوبِهِمْ ۗ وَٱللَّهُ

تُحْيِۦ وَتُمِيتُ ۗ وَٱللَّهُ بِمَا تَعْمَلُونَ بَصِيرٌ ۝ وَلَئِن قُتِلْتُمْ فِى سَبِيلِ ٱللَّهِ أَوْ مُتُّمْ لَمَغْفِرَةٌ مِّنَ ٱللَّهِ وَرَحْمَةٌ خَيْرٌ مِّمَّا يَجْمَعُونَ ۝ وَلَئِن مُّتُّمْ أَوْ قُتِلْتُمْ لَإِلَى ٱللَّهِ تُحْشَرُونَ ۝ فَبِمَا رَحْمَةٍ مِّنَ ٱللَّهِ لِنتَ لَهُمْ ۖ وَلَوْ كُنتَ فَظًّا غَلِيظَ ٱلْقَلْبِ لَٱنفَضُّوا۟ مِنْ حَوْلِكَ ۖ فَٱعْفُ عَنْهُمْ وَٱسْتَغْفِرْ لَهُمْ وَشَاوِرْهُمْ فِى ٱلْأَمْرِ ۖ فَإِذَا عَزَمْتَ فَتَوَكَّلْ عَلَى ٱللَّهِ ۚ إِنَّ ٱللَّهَ يُحِبُّ ٱلْمُتَوَكِّلِينَ ۝ إِن يَنصُرْكُمُ ٱللَّهُ فَلَا غَالِبَ لَكُمْ ۖ وَإِن يَخْذُلْكُمْ فَمَن ذَا ٱلَّذِى يَنصُرُكُم مِّنۢ بَعْدِهِۦ ۗ وَعَلَى ٱللَّهِ فَلْيَتَوَكَّلِ ٱلْمُؤْمِنُونَ ۝ وَمَا كَانَ لِنَبِىٍّ أَن يَغُلَّ ۚ وَمَن يَغْلُلْ يَأْتِ بِمَا غَلَّ يَوْمَ ٱلْقِيَٰمَةِ ۚ ثُمَّ تُوَفَّىٰ كُلُّ نَفْسٍ مَّا كَسَبَتْ وَهُمْ لَا يُظْلَمُونَ ۝ أَفَمَنِ ٱتَّبَعَ رِضْوَٰنَ ٱللَّهِ كَمَنۢ بَآءَ بِسَخَطٍ مِّنَ ٱللَّهِ وَمَأْوَىٰهُ جَهَنَّمُ ۚ وَبِئْسَ ٱلْمَصِيرُ ۝ هُمْ دَرَجَٰتٌ عِندَ ٱللَّهِ ۗ وَٱللَّهُ بَصِيرٌۢ بِمَا يَعْمَلُونَ ۝ لَقَدْ مَنَّ ٱللَّهُ عَلَى ٱلْمُؤْمِنِينَ إِذْ بَعَثَ فِيهِمْ رَسُولًا مِّنْ أَنفُسِهِمْ يَتْلُوا۟ عَلَيْهِمْ ءَايَٰتِهِۦ وَيُزَكِّيهِمْ وَيُعَلِّمُهُمُ ٱلْكِتَٰبَ وَٱلْحِكْمَةَ وَإِن كَانُوا۟ مِن قَبْلُ لَفِى ضَلَٰلٍ مُّبِينٍ ۝ أَوَلَمَّآ أَصَٰبَتْكُم مُّصِيبَةٌ قَدْ أَصَبْتُم مِّثْلَيْهَا قُلْتُمْ أَنَّىٰ هَٰذَا ۖ قُلْ هُوَ مِنْ عِندِ أَنفُسِكُمْ ۗ إِنَّ ٱللَّهَ عَلَىٰ كُلِّ شَىْءٍ قَدِيرٌ ۝ وَمَآ أَصَٰبَكُمْ يَوْمَ ٱلْتَقَى ٱلْجَمْعَانِ فَبِإِذْنِ ٱللَّهِ وَلِيَعْلَمَ ٱلْمُؤْمِنِينَ ۝ وَلِيَعْلَمَ ٱلَّذِينَ نَافَقُوا۟ ۚ وَقِيلَ لَهُمْ تَعَالَوْا۟ قَٰتِلُوا۟ فِى سَبِيلِ ٱللَّهِ أَوِ ٱدْفَعُوا۟ ۖ قَالُوا۟ لَوْ نَعْلَمُ قِتَالًا لَّٱتَّبَعْنَٰكُمْ ۗ هُمْ لِلْكُفْرِ يَوْمَئِذٍ أَقْرَبُ مِنْهُمْ لِلْإِيمَٰنِ ۚ يَقُولُونَ بِأَفْوَٰهِهِم مَّا لَيْسَ فِى قُلُوبِهِمْ ۗ وَٱللَّهُ أَعْلَمُ بِمَا يَكْتُمُونَ ۝ ٱلَّذِينَ قَالُوا۟ لِإِخْوَٰنِهِمْ وَقَعَدُوا۟ لَوْ أَطَاعُونَا مَا قُتِلُوا۟ ۗ قُلْ فَٱدْرَءُوا۟ عَنْ أَنفُسِكُمُ ٱلْمَوْتَ إِن كُنتُمْ صَٰدِقِينَ ۝ وَلَا تَحْسَبَنَّ ٱلَّذِينَ قُتِلُوا۟ فِى سَبِيلِ ٱللَّهِ أَمْوَٰتًۢا ۚ بَلْ أَحْيَآءٌ عِندَ رَبِّهِمْ يُرْزَقُونَ ۝ فَرِحِينَ بِمَآ ءَاتَىٰهُمُ ٱللَّهُ مِن فَضْلِهِۦ وَيَسْتَبْشِرُونَ بِٱلَّذِينَ لَمْ يَلْحَقُوا۟ بِهِم مِّنْ خَلْفِهِمْ أَلَّا

خَوْفٌ عَلَيْهِمْ وَلَا هُمْ يَحْزَنُونَ ۝ يَسْتَبْشِرُونَ بِنِعْمَةٍ مِّنَ ٱللَّهِ وَفَضْلٍ وَأَنَّ ٱللَّهَ لَا يُضِيعُ أَجْرَ ٱلْمُؤْمِنِينَ ۝ ٱلَّذِينَ ٱسْتَجَابُواْ لِلَّهِ وَٱلرَّسُولِ مِنۢ بَعْدِ مَآ أَصَابَهُمُ ٱلْقَرْحُۚ لِلَّذِينَ أَحْسَنُواْ مِنْهُمْ وَٱتَّقَوْاْ أَجْرٌ عَظِيمٌ ۝ ٱلَّذِينَ قَالَ لَهُمُ ٱلنَّاسُ إِنَّ ٱلنَّاسَ قَدْ جَمَعُواْ لَكُمْ فَٱخْشَوْهُمْ فَزَادَهُمْ إِيمَٰنًا وَقَالُواْ حَسْبُنَا ٱللَّهُ وَنِعْمَ ٱلْوَكِيلُ ۝ فَٱنقَلَبُواْ بِنِعْمَةٍ مِّنَ ٱللَّهِ وَفَضْلٍ لَّمْ يَمْسَسْهُمْ سُوٓءٌ وَٱتَّبَعُواْ رِضْوَٰنَ ٱللَّهِۗ وَٱللَّهُ ذُو فَضْلٍ عَظِيمٍ ۝ إِنَّمَا ذَٰلِكُمُ ٱلشَّيْطَٰنُ يُخَوِّفُ أَوْلِيَآءَهُۥ فَلَا تَخَافُوهُمْ وَخَافُونِ إِن كُنتُم مُّؤْمِنِينَ ۝ وَلَا يَحْزُنكَ ٱلَّذِينَ يُسَٰرِعُونَ فِى ٱلْكُفْرِۚ إِنَّهُمْ لَن يَضُرُّواْ ٱللَّهَ شَيْـًٔاۗ يُرِيدُ ٱللَّهُ أَلَّا يَجْعَلَ لَهُمْ حَظًّا فِى ٱلْءَاخِرَةِۖ وَلَهُمْ عَذَابٌ عَظِيمٌ ۝ إِنَّ ٱلَّذِينَ ٱشْتَرَوُاْ ٱلْكُفْرَ بِٱلْإِيمَٰنِ لَن يَضُرُّواْ ٱللَّهَ شَيْـًٔا وَلَهُمْ عَذَابٌ أَلِيمٌ ۝ وَلَا يَحْسَبَنَّ ٱلَّذِينَ كَفَرُوٓاْ أَنَّمَا نُمْلِى لَهُمْ خَيْرٌ لِّأَنفُسِهِمْۚ إِنَّمَا نُمْلِى لَهُمْ لِيَزْدَادُوٓاْ إِثْمًاۚ وَلَهُمْ عَذَابٌ مُّهِينٌ ۝ مَّا كَانَ ٱللَّهُ لِيَذَرَ ٱلْمُؤْمِنِينَ عَلَىٰ مَآ أَنتُمْ عَلَيْهِ حَتَّىٰ يَمِيزَ ٱلْخَبِيثَ مِنَ ٱلطَّيِّبِۗ وَمَا كَانَ ٱللَّهُ لِيُطْلِعَكُمْ عَلَى ٱلْغَيْبِ وَلَٰكِنَّ ٱللَّهَ يَجْتَبِى مِن رُّسُلِهِۦ مَن يَشَآءُۖ فَـَٔامِنُواْ بِٱللَّهِ وَرُسُلِهِۦۚ وَإِن تُؤْمِنُواْ وَتَتَّقُواْ فَلَكُمْ أَجْرٌ عَظِيمٌ ۝ وَلَا يَحْسَبَنَّ ٱلَّذِينَ يَبْخَلُونَ بِمَآ ءَاتَىٰهُمُ ٱللَّهُ مِن فَضْلِهِۦ هُوَ خَيْرًا لَّهُمۖ بَلْ هُوَ شَرٌّ لَّهُمْۖ سَيُطَوَّقُونَ مَا بَخِلُواْ بِهِۦ يَوْمَ ٱلْقِيَٰمَةِۗ وَلِلَّهِ مِيرَٰثُ ٱلسَّمَٰوَٰتِ وَٱلْأَرْضِۗ وَٱللَّهُ بِمَا تَعْمَلُونَ خَبِيرٌ ۝ لَّقَدْ سَمِعَ ٱللَّهُ قَوْلَ ٱلَّذِينَ قَالُوٓاْ إِنَّ ٱللَّهَ فَقِيرٌ وَنَحْنُ أَغْنِيَآءُۘ سَنَكْتُبُ مَا قَالُواْ وَقَتْلَهُمُ ٱلْأَنۢبِيَآءَ بِغَيْرِ حَقٍّ وَنَقُولُ ذُوقُواْ عَذَابَ ٱلْحَرِيقِ ۝ ذَٰلِكَ بِمَا قَدَّمَتْ أَيْدِيكُمْ وَأَنَّ ٱللَّهَ لَيْسَ بِظَلَّٰمٍ لِّلْعَبِيدِ ۝ ٱلَّذِينَ قَالُوٓاْ إِنَّ ٱللَّهَ عَهِدَ إِلَيْنَآ أَلَّا نُؤْمِنَ لِرَسُولٍ حَتَّىٰ يَأْتِيَنَا بِقُرْبَانٍ تَأْكُلُهُ ٱلنَّارُۗ قُلْ قَدْ جَآءَكُمْ رُسُلٌ مِّن قَبْلِى بِٱلْبَيِّنَٰتِ

وَبِٱلَّذِى قُلْتُمْ فَلِمَ قَتَلْتُمُوهُمْ إِن كُنتُمْ صَـٰدِقِينَ ۝ فَإِن كَذَّبُوكَ فَقَدْ كُذِّبَ رُسُلٌ مِّن قَبْلِكَ جَآءُو بِٱلْبَيِّنَـٰتِ وَٱلزُّبُرِ وَٱلْكِتَـٰبِ ٱلْمُنِيرِ ۝ كُلُّ نَفْسٍ ذَآئِقَةُ ٱلْمَوْتِ ۗ وَإِنَّمَا تُوَفَّوْنَ أُجُورَكُمْ يَوْمَ ٱلْقِيَـٰمَةِ ۖ فَمَن زُحْزِحَ عَنِ ٱلنَّارِ وَأُدْخِلَ ٱلْجَنَّةَ فَقَدْ فَازَ ۗ وَمَا ٱلْحَيَوٰةُ ٱلدُّنْيَآ إِلَّا مَتَـٰعُ ٱلْغُرُورِ ۝ لَتُبْلَوُنَّ فِىٓ أَمْوَٰلِكُمْ وَأَنفُسِكُمْ وَلَتَسْمَعُنَّ مِنَ ٱلَّذِينَ أُوتُوا۟ ٱلْكِتَـٰبَ مِن قَبْلِكُمْ وَمِنَ ٱلَّذِينَ أَشْرَكُوٓا۟ أَذًى كَثِيرًا ۚ وَإِن تَصْبِرُوا۟ وَتَتَّقُوا۟ فَإِنَّ ذَٰلِكَ مِنْ عَزْمِ ٱلْأُمُورِ ۝ وَإِذْ أَخَذَ ٱللَّهُ مِيثَـٰقَ ٱلَّذِينَ أُوتُوا۟ ٱلْكِتَـٰبَ لَتُبَيِّنُنَّهُۥ لِلنَّاسِ وَلَا تَكْتُمُونَهُۥ فَنَبَذُوهُ وَرَآءَ ظُهُورِهِمْ وَٱشْتَرَوْا۟ بِهِۦ ثَمَنًا قَلِيلًا ۖ فَبِئْسَ مَا يَشْتَرُونَ ۝ لَا تَحْسَبَنَّ ٱلَّذِينَ يَفْرَحُونَ بِمَآ أَتَوا۟ وَّيُحِبُّونَ أَن يُحْمَدُوا۟ بِمَا لَمْ يَفْعَلُوا۟ فَلَا تَحْسَبَنَّهُم بِمَفَازَةٍ مِّنَ ٱلْعَذَابِ ۖ وَلَهُمْ عَذَابٌ أَلِيمٌ ۝ وَلِلَّهِ مُلْكُ ٱلسَّمَـٰوَٰتِ وَٱلْأَرْضِ ۗ وَٱللَّهُ عَلَىٰ كُلِّ شَىْءٍ قَدِيرٌ ۝ إِنَّ فِى خَلْقِ ٱلسَّمَـٰوَٰتِ وَٱلْأَرْضِ وَٱخْتِلَـٰفِ ٱلَّيْلِ وَٱلنَّهَارِ لَـَٔايَـٰتٍ لِّأُو۟لِى ٱلْأَلْبَـٰبِ ۝ ٱلَّذِينَ يَذْكُرُونَ ٱللَّهَ قِيَـٰمًا وَقُعُودًا وَعَلَىٰ جُنُوبِهِمْ وَيَتَفَكَّرُونَ فِى خَلْقِ ٱلسَّمَـٰوَٰتِ وَٱلْأَرْضِ رَبَّنَا مَا خَلَقْتَ هَـٰذَا بَـٰطِلًا سُبْحَـٰنَكَ فَقِنَا عَذَابَ ٱلنَّارِ ۝ رَبَّنَآ إِنَّكَ مَن تُدْخِلِ ٱلنَّارَ فَقَدْ أَخْزَيْتَهُۥ ۖ وَمَا لِلظَّـٰلِمِينَ مِنْ أَنصَارٍ ۝ رَّبَّنَآ إِنَّنَا سَمِعْنَا مُنَادِيًا يُنَادِى لِلْإِيمَـٰنِ أَنْ ءَامِنُوا۟ بِرَبِّكُمْ فَـَٔامَنَّا ۚ رَبَّنَا فَٱغْفِرْ لَنَا ذُنُوبَنَا وَكَفِّرْ عَنَّا سَيِّـَٔاتِنَا وَتَوَفَّنَا مَعَ ٱلْأَبْرَارِ ۝ رَبَّنَا وَءَاتِنَا مَا وَعَدتَّنَا عَلَىٰ رُسُلِكَ وَلَا تُخْزِنَا يَوْمَ ٱلْقِيَـٰمَةِ ۗ إِنَّكَ لَا تُخْلِفُ ٱلْمِيعَادَ ۝ فَٱسْتَجَابَ لَهُمْ رَبُّهُمْ أَنِّى لَآ أُضِيعُ عَمَلَ عَـٰمِلٍ مِّنكُم مِّن ذَكَرٍ أَوْ أُنثَىٰ ۖ بَعْضُكُم مِّنۢ بَعْضٍ ۖ فَٱلَّذِينَ هَاجَرُوا۟ وَأُخْرِجُوا۟ مِن دِيَـٰرِهِمْ وَأُوذُوا۟ فِى سَبِيلِى وَقَـٰتَلُوا۟ وَقُتِلُوا۟ لَأُكَفِّرَنَّ عَنْهُمْ سَيِّـَٔاتِهِمْ وَلَأُدْخِلَنَّهُمْ جَنَّـٰتٍ تَجْرِى مِن تَحْتِهَا

ٱلْأَنْهَـٰرُ ثَوَابًا مِّنْ عِندِ ٱللَّهِ ۗ وَٱللَّهُ عِندَهُۥ حُسْنُ ٱلثَّوَابِ ۝١٩٥ لَا يَغُرَّنَّكَ تَقَلُّبُ ٱلَّذِينَ كَفَرُوا۟ فِى ٱلْبِلَـٰدِ ۝١٩٦ مَتَـٰعٌ قَلِيلٌ ثُمَّ مَأْوَىٰهُمْ جَهَنَّمُ ۚ وَبِئْسَ ٱلْمِهَادُ ۝١٩٧ لَـٰكِنِ ٱلَّذِينَ ٱتَّقَوْا۟ رَبَّهُمْ لَهُمْ جَنَّـٰتٌ تَجْرِى مِن تَحْتِهَا ٱلْأَنْهَـٰرُ خَـٰلِدِينَ فِيهَا نُزُلًا مِّنْ عِندِ ٱللَّهِ ۗ وَمَا عِندَ ٱللَّهِ خَيْرٌ لِّلْأَبْرَارِ ۝١٩٨ وَإِنَّ مِنْ أَهْلِ ٱلْكِتَـٰبِ لَمَن يُؤْمِنُ بِٱللَّهِ وَمَآ أُنزِلَ إِلَيْكُمْ وَمَآ أُنزِلَ إِلَيْهِمْ خَـٰشِعِينَ لِلَّهِ لَا يَشْتَرُونَ بِـَٔايَـٰتِ ٱللَّهِ ثَمَنًا قَلِيلًا ۗ أُو۟لَـٰٓئِكَ لَهُمْ أَجْرُهُمْ عِندَ رَبِّهِمْ ۗ إِنَّ ٱللَّهَ سَرِيعُ ٱلْحِسَابِ ۝١٩٩ يَـٰٓأَيُّهَا ٱلَّذِينَ ءَامَنُوا۟ ٱصْبِرُوا۟ وَصَابِرُوا۟ وَرَابِطُوا۟ وَٱتَّقُوا۟ ٱللَّهَ لَعَلَّكُمْ تُفْلِحُونَ ۝٢٠٠

(Al-i-'Imran 093-200)

Chapter (Surah) 4: An-Nisaa 001-023

بِسْمِ ٱللَّهِ ٱلرَّحْمَـٰنِ ٱلرَّحِيمِ

يَـٰٓأَيُّهَا ٱلنَّاسُ ٱتَّقُوا۟ رَبَّكُمُ ٱلَّذِى خَلَقَكُم مِّن نَّفْسٍ وَٰحِدَةٍ وَخَلَقَ مِنْهَا زَوْجَهَا وَبَثَّ مِنْهُمَا رِجَالًا كَثِيرًا وَنِسَآءً ۚ وَٱتَّقُوا۟ ٱللَّهَ ٱلَّذِى تَسَآءَلُونَ بِهِۦ وَٱلْأَرْحَامَ ۚ إِنَّ ٱللَّهَ كَانَ عَلَيْكُمْ رَقِيبًا ۝١ وَءَاتُوا۟ ٱلْيَتَـٰمَىٰٓ أَمْوَٰلَهُمْ ۖ وَلَا تَتَبَدَّلُوا۟ ٱلْخَبِيثَ بِٱلطَّيِّبِ ۖ وَلَا تَأْكُلُوٓا۟ أَمْوَٰلَهُمْ إِلَىٰٓ أَمْوَٰلِكُمْ ۚ إِنَّهُۥ كَانَ حُوبًا كَبِيرًا ۝٢ وَإِنْ خِفْتُمْ أَلَّا تُقْسِطُوا۟ فِى ٱلْيَتَـٰمَىٰ فَٱنكِحُوا۟ مَا طَابَ لَكُم مِّنَ ٱلنِّسَآءِ مَثْنَىٰ وَثُلَـٰثَ وَرُبَـٰعَ ۖ فَإِنْ خِفْتُمْ أَلَّا تَعْدِلُوا۟ فَوَٰحِدَةً أَوْ مَا مَلَكَتْ أَيْمَـٰنُكُمْ ۚ ذَٰلِكَ أَدْنَىٰٓ أَلَّا تَعُولُوا۟ ۝٣ وَءَاتُوا۟ ٱلنِّسَآءَ صَدُقَـٰتِهِنَّ نِحْلَةً ۚ فَإِن طِبْنَ لَكُمْ عَن شَىْءٍ مِّنْهُ نَفْسًا فَكُلُوهُ هَنِيٓـًٔا مَّرِيٓـًٔا ۝٤ وَلَا تُؤْتُوا۟ ٱلسُّفَهَآءَ أَمْوَٰلَكُمُ ٱلَّتِى جَعَلَ ٱللَّهُ لَكُمْ قِيَـٰمًا وَٱرْزُقُوهُمْ فِيهَا وَٱكْسُوهُمْ وَقُولُوا۟ لَهُمْ قَوْلًا مَّعْرُوفًا ۝٥ وَٱبْتَلُوا۟ ٱلْيَتَـٰمَىٰ حَتَّىٰٓ إِذَا بَلَغُوا۟ ٱلنِّكَاحَ فَإِنْ ءَانَسْتُم مِّنْهُمْ رُشْدًا فَٱدْفَعُوٓا۟ إِلَيْهِمْ أَمْوَٰلَهُمْ

وَلَا تَأْكُلُوهَا إِسْرَافًا وَبِدَارًا أَن يَكْبَرُوا ۚ وَمَن كَانَ غَنِيًّا فَلْيَسْتَعْفِفْ ۖ وَمَن كَانَ فَقِيرًا فَلْيَأْكُلْ بِالْمَعْرُوفِ ۚ فَإِذَا دَفَعْتُمْ إِلَيْهِمْ أَمْوَٰلَهُمْ فَأَشْهِدُوا۟ عَلَيْهِمْ ۚ وَكَفَىٰ بِٱللَّهِ حَسِيبًا ۝ لِّلرِّجَالِ نَصِيبٌ مِّمَّا تَرَكَ ٱلْوَٰلِدَانِ وَٱلْأَقْرَبُونَ وَلِلنِّسَاءِ نَصِيبٌ مِّمَّا تَرَكَ ٱلْوَٰلِدَانِ وَٱلْأَقْرَبُونَ مِمَّا قَلَّ مِنْهُ أَوْ كَثُرَ ۚ نَصِيبًا مَّفْرُوضًا ۝ وَإِذَا حَضَرَ ٱلْقِسْمَةَ أُو۟لُوا۟ ٱلْقُرْبَىٰ وَٱلْيَتَٰمَىٰ وَٱلْمَسَٰكِينُ فَٱرْزُقُوهُم مِّنْهُ وَقُولُوا۟ لَهُمْ قَوْلًا مَّعْرُوفًا ۝ وَلْيَخْشَ ٱلَّذِينَ لَوْ تَرَكُوا۟ مِنْ خَلْفِهِمْ ذُرِّيَّةً ضِعَٰفًا خَافُوا۟ عَلَيْهِمْ فَلْيَتَّقُوا۟ ٱللَّهَ وَلْيَقُولُوا۟ قَوْلًا سَدِيدًا ۝ إِنَّ ٱلَّذِينَ يَأْكُلُونَ أَمْوَٰلَ ٱلْيَتَٰمَىٰ ظُلْمًا إِنَّمَا يَأْكُلُونَ فِى بُطُونِهِمْ نَارًا ۖ وَسَيَصْلَوْنَ سَعِيرًا ۝ يُوصِيكُمُ ٱللَّهُ فِىٓ أَوْلَٰدِكُمْ ۖ لِلذَّكَرِ مِثْلُ حَظِّ ٱلْأُنثَيَيْنِ ۚ فَإِن كُنَّ نِسَاءً فَوْقَ ٱثْنَتَيْنِ فَلَهُنَّ ثُلُثَا مَا تَرَكَ ۖ وَإِن كَانَتْ وَٰحِدَةً فَلَهَا ٱلنِّصْفُ ۚ وَلِأَبَوَيْهِ لِكُلِّ وَٰحِدٍ مِّنْهُمَا ٱلسُّدُسُ مِمَّا تَرَكَ إِن كَانَ لَهُۥ وَلَدٌ ۚ فَإِن لَّمْ يَكُن لَّهُۥ وَلَدٌ وَوَرِثَهُۥٓ أَبَوَاهُ فَلِأُمِّهِ ٱلثُّلُثُ ۚ فَإِن كَانَ لَهُۥٓ إِخْوَةٌ فَلِأُمِّهِ ٱلسُّدُسُ ۚ مِنۢ بَعْدِ وَصِيَّةٍ يُوصِى بِهَآ أَوْ دَيْنٍ ۗ ءَابَآؤُكُمْ وَأَبْنَآؤُكُمْ لَا تَدْرُونَ أَيُّهُمْ أَقْرَبُ لَكُمْ نَفْعًا ۚ فَرِيضَةً مِّنَ ٱللَّهِ ۗ إِنَّ ٱللَّهَ كَانَ عَلِيمًا حَكِيمًا ۝ وَلَكُمْ نِصْفُ مَا تَرَكَ أَزْوَٰجُكُمْ إِن لَّمْ يَكُن لَّهُنَّ وَلَدٌ ۚ فَإِن كَانَ لَهُنَّ وَلَدٌ فَلَكُمُ ٱلرُّبُعُ مِمَّا تَرَكْنَ ۚ مِنۢ بَعْدِ وَصِيَّةٍ يُوصِينَ بِهَآ أَوْ دَيْنٍ ۚ وَلَهُنَّ ٱلرُّبُعُ مِمَّا تَرَكْتُمْ إِن لَّمْ يَكُن لَّكُمْ وَلَدٌ ۚ فَإِن كَانَ لَكُمْ وَلَدٌ فَلَهُنَّ ٱلثُّمُنُ مِمَّا تَرَكْتُم ۚ مِّنۢ بَعْدِ وَصِيَّةٍ تُوصُونَ بِهَآ أَوْ دَيْنٍ ۗ وَإِن كَانَ رَجُلٌ يُورَثُ كَلَٰلَةً أَوِ ٱمْرَأَةٌ وَلَهُۥٓ أَخٌ أَوْ أُخْتٌ فَلِكُلِّ وَٰحِدٍ مِّنْهُمَا ٱلسُّدُسُ ۚ فَإِن كَانُوٓا۟ أَكْثَرَ مِن ذَٰلِكَ فَهُمْ شُرَكَآءُ فِى ٱلثُّلُثِ ۚ مِنۢ بَعْدِ وَصِيَّةٍ يُوصَىٰ بِهَآ أَوْ دَيْنٍ غَيْرَ مُضَآرٍّ ۚ وَصِيَّةً مِّنَ ٱللَّهِ ۗ وَٱللَّهُ عَلِيمٌ حَلِيمٌ ۝

تِلْكَ حُدُودُ ٱللَّهِ ۚ وَمَن يُطِعِ ٱللَّهَ وَرَسُولَهُ يُدْخِلْهُ جَنَّٰتٍ تَجْرِى مِن تَحْتِهَا ٱلْأَنْهَٰرُ خَٰلِدِينَ فِيهَا ۚ وَذَٰلِكَ ٱلْفَوْزُ ٱلْعَظِيمُ ۞ وَمَن يَعْصِ ٱللَّهَ وَرَسُولَهُ وَيَتَعَدَّ حُدُودَهُ يُدْخِلْهُ نَارًا خَٰلِدًا فِيهَا وَلَهُۥ عَذَابٌ مُّهِينٌ ۞ وَٱلَّٰتِى يَأْتِينَ ٱلْفَٰحِشَةَ مِن نِّسَآئِكُمْ فَٱسْتَشْهِدُوا۟ عَلَيْهِنَّ أَرْبَعَةً مِّنكُمْ ۖ فَإِن شَهِدُوا۟ فَأَمْسِكُوهُنَّ فِى ٱلْبُيُوتِ حَتَّىٰ يَتَوَفَّىٰهُنَّ ٱلْمَوْتُ أَوْ يَجْعَلَ ٱللَّهُ لَهُنَّ سَبِيلًا ۞ وَٱلَّذَانِ يَأْتِيَٰنِهَا مِنكُمْ فَـَٔاذُوهُمَا ۖ فَإِن تَابَا وَأَصْلَحَا فَأَعْرِضُوا۟ عَنْهُمَآ ۗ إِنَّ ٱللَّهَ كَانَ تَوَّابًا رَّحِيمًا ۞ إِنَّمَا ٱلتَّوْبَةُ عَلَى ٱللَّهِ لِلَّذِينَ يَعْمَلُونَ ٱلسُّوٓءَ بِجَهَٰلَةٍ ثُمَّ يَتُوبُونَ مِن قَرِيبٍ فَأُو۟لَٰٓئِكَ يَتُوبُ ٱللَّهُ عَلَيْهِمْ ۗ وَكَانَ ٱللَّهُ عَلِيمًا حَكِيمًا ۞ وَلَيْسَتِ ٱلتَّوْبَةُ لِلَّذِينَ يَعْمَلُونَ ٱلسَّيِّـَٔاتِ حَتَّىٰٓ إِذَا حَضَرَ أَحَدَهُمُ ٱلْمَوْتُ قَالَ إِنِّى تُبْتُ ٱلْـَٰٔنَ وَلَا ٱلَّذِينَ يَمُوتُونَ وَهُمْ كُفَّارٌ ۚ أُو۟لَٰٓئِكَ أَعْتَدْنَا لَهُمْ عَذَابًا أَلِيمًا ۞ يَٰٓأَيُّهَا ٱلَّذِينَ ءَامَنُوا۟ لَا يَحِلُّ لَكُمْ أَن تَرِثُوا۟ ٱلنِّسَآءَ كَرْهًا ۖ وَلَا تَعْضُلُوهُنَّ لِتَذْهَبُوا۟ بِبَعْضِ مَآ ءَاتَيْتُمُوهُنَّ إِلَّآ أَن يَأْتِينَ بِفَٰحِشَةٍ مُّبَيِّنَةٍ ۚ وَعَاشِرُوهُنَّ بِٱلْمَعْرُوفِ ۚ فَإِن كَرِهْتُمُوهُنَّ فَعَسَىٰٓ أَن تَكْرَهُوا۟ شَيْـًٔا وَيَجْعَلَ ٱللَّهُ فِيهِ خَيْرًا كَثِيرًا ۞ وَإِنْ أَرَدتُّمُ ٱسْتِبْدَالَ زَوْجٍ مَّكَانَ زَوْجٍ وَءَاتَيْتُمْ إِحْدَىٰهُنَّ قِنطَارًا فَلَا تَأْخُذُوا۟ مِنْهُ شَيْـًٔا ۚ أَتَأْخُذُونَهُۥ بُهْتَٰنًا وَإِثْمًا مُّبِينًا ۞ وَكَيْفَ تَأْخُذُونَهُۥ وَقَدْ أَفْضَىٰ بَعْضُكُمْ إِلَىٰ بَعْضٍ وَأَخَذْنَ مِنكُم مِّيثَٰقًا غَلِيظًا ۞ وَلَا تَنكِحُوا۟ مَا نَكَحَ ءَابَآؤُكُم مِّنَ ٱلنِّسَآءِ إِلَّا مَا قَدْ سَلَفَ ۚ إِنَّهُۥ كَانَ فَٰحِشَةً وَمَقْتًا وَسَآءَ سَبِيلًا ۞ حُرِّمَتْ عَلَيْكُمْ أُمَّهَٰتُكُمْ وَبَنَاتُكُمْ وَأَخَوَٰتُكُمْ وَعَمَّٰتُكُمْ وَخَٰلَٰتُكُمْ وَبَنَاتُ ٱلْأَخِ وَبَنَاتُ ٱلْأُخْتِ وَأُمَّهَٰتُكُمُ ٱلَّٰتِىٓ أَرْضَعْنَكُمْ وَأَخَوَٰتُكُم مِّنَ ٱلرَّضَٰعَةِ وَأُمَّهَٰتُ نِسَآئِكُمْ وَرَبَٰٓئِبُكُمُ

$$ \text{اللَّاتِي فِي حُجُورِكُم مِّن نِّسَآئِكُمُ اللَّاتِي دَخَلْتُم بِهِنَّ فَإِن لَّمْ تَكُونُواْ دَخَلْتُم بِهِنَّ فَلَا جُنَاحَ عَلَيْكُمْ وَحَلَائِلُ أَبْنَآئِكُمُ الَّذِينَ مِنْ أَصْلَابِكُمْ وَأَن تَجْمَعُواْ بَيْنَ الْأُخْتَيْنِ إِلَّا مَا قَدْ سَلَفَ إِنَّ اللَّهَ كَانَ غَفُورًا رَّحِيمًا ﴿٢٣﴾ } $$

(An-Nisaa 001-023)

INTRODUCTION TO CHAPTER (SURAH) 3: AL-I-'IMRAN (THE FAMILY OF IMRAN)

Ibn Kathir's Introduction

Surah Al `Imran was revealed in Al-Madinah, as evident by the fact that the first eighty-three Ayat in it relate to the delegation from Najran that arrived in Al-Madinah on the ninth year of Hijrah (632 CE). We will elaborate on this subject when we explain the Ayah about the Mubahalah (3:61) in this Surah, Allah willing. We should also state that we mentioned the virtues of Surah Al `Imran along with the virtues of Surat Al-Baqarah in the beginning of the Tafsir of Surat Al-Baqarah

CHAPTER (SURAH) 3: AL-I-'IMRAN (THE FAMILY OF 'IMRAN), VERSES 093-200

Surah: 3 Ayah: 93, Ayah: 94 & Ayah: 95

$$ \text{﴿ كُلُّ الطَّعَامِ كَانَ حِلًّا لِّبَنِي إِسْرَائِيلَ إِلَّا مَا حَرَّمَ إِسْرَائِيلُ عَلَىٰ نَفْسِهِ مِن قَبْلِ أَن تُنَزَّلَ التَّوْرَاةُ قُلْ فَأْتُواْ بِالتَّوْرَاةِ فَاتْلُوهَا إِن كُنتُمْ صَادِقِينَ ﴿٩٣﴾ ﴾} $$

93. All food was lawful to the Children of Israel, except what Israel made unlawful for himself before the Taurât (Torah) was revealed. Say (O Muhammad (peace be upon him)) "Bring here the Taurât (Torah) and recite it, if you are truthful."

$$ \text{﴿ فَمَنِ افْتَرَىٰ عَلَى اللَّهِ الْكَذِبَ مِنْ بَعْدِ ذَٰلِكَ فَأُوْلَٰئِكَ هُمُ الظَّالِمُونَ ﴿٩٤﴾ ﴾} $$

94. Then after that, whosoever shall invent a lie against Allâh, ... such shall indeed be the Zâlimûn (disbelievers).

$$ \text{﴿ قُلْ صَدَقَ اللَّهُ فَاتَّبِعُواْ مِلَّةَ إِبْرَاهِيمَ حَنِيفًا وَمَا كَانَ مِنَ الْمُشْرِكِينَ ﴿٩٥﴾ ﴾} $$

95. Say (O Muhammad (peace be upon him)) "Allâh has spoken the truth; follow the religion of Ibrâhim (Abraham) Hanifa (Islâmic Monotheism, i.e. he used to worship Allâh Alone), and he was not of Al-Mushrikûn." (See V.2:105)

Chapter 3: Al-i-'Imran (The Family oF Imran), Verses 093-200

Transliteration

93. Kullu alttaAAami kana hillan libanee isra-eela illa ma harrama isra-eelu AAala nafsihi min qabli an tunazzala alttawratu qul fa/too bialttawrati faotlooha in kuntum sadiqeena 94. Famani iftara AAala Allahi alkathiba min baAAdi thalika faola-ika humu althalimoona 95. Qul sadaqa Allahu faittabiAAoo millata ibraheema haneefan wama kana mina almushrikeena

Tafsir Ibn Kathir

The Questions that the Jews Asked Our Prophet

Imam Ahmad recorded that Ibn `Abbas said, "A group of Jews came to Allah's Prophet and said, `Talk to us about some things we will ask you and which only a Prophet would know.' He said, `Ask me about whatever you wish. However, give your pledge to Allah, similar to the pledge that Ya`qub took from his children, that if I tell you something and you recognize its truth, you will follow me in Islam.' They said, `Agreed.' The Prophet said, `Ask me about whatever you wish.' They said, `Tell us about four matters: 1. What kinds of food did Isra'il prohibit for himself 2. What about the sexual discharge of the woman and the man, and what role does each play in producing male or female offspring 3. Tell us about the condition of the unlettered Prophet during sleep, 4. And who is his Wali (supporter) among the angels' The Prophet took their covenant that they will follow him if he answers these questions, and they agreed. He said, `I ask you by He Who sent down the Tawrah to Musa, do you not know that Isra'il once became very ill When his illness was prolonged, he vowed to Allah that if He cures His illness, he would prohibit the best types of drink and food for himself. Was not the best food to him camel meat and the best drink camel milk' They said, `Yes, by Allah.' The Messenger said, `O Allah, be Witness against them.' The Prophet then said, `I ask you by Allah, other than Whom there is no deity (worthy of worship), Who sent down the Tawrah to Musa, do you not know that man's discharge is thick and white and woman's is yellow and thin If any of these fluids becomes dominant, the offspring will take its sex and resemblance by Allah's leave. Hence, if the man's is more than the woman's, the child will be male, by Allah's leave. If the woman's discharge is more than the man's, then the child will be female, by Allah's leave.' They said, `Yes.' He said, `O Allah, be Witness against them.' He then said, `I ask you by He Who sent down the Tawrah to Musa, do you not know that the eyes of this unlettered Prophet sleep, but his heart does not sleep' They said, `Yes, by Allah!' He said, `O Allah, be Witness.' They said, `Tell us now about your Wali among the angels, for this is when we either follow or shun you.' He said, `My Wali (who brings down the revelation from Allah) is Jibril, and Allah never sent a Prophet, but Jibril is his Wali.' They said, `We then shun you. Had you a Wali other than Jibril, we would have followed you.' On that, Allah, the Exalted revealed,

(Say: "Whoever is an enemy to Jibril...") (2:97)."

Allah's statement,

(before the Tawrah was revealed) (3:93), means, Isra'il forbade that for himself before the Tawrah was revealed. There are two objectives behind revealing this segment of the Ayah. First, he forbade himself the most delightful things for Allah's sake. This practice was allowed during his period of Law, and is, thus, suitable that it is mentioned after Allah's statement,

(By no means shall you attain Al-Birr, unless you spend of that which you love) (3:92).

What we are allowed in our Law is to spend in Allah's obedience from what we like and covet (but not to prohibit what Allah has allowed). Allah said in other Ayat;

(And gives his wealth, in spite of love for it,) (2:177), and;

(And they give food, in spite of their love for it,) (76:8).

The second reason is that after Allah refuted the false Christian beliefs and allegations about `Isa and his mother. Allah started refuting the Jews here, may Allah curse them, by stating that the abrogation of the Law, that they denied occurs, already occurred in their Law. For instance, Allah has stated in their Book, the Tawrah, that when Nuh departed from the ark, Allah allowed him to eat the meat of all types of animals. Afterwards, Isra'il forbade the meat and milk of camels for himself, and his children imitated this practice after him. The Tawrah later on prohibited this type of food, and added several more types of prohibitions. Allah allowed Adam to marry his daughters to his sons, and this practice was later forbidden. The Law of Ibrahim allowed the man to take female servants as companions along with his wife, as Ibrahim did when he took Hajar, while he was married to Sarah. Later on, the Tawrah prohibited this practice. It was previously allowed to take two sisters as wives at the same time, as Ya`qub married two sisters at the same time. Later on, this practice was prohibited in the Tawrah. All these examples are in the Tawrah and constitute a Naskh (abrogation) of the Law. Therefore, let the Jews consider what Allah legislated for `Isa and if such legislation falls under the category of abrogation or not. Why do they not then follow `Isa in this regard Rather, the Jews defied and rebelled against `Isa and against the correct religion that Allah sent Muhammad with.

This is why Allah said,

(All food was lawful to the Children of Israel, except what Isra'il made unlawful for himself before the Tawrah was revealed) (3:93) meaning, before the Tawrah was revealed, all types of foods were allowed, except what Isra'il prohibited for himself. Allah then said,

(Say: "Bring here the Tawrah and recite it, if you are truthful."),

for the Tawrah affirms what we are stating here. Allah said next,

(Then after that, whosoever shall invent a lie against Allah, then these it is that are the wrongdoers.) (3:94), in reference to those who lie about Allah and claim that He made the Sabbath and the Tawrah eternal. They are those who claim that Allah did not send another Prophet calling to Allah with the proofs and evidences, although evidence indicates that abrogation, as we have described, occurred before in the Tawrah,

Chapter 3: Al-i-'Imran (The Family of Imran), Verses 093-200

(then these it is that are the wrongdoers.)

Allah then said,

(Say, "Allah has spoken the truth;") (3:95) meaning, O Muhammad, say that Allah has said the truth in what He conveyed and legislated in the Qur'an,

(follow the religion of Ibrahim the Hanif, and he was not of the idolators.") (3:95).

Therefore, follow the religion of Ibrahim that Allah legislated in the Qur'an. Indeed, this is the truth, there is no doubt in it, and the perfect way, and no Prophet has brought a more complete, clear, plain and perfect way than he did. Allah said in other Ayat,

(Say: "Truly, my Lord has guided me to a straight path, a right religion, the religion of Ibrahim, the Hanif, and he was not of the idolators.") (6:161)

and,

(Then, We have sent the revelation to you (saying): "Follow the religion of Ibrahim, the Hanif, and he was not of the idolators.) (16:123).

Surah: 3 Ayah: 96 & Ayah: 97

﴿ إِنَّ أَوَّلَ بَيْتٍ وُضِعَ لِلنَّاسِ لَلَّذِي بِبَكَّةَ مُبَارَكًا وَهُدًى لِّلْعَالَمِينَ ۞ ﴾

96. Verily, the first House (of worship) appointed for mankind was that at Bakkah (Makkah), full of blessing, and a guidance for Al-'Alamîn (the mankind and jinn).

﴿ فِيهِ ءَايَاتٌ بَيِّنَاتٌ مَّقَامُ إِبْرَاهِيمَ وَمَن دَخَلَهُ كَانَ ءَامِنًا وَلِلَّهِ عَلَى ٱلنَّاسِ حِجُّ ٱلْبَيْتِ مَنِ ٱسْتَطَاعَ إِلَيْهِ سَبِيلًا وَمَن كَفَرَ فَإِنَّ ٱللَّهَ غَنِيٌّ عَنِ ٱلْعَالَمِينَ ۞ ﴾

97. In it are manifest signs (for example), the Maqâm (place) of Ibrâhim (Abraham); whosoever enters it, he attains security. And Hajj (pilgrimage to Makkah) to the House (Ka'bah) is a duty that mankind owes to Allâh, those who can afford the expenses (for one's conveyance, provision and residence); and whoever disbelieves (i.e. denies Hajj (pilgrimage to Makkah), then he is a disbeliever of Allâh), then Allâh stands not in need of any of the 'Alamîn (mankind, jinn and all that exists).

Transliteration

96. Inna awwala baytin wudiAAa lilnnasi lallathee bibakkata mubarakan wahudan lilAAalameena 97. Feehi ayatun bayyinatun maqamu ibraheema waman dakhalahu kana aminan walillahi AAala alnnasi hijju albayti mani istataAAa ilayhi sabeelan waman kafara fa-inna Allaha ghaniyyun AAani alAAalameena

Tafsir Ibn Kathir

The Ka`bah is the First House of Worship

Allah said,

(Verily, the first House appointed for mankind) for all people, for their acts of worship and religious rituals. They go around the House (in Tawaf), pray in its vicinity and remain in its area in I`tikaf.

(was that at Bakkah,) meaning, the Ka`bah that was built by Ibrahim Al-Khalil, whose religion the Jews and Christians claim they follow. However, they do not perform Hajj to the house that Ibrahim built by Allah's command, and to which he invited the people to perform Hajj. Allah said next,

(full of blessing), sanctified,

(and a guidance for Al-`Alamin.)

Imam Ahmad recorded that Abu Dharr said; "I said, `O Allah's Messenger! Which Masjid was the first to be built on the surface of the earth' He said, `Al-Masjid Al-Haram (in Makkah).' I said, `Which was built next' He replied `Al-Masjid Al-Aqsa (in Jerusalem).' I said, `What was the period of time between building the two' He said, `Forty years.' He added,

«ثُمَّ حَيْثُ أَدْرَكْتَ الصَّلَاةَ فَصَلِّ، فَكُلُّهَا مَسْجِدٌ»

(Wherever (you may be, and) the prayer becomes due, perform the prayer there, for the whole earth was made a Masjid.)" Al-Bukhari and Muslim also collected this Hadith.

The Names of Makkah, Such As `Bakkah

Allah said,

(was that at Bakkah), where Bakkah is one of the names of Makkah. Bakkah means, `it brings Buka' (crying, weeping) to the tyrants and arrogant, meaning they cry and become humble in its vicinity. It was also said that Makkah was called Bakkah because people do Buka next to it, meaning they gather around it. There are many names for Makkah, such as Bakkah, Al-Bayt Al-`Atiq (the Ancient House), Al-Bayt Al-Haram (the Sacred House), Al-Balad Al-Amin (the City of Safety) and Al-Ma'mun (Security). Makkah's names include Umm Rahm (Mother of Mercy), Umm Al-Qura (Mother of the Towns), Salah, (as well as others).

The Station of Ibrahim

Allah's statement,

(In it are manifest signs) (3:97), means, clear signs that Ibrahim built the Ka`bah and that Allah has honored and blessed it. Allah then said,

Chapter 3: Al-i-'Imran (The Family of Imran), Verses 093-200

(the Maqam (station) of Ibrahim) When the building (the Ka`bah) was raised, Ibrahim stood on; the Maqam so that he could raise the walls higher, while his son Isma`il was handing the stones to him. We should mention that the Maqam used to be situated right next to the House. Later, and during his reign, `Umar bin Al-Khattab moved the Maqam farther to the east, so that those who go around the House in Tawaf are able to perform it easily, without disturbing those who pray next to the Maqam after finishing their Tawaf. Allah commanded us to pray next to the Maqam;

(And take you (people) the Maqam (station) of Ibrahim as a place of prayer) (2:125).

We mentioned the Hadiths about this subject before, and all the thanks are due to Allah. Al-`Awfi said that, Ibn `Abbas commented on Allah's statement,

(In it are manifest signs, the Maqam of Ibrahim;)

"Such as the Maqam and Al-Mash`ar (Al-Haram)." Mujahid said, "The impression of Ibrahim's feet remains on the Maqam as a clear sign." It was reported that `Umar bin `Abdul-`Aziz, Al-Hasan, Qatadah, As-Suddi, Muqatil bin Hayyan and others said similarly.

Al-Haram, the Sacred Area, is a Safe Area

Allah said,

(whosoever enters it, he attains security,) (3:97) meaning, the Haram of Makkah is a safe refuge for those in a state of fear. There in its vicinity, they will be safe, just as was the case during the time of Jahiliyyah. Al-Hasan Al-Basri said, "(During the time of Jahiliyyah) a man would commit murder, then wear a piece of wool around his neck and enter the Haram. And even when the son of the murdered person would meet him, he would not make a move against him, until he left the sanctuary." Allah said,

(Have they not seen that We have made (Makkah) a secure sanctuary, while men are being snatched away from all around them) (29:67), and,

(So let them worship (Allah) the Lord of this House (the Ka`bah). (He) Who has fed them against hunger, and has made them safe from fear) (106:3-4).

It is not allowed for anyone to hunt in the Haram or to drive game out of its den to be hunted, or cut the trees in its vicinity, or pick its grass, as the Hadiths of the Prophet and the statements of the Companions testify. The Two Sahihs recorded (this being the wording of Muslim) that Ibn `Abbas said, "On the day of the conquest of Makkah, the Messenger of Allah said,

«لَا هِجْرَةَ، وَلكِنْ جِهَادٌ وَنِيَّةٌ، وَإِذَا اسْتُنْفِرْتُمْ فَانْفِرُوا»

(There is no more Hijrah (migration to Makkah), only Jihad and good intention. If you were mobilized, then march forth.)

He also said on the day of the conquest of Makkah,

«إِنَّ هَذَا الْبَلَدَ حَرَّمَهُ اللهُ يَوْمَ خَلَقَ السَّمَوَاتِ وَالْأَرْضَ، فَهُوَ حَرَامٌ بِحُرْمَةِ اللهِ إِلَى يَوْمِ الْقِيَامَةِ، وَإِنَّهُ لَمْ يَحِلَّ الْقِتَالُ فِيهِ لِأَحَدٍ قَبْلِي، وَلَمْ يَحِلَّ لِي إِلَّا فِي سَاعَةٍ مِنْ نَهَارٍ، فَهُوَ حَرَامٌ بِحُرْمَةِ اللهِ إِلَى يَوْمِ الْقِيَامَةِ، لَا يُعْضَدُ شَوْكُهُ، وَلَا يُنَفَّرُ صَيْدُهُ، وَلَا يَلْتَقِطُ لُقَطَتَهَا إِلَّا مَنْ عَرَّفَهَا، وَلَا يُخْتَلَى خَلَاهَا»

(Beware! Allah made this town (Makkah) a sanctuary when He created the heavens and earth, and it is sacred by Allah's decree until the Day of Resurrection. Fighting in Makkah was not permitted for anyone before me, and it was made legal for me for only a few hours or so on that day. No doubt it is at this moment a sanctuary by Allah's decree until the Day of Resurrection. It is not allowed to uproot its thorny shrubs, hunt its game, pick up its lost objects, except by announcing it, or to uproot its trees.)

Al-`Abbas said, `Except the lemon grass, O Allah's Messenger, as they use it in their houses and graves.' The Prophet said:

«إِلَّا الْإِذْخِرَ»

(Except lemongrass)."

The Two Sahihs also recorded that Abu Shurayh Al-`Adawi said that he said to `Amr bin Sa`id while he was sending the troops to Makkah (to fight `Abdullah bin Az-Zubayr), "O Commander! Allow me to tell you what Allah's Messenger said on the day following the conquest of Makkah. My ears heard it and my heart memorized it thoroughly, and I saw the Prophet with my own eyes when he, after glorifying and praising Allah, said,

«إِنَّ مَكَّةَ حَرَّمَهَا اللهُ، وَلَمْ يُحَرِّمْهَا النَّاسُ، فَلَا يَحِلُّ لِامْرِئٍ يُؤْمِنُ بِاللهِ وَالْيَوْمِ الْآخِرِ أَنْ يَسْفِكَ بِهَا دَمًا، وَلَا يَعْضِدَ بِهَا شَجَرَةً، فَإِنْ أَحَدٌ تَرَخَّصَ بِقِتَالِ رَسُولِ اللهِ صلى الله عليه وسلم فِيهَا فَقُولُوا لَهُ: إِنَّ اللهَ أَذِنَ لِرَسُولِهِ وَلَمْ يَأْذَنْ لَكُمْ، وَإِنَّمَا أَذِنَ لِي فِيهَا سَاعَةً مِنْ نَهَارٍ، وَقَدْ عَادَتْ حُرْمَتُهَا الْيَوْمَ كَحُرْمَتِهَا بِالْأَمْسِ فَلْيُبَلِّغِ الشَّاهِدُ الْغَائِبَ»

(Allah, not the people, made Makkah a sanctuary. Therefore, anybody who has belief in Allah and the Last Day, should neither shed blood in it nor cut down its trees. If anybody argues that fighting in it is permissible on the basis that Allah's Messenger fought in Makkah, say to him, `Allah allowed His Messenger and did not allow you.' Allah allowed me only for a few hours on that day (of the conquest), and today its sanctity is as valid as it was before. So, those who are present, should inform those who are absent of this fact.).''

Abu Shurayh was asked, "What did `Amr reply'' He said that `Amr said, "O Abu Shurayh! I know better than you in this respect; Makkah does not give protection to a sinner, a murderer or a thief.''

Jabir bin `Abdullah said, "I heard the Messenger of Allah saying,

«لَا يَحِلُّ لِأَحَدِكُمْ أَنْ يَحْمِلَ بِمَكَّةَ السِّلَاحَ»

(None of you is allowed to carry a weapon in Makkah.) Muslim recorded this Hadith.

`Abdullah bin `Adi bin Al-Hamra' Az-Zuhri said that he heard the Messenger of Allah say while standing at Al-Hazwarah in the marketplace of Makkah,

«وَاللهِ إِنَّكِ لَخَيْرُ أَرْضِ اللهِ، وَأَحَبُّ أَرْضِ اللهِ إِلَى اللهِ، وَلَوْلَا أَنِّي أُخْرِجْتُ مِنْكِ مَا خَرَجْتُ»

(By Allah! You are the best of Allah's land and the most beloved land to Allah. Had it not been for the fact that I was driven out of you, I would not have left you.)

Imam Ahmad collected this Hadith and this is his wording. At-Tirmidhi, An-Nasa'i and Ibn Majah also collected it. At-Tirmidhi said, "Hasan Sahih.''

The Necessity of Performing Hajj

Allah said,

(And Hajj to the House is a duty that mankind owes to Allah, for those who are able to undertake the journey) (3:97).

This Ayah established the obligation of performing Hajj. There are many Hadiths that mention it as one of the pillars and fundamentals of Islam, and this is agreed upon by the Muslims. According to texts and the consensus of the scholars, it is only obligatory for the adult Muslim to perform it once during his lifetime. Imam Ahmad recorded that Abu Hurayrah said that the Messenger of Allah once gave a speech in which he said,

«أَيُّهَا النَّاسُ قَدْ فُرِضَ عَلَيْكُمُ الْحَجُّ فَحُجُّوا»

(O people! Hajj has been enjoined on you, therefore, perform Hajj.)

A man asked, "Is it every year, O Allah's Messenger" The Prophet remained silent until the man repeated the question three times and he then said,

«لَوْ قُلْتُ: نَعَمْ لَوَجَبَتْ وَلَمَا اسْتَطَعْتُمْ»

(Had I said yes, it would have become an obligation and you would not have been able to fulfill it.) He said next,

«ذَرُونِي مَا تَرَكْتُكُمْ فَإِنَّمَا هَلَكَ مَنْ كَانَ قَبْلَكُمْ بِكَثْرَةِ سُؤَالِهِمْ وَاخْتِلَافِهِمْ عَلَى أَنْبِيَائِهِمْ، وَإِذَا أَمَرْتُكُمْ بِشَيْءٍ فَأْتُوا مِنْهُ مَا اسْتَطَعْتُمْ، وَإِذَا نَهَيْتُكُمْ عَنْ شَيْءٍ فَدَعُوهُ»

(Leave me as I leave you, those before you were destroyed because of their many questions and disputing with their Prophets. If I command you with something, perform it as much as you can. If I forbid something for you, then refrain from it.) Muslim recorded similarly.

Meaning of `Afford' in the Ayah

There are several categories of "the ability to under take the journey". There is the physical ability of the person himself and the ability that is related to other things as mentioned in the books of jurisprudence. Abu `Isa At-Tirmidhi recorded that Ibn `Umar said, "A man stood up and asked the Messenger of Allah , `O Messenger of Allah! Who is the pilgrim' He said, `He who has untidy hair and clothes.' Another man asked, `Which Hajj is better, O Messenger of Allah' He said, `The noisy (with supplication to Allah) and bloody (with sacrifice).' Another man asked, `What is the ability to undertake the journey, O Messenger of Allah' He said, `Having provision and a means of transportation.'" This is the narration that Ibn Majah collected. Al-Hakim narrated that Anas said that the Messenger of Allah was asked about Allah's statement,

(for those who are able to undertake the journey;) (3:97) "What does `able to undertake the journey' mean" The Prophet answered, "Having sufficient provision and a means of transportation." Al-Hakim stated that this Hadith's chain of narration is authentic, following the guidelines of Muslim in his Sahih, but the Two Sahihs did not collect it. Ahmad recorded that Ibn `Abbas said that the Messenger of Allah said,

«مَنْ أَرَادَ الْحَجَّ فَلْيَتَعَجَّلْ»

(Whoever intends to perform Hajj, let him rush to perform it.) Abu Dawud also collected this Hadith.

The One who Denies the Necessity of Hajj Becomes a Disbeliever

Allah said,

(...and whoever disbelieves, then Allah stands not in need of any of the `Alamin) (3:97).

Ibn `Abbas, Mujahid and several others commented on this Ayah, "Whoever denies the necessity of Hajj becomes disbeliever, and Allah is far Richer than to need him." Al-Hafiz Abu Bakr Al-Isma`ili recorded that `Umar bin Al-Khattab said, "Whoever can afford Hajj but did not perform it, there is no difference in his case if he dies while Jew or Christian." This has an authentic chain of narration leading to `Umar.

Surah: 3 Ayah: 98 & Ayah: 99

﴿ قُلْ يَا أَهْلَ الْكِتَابِ لِمَ تَكْفُرُونَ بِآيَاتِ اللَّهِ وَاللَّهُ شَهِيدٌ عَلَى مَا تَعْمَلُونَ ۝ ﴾

98. Say: "O people of the Scripture (Jews and Christians)! Why do you reject the Ayât of Allâh (proofs, evidences, verses, lessons, signs, revelations, etc.) while Allâh is Witness to what you do?"

﴿ قُلْ يَا أَهْلَ الْكِتَابِ لِمَ تَصُدُّونَ عَن سَبِيلِ اللَّهِ مَنْ ءَامَنَ تَبْغُونَهَا عِوَجًا وَأَنتُمْ شُهَدَاءُ وَمَا اللَّهُ بِغَافِلٍ عَمَّا تَعْمَلُونَ ۝ ﴾

99. Say: "O people of the Scripture (Jews and Christians)! Why do you stop those who have believed, from the Path of Allâh, seeking to make it seem crooked, while you (yourselves) are witnesses (to Muhammad (peace be upon him) as a Messenger of Allâh and Islâm (Allâh's Religion, i.e. to worship none but Him Alone)) And Allâh is not unaware of what you do."

Transliteration

98. Qul ya ahla alkitabi lima takfuroona bi-ayati Allahi waAllahu shaheedun AAala ma taAAmaloona 99. Qul ya ahla alkitabi lima tasuddoona AAan sabeeli Allahi man amana tabghoonaha AAiwajan waantum shuhadao wama Allahu bighafilin AAamma taAAmaloona

Tafsir Ibn Kathir

Chastising the People of the Book for Their Disbelief and Blocking the Path of Allah

In this Ayah Allah criticizes the disbelieving People of the Book for refusing the truth, rejecting Allah's Ayat and hindering those who seek to believe from His path, although they know that what the Messenger was sent with is the truth from Allah. They learned this from the previous Prophets and honorable Messengers, may Allah's peace and blessings be on them all. They all brought the glad tidings and the good news of the coming of the unlettered, Arab, Hashimi Prophet from Makkah, the master of the Children of Adam, the Final Prophet and the Messenger of the Lord of heavens and earth. Allah has warned the People of the Book against this behavior, stating that He is Witness over what they do, indicating their defiance of the knowledge conveyed to them by the Prophets. They rejected, denied and refused the very Messenger whom they were ordered to convey the glad tidings about his coming. Allah states that He is never unaware of what they do, and He will hold them responsible for their actions,

(The Day whereon neither wealth nor sons will avail) (26:88).

Surah: 3 Ayah: 100 & Ayah: 101

﴿ يَٰٓأَيُّهَا ٱلَّذِينَ ءَامَنُوٓا۟ إِن تُطِيعُوا۟ فَرِيقًا مِّنَ ٱلَّذِينَ أُوتُوا۟ ٱلْكِتَٰبَ يَرُدُّوكُم بَعْدَ إِيمَٰنِكُمْ كَٰفِرِينَ ﴾

100. O you who believe! If you obey a group of those who were given the Scripture (Jews and Christians), they would (indeed) render you disbelievers after you have believed!

﴿ وَكَيْفَ تَكْفُرُونَ وَأَنتُمْ تُتْلَىٰ عَلَيْكُمْ ءَايَٰتُ ٱللَّهِ وَفِيكُمْ رَسُولُهُۥ ۗ وَمَن يَعْتَصِم بِٱللَّهِ فَقَدْ هُدِىَ إِلَىٰ صِرَٰطٍ مُّسْتَقِيمٍ ﴾

101. And how would you disbelieve, while unto you are recited the Verses of Allâh, and among you is His Messenger (Muhammad (peace be upon him)) And whoever holds firmly to Allâh, (i.e. follows Islâm - Allâh's Religion, and obeys all that Allâh has ordered, practically), then he is indeed guided to the Right Path.

Transliteration

100. Ya ayyuha allatheena amanoo in tuteeAAoo fareeqan mina allatheena ootoo alkitabu yaruddookum baAAda eemanikum kafireena 101. Wakayfa takfuroona waantum tutla AAalaykum ayatu Allahi wafeekum rasooluhu waman yaAAtasim biAllahi faqad hudiya ila siratin mustaqeemin

Tafsir Ibn Kathir

Warning Muslims Against Imitating People of the Scriptures

Allah warns His believing servants against obeying the People of the Book, who envy the believers for the favor that Allah gave them by sending His Messenger . Similarly, Allah said,

(Many of the People of the Scripture (Jews and Christians) wish that they could turn you away as disbelievers after you have believed, out of their own envy) (2:109).

In this Ayah (3:100), Allah said,

(If you obey a group of those who were given the Scripture (Jews and Christians), they would (indeed) render you disbelievers after you have believed!), then said,

(And how would you disbelieve, while unto you are recited the verses of Allah, and among you is His Messenger), meaning, disbelief is far from touching you, since the Ayat of Allah are being sent down on His Messenger day and night, and he recites and conveys them to you. Similarly, Allah said,

(And what is the matter with you that you believe not in Allah! While the Messenger invites you to believe in your Lord; and He has indeed taken your covenant, if you are real believers) (57:8). A Hadith states that one day, the Prophet said to his Companions,

«أَيُّ الْمُؤْمِنِينَ أَعْجَبُ إِلَيْكُمْ إِيمَانًا؟»

("Who among the faithful believers do you consider has the most amazing faith" They said, "The angels." He said,

«وَكَيْفَ لَا يُؤْمِنُونَ وَهُمْ عِنْدَ رَبِّهِم»

"Why would they not believe, since they are with their Lord" They mentioned the Prophets, and the Prophet said,

«وَكَيْفَ لَا يُؤْمِنُونَ وَالْوَحْيُ يَنْزِلُ عَلَيْهِمْ؟»

"Why would they not believe while the revelation is sent down to them" They said, "Then, we are." He said,

«وَكَيْفَ لَا تُؤْمِنُونَ وَأَنَا بَيْنَ أَظْهُرِكُمْ؟»

"Why would not you believe when I am among you" They asked, "Who has the most amazing faith" The Prophet said,

«قَوْمٌ يَجِيئُونَ مِنْ بَعْدِكُمْ يَجِدُونَ صُحُفًا يُؤْمِنُونَ بِمَا فِيهَا»

"A people who will come after you and who will find only books that they will believe in.")

Allah said next,

(And whoever depends upon Allah, then he is indeed guided to the right path) (3:101) for trusting and relying on Allah are the basis of achieving the right guidance and staying away from the path of wickedness. They also represent the tool to acquiring guidance and truth and achieving the righteous aims.

Surah: 3 Ayah: 102 & Ayah: 103

﴿ يَٰٓأَيُّهَا ٱلَّذِينَ ءَامَنُوا۟ ٱتَّقُوا۟ ٱللَّهَ حَقَّ تُقَاتِهِۦ وَلَا تَمُوتُنَّ إِلَّا وَأَنتُم مُّسْلِمُونَ ۝ ﴾

102. O you who believe! Fear Allâh (by doing all that He has ordered and by abstaining from all that He has forbidden) as He should be feared. (Obey Him, be thankful to Him, and remember Him always), and die not except in a state of Islâm (as Muslims (with complete submission to Allâh)).

﴿ وَٱعْتَصِمُوا۟ بِحَبْلِ ٱللَّهِ جَمِيعًا وَلَا تَفَرَّقُوا۟ وَٱذْكُرُوا۟ نِعْمَتَ ٱللَّهِ عَلَيْكُمْ إِذْ كُنتُمْ أَعْدَآءً فَأَلَّفَ بَيْنَ قُلُوبِكُمْ فَأَصْبَحْتُم بِنِعْمَتِهِۦٓ إِخْوَٰنًا وَكُنتُمْ عَلَىٰ شَفَا حُفْرَةٍ مِّنَ ٱلنَّارِ فَأَنقَذَكُم مِّنْهَا كَذَٰلِكَ يُبَيِّنُ ٱللَّهُ لَكُمْ ءَايَٰتِهِۦ لَعَلَّكُمْ تَهْتَدُونَ ۝ ﴾

103. And hold fast, all of you together, to the Rope of Allâh (i.e. this Qur'ân), and be not divided among yourselves, and remember Allâh's Favor on you, for you were enemies one to another but He joined your hearts together, so that, by His Grace, you became brethren (in Islâmic Faith), and you were on the brink of a pit of Fire, and He saved you from it. Thus Allâh makes His Ayât (proofs, evidences, verses, lessons, signs, revelations, etc.,) clear to you, that you may be guided.

Transliteration

102. Ya ayyuha allatheena amanoo ittaqoo Allaha haqqa tuqatihi wala tamootunna illa waantum muslimoona 103. WaiAAtasimoo bihabli Allahi jameeAAan wala tafarraqoo waothkuroo niAAmata Allahi AAalaykum ith kuntum aAAdaan faallafa bayna quloobikum faasbahtum biniAAmatihi ikhwanan wakuntum AAala shafa hufratin mina alnnari faanqathakum minha kathalika yubayyinu Allahu lakum ayatihi laAAallakum tahtadoona

Tafsir Ibn Kathir

Meaning of Taqwa of Allah

Ibn Abi Hatim recorded that `Abdullah bin Mas`ud commented on the Ayah,

(Have Taqwa of Allah as is His due,)

"That He is obeyed and not defied, remembered and not forgotten and appreciated and not unappreciated." This has an authentic chain of narration to `Abdullah bin Mas`ud. Al-Hakim collected this Hadith in his Mustadrak, from Ibn Mas`ud, who related it to the Prophet . Al-Hakim said, "It is authentic according to the criteria of the Two Shaykhs (Al-Bukhari and Muslim), and they did not record it." This is what he said, but it appears that it is only a statement of `Abdullah bin Mas`ud, and Allah knows best. It was also reported that Anas said, "The servant will not have Taqwa of Allah as is His due until he keeps his tongue idle." Allah's statement, (and die not except as (true) Muslims) (3:102), means, preserve your Islam while you are well and safe, so that you die as a Muslim. The Most Generous Allah has made it His decision that whatever state one lives in, that is what he dies upon and is resurrected upon. We seek refuge from dying on other than Islam.

Imam Ahmad recorded that Mujahid said, "The people were circling around the Sacred House when Ibn `Abbas was sitting, holding a bent-handled walking stick. Ibn `Abbas said, The Messenger of Allah (recited),

(Have Taqwa of Allah as is His due, die not except as (true) Muslims.) (3:102), (then he said;)

«وَلَوْ أَنَّ قَطْرَةً مِنَ الزَّقُّومِ قُطِرَتْ لَأَمَرَّتْ عَلَى أَهْلِ الْأَرْضِ عِيشَتَهُمْ، فَكَيْفَ بِمَنْ لَيْسَ لَهُ طَعَامٌ إِلَّا الزَّقُّومُ؟»

(Verily, if a drop of Zaqqum (a tree in Hell) falls, it will spoil life for the people of earth. What about those whose food is only from Zaqqum)"

This was recorded by At-Tirmidhi, An-Nasa'i, Ibn Majah, Ibn Hibban in his Sahih and Al-Hakim his Mustadrak. At-Tirmidhi said, "Hasan Sahih"' while Al-Hakim said; "It meets the conditions of the Two Sahihs and they did not record it."

Imam Ahmad recorded that Jabir said that three nights before the Messenger of Allah died he heard him saying;

«لَا يَمُوتَنَّ أَحَدُكُمْ إِلَّا وَهُوَ يُحْسِنُ الظَّنَّ بِاللهِ عَزَّ وَجَل»

(None of you should die except while having sincere trust in Allah, the Exalted and Most Honorable.) Muslim also recorded it. The Two Sahihs record that Abu Hurayrah said that the Messenger of Allah said,

«يَقُولُ اللهُ: أَنَا عِنْدَ ظَنِّ عَبْدِي بِي»

(Allah said, "I am as My servant thinks of Me.")

The Necessity of Holding to the Path of Allah and the Community of the Believers

Allah said next,

(And hold fast, all of you together, to the Rope of Allah, and be not divided among yourselves.) It was said that, (to the Rope of Allah) refers to Allah's covenant, just as Allah said in the following Ayah,

(Indignity is put over them wherever they may be, except when under a covenant (of protection) from Allah, and from men;) (3:112), in reference to pledges and peace treaties.

Allah's statement

(and be not divided among yourselves), orders sticking to the community of the believers and forbids division. There are several Hadiths that require adhering to the Jama`ah (congregation of believers) and prohibit division. Muslim recorded that Abu Hurayrah said that the Messenger of Allah said,

«إِنَّ اللهَ يَرْضَى لَكُمْ ثَلَاثًا، وَيَسْخَطُ لَكُمْ ثَلَاثًا: يَرْضَى لَكُمْ أَنْ تَعْبُدُوهُ وَلَا تُشْرِكُوا بِهِ شَيْئًا، وَأَنْ تَعْتَصِمُوا بِحَبْلِ اللهِ جَمِيعًا وَلَا تَفَرَّقُوا، وَأَنْ تَنَاصَحُوا مَنْ وَلَّاهُ اللهُ أَمْرَكُمْ. وَيَسْخَطُ لَكُمْ ثَلَاثًا: قِيلَ وَقَالَ، وَكَثْرَةَ السُّؤَالِ، وَإِضَاعَةَ الْمَالِ»

(It pleases Allah for you to acquire three qualities and displeases Him that you acquire three characteristics. It pleases Him that you worship Him Alone and not associate anything or anyone with Him in worship, that you hold on to the Rope of Allah altogether and do not divide, and that you advise whoever Allah appoints as your Leader. The three that displease Him are that you say, `It was said,' and, `So-and-so said,' asking many unnecessary questions and wasting money.)

Allah said,

(and remember Allah's favor on you, for you were enemies one to another but He joined your hearts together, so that, by His grace, you became brethren) (3:103).

This was revealed about the Aws and Khazraj. During the time of Jahiliyyah, the Aws and Khazraj were at war and had great hatred, enmity and ill feelings towards each other, causing long conflicts and battles to occur between them. When Allah brought Islam, those among them who embraced it became brothers who loved each other by Allah's grace, having good ties for Allah's sake and helping each other in righteousness and piety. Allah said,

(He it is Who has supported you with His Help and with the believers. And He has united their hearts. If you had spent all that is in the earth, you could not have united their hearts, but Allah has united them)(8:62,63), until the end of the Ayah. Before Islam, their disbelief had them standing at the edge of a pit of the Fire, but Allah saved them from it and delivered them to faith. The Messenger of Allah reminded the Ansar (from both Aws and Khazraj) of this bounty when he was dividing the war booty of Hunayn. During that time, some Ansar did not like the way the booty was divided, since they did not get what the others did, although that was what Allah directed His Prophet to do. The Messenger of Allah gave them a speech, in which he said,

«يَا مَعْشَرَ الْأَنْصَارِ أَلَمْ أَجِدْكُمْ ضُلَّالًا فَهَدَاكُمُ اللهُ بِي، وَكُنْتُمْ مُتَفَرِّقِينَ فَأَلَّفَكُمُ اللهُ بِي، وَعَالَةً فَأَغْنَاكُمُ اللهُ بِي؟»

(O Ansar! Did I not find you misguided and Allah directed you to guidance because of me Were you not divided beforehand and Allah united you around me Were you not poor and Allah enriched you because of me)

Whenever the Prophet asked them a question, they would answer, "Indeed, Allah and His Messenger have granted us bounty."

Surah: 3 Ayah: 104, Ayah: 105, Ayah: 106, Ayah: 107, Ayah: 108 & Ayah: 109

﴿ وَلْتَكُن مِّنكُمْ أُمَّةٌ يَدْعُونَ إِلَى ٱلْخَيْرِ وَيَأْمُرُونَ بِٱلْمَعْرُوفِ وَيَنْهَوْنَ عَنِ ٱلْمُنكَرِ ۚ وَأُوْلَٰٓئِكَ هُمُ ٱلْمُفْلِحُونَ ﴾

104. Let there arise out of you a group of people inviting to all that is good (Islâm), enjoining Al-Ma'rûf (i.e. Islâmic Monotheism and all that Islâm orders one to do) and forbidding Al-Munkar (polytheism and disbelief and all that Islâm has forbidden). And it is they who are the successful.

﴿ وَلَا تَكُونُوا۟ كَٱلَّذِينَ تَفَرَّقُوا۟ وَٱخْتَلَفُوا۟ مِنۢ بَعْدِ مَا جَآءَهُمُ ٱلْبَيِّنَٰتُ ۚ وَأُوْلَٰٓئِكَ لَهُمْ عَذَابٌ عَظِيمٌ ﴾

105. And be not as those who divided and differed among themselves after the clear proofs had come to them. It is they for whom there is an awful torment.

﴿ يَوْمَ تَبْيَضُّ وُجُوهٌ وَتَسْوَدُّ وُجُوهٌ ۚ فَأَمَّا ٱلَّذِينَ ٱسْوَدَّتْ وُجُوهُهُمْ أَكَفَرْتُم بَعْدَ إِيمَٰنِكُمْ فَذُوقُوا۟ ٱلْعَذَابَ بِمَا كُنتُمْ تَكْفُرُونَ ﴾

106. On the Day (i.e. the Day of Resurrection) when some faces will become white and some faces will become black; as for those whose faces will become black (to them will be said): "Did you reject Faith after accepting it? Then taste the torment (in Hell) for rejecting Faith."

﴿ وَأَمَّا ٱلَّذِينَ ٱبْيَضَّتْ وُجُوهُهُمْ فَفِى رَحْمَةِ ٱللَّهِ هُمْ فِيهَا خَٰلِدُونَ ﴾

107. And for those whose faces will become white, they will be in Allâh's Mercy (Paradise), therein they shall dwell forever.

﴿ تِلْكَ ءَايَـتُ ٱللَّهِ نَتْلُوهَا عَلَيْكَ بِٱلْحَقِّ وَمَا ٱللَّهُ يُرِيدُ ظُلْماً لِّلْعَـلَمِينَ ۝ ﴾

108. These are the Verses of Allâh: We recite them to you (O Muhammad (peace be upon him)) in truth, and Allâh wills no injustice to the 'Alâmîn (mankind, jinn and all that exists).

﴿ وَلِلَّهِ مَا فِى ٱلسَّمَـوَتِ وَمَا فِى ٱلْأَرْضِ وَإِلَى ٱللَّهِ تُرْجَعُ ٱلْأُمُورُ ۝ ﴾

109. And to Allâh belongs all that is in the heavens and all that is in the earth. And all matters go back (for decision) to Allâh.

Transliteration

104. Waltakun minkum ommatun yadAAoona ila alkhayri waya/muroona bialmaAAroofi wayanhawna AAani almunkari waola-ika humu almuflihoona 105. Wala takoonoo kaallatheena tafarraqoo waikhtalafoo min baAAdi ma jaahumu albayyinatu waolaika lahum AAathabun AAatheemun 106. Yawma tabyaddu wujoohun wataswaddu wujoohun faamma allatheena iswaddat wujoohuhum akafartum baAAda eemanikum fathooqoo alAAathaba bima kuntum takfuroona 107. Waamma allatheena ibyaddat wujoohuhum fafee rahmati Allahi hum feeha khalidoona 108. Tilka ayatu Allahi natlooha AAalayka bialhaqqi wama Allahu yureedu thulman lilAAalameena 109. Walillahi ma fee alssamawati wama fee al-ardi wa-ila Allahi turjaAAu al-omooru

Tafsir Ibn Kathir

The Command to Establish the Invitation to Allah

Allah said,

(Let there arise out of you a group of people)

that calls to righteousness, enjoins all that is good and forbids evil in the manner Allah commanded,

(And it is they who are the successful.)

Ad-Dahhak said, "They are a special group of the Companions and a special group of those after them, that is those who perform Jihad and the scholars."

The objective of this Ayah is that there should be a segment of this Muslim Ummah fulfilling this task, even though it is also an obligation on every member of this Ummah, each according to his ability. Muslim recorded that Abu Hurayrah said that the Messenger of Allah said,

«مَنْ رَأَى مِنْكُمْ مُنْكَرًا فَلْيُغَيِّرْهُ بِيَدِهِ، فَإِنْ لَمْ يَسْتَطِعْ فَبِلِسَانِهِ، فَإِنْ لَمْ يَسْتَطِعْ فَبِقَلْبِهِ، وَذَلِكَ أَضْعَفُ الْإِيمَانِ»

(Whoever among you witnesses an evil, let him change it with his hand. If he is unable, then let him change it with his tongue. If he is unable, then let him change it with his heart, and this is the weakest faith.) In another narration, The Prophet said,

«وَلَيْسَ وَرَاءَ ذَلِكَ مِنَ الْإِيمَانِ حَبَّةُ خَرْدَلٍ»

(There is no faith beyond that, not even the weight of a mustard seed.)

Imam Ahmad recorded that Hudhayfah bin Al-Yaman said that the Prophet said,

«وَالَّذِي نَفْسِي بِيَدِهِ، لَتَأْمُرُنَّ بِالْمَعْرُوفِ، وَلَتَنْهَوُنَّ عَنِ الْمُنْكَرِ، أَوْ لَيُوشِكَنَّ اللهُ أَنْ يَبْعَثَ عَلَيْكُمْ عِقَابًا مِنْ عِنْدِهِ، ثُمَّ لَتَدْعُنَّهُ فَلَا يَسْتَجِيبُ لَكُمْ»

(By He in Whose Hand is my soul! You will enjoin righteousness and forbid evil, or Allah shall send down a punishment from Him to you. Then, you will supplicate to Him, but He will not accept your supplication.)

At-Tirmidhi also collected this Hadith and said, "Hasan". There are many other Hadiths and Ayat on this subject, which will be explained later.

The Prohibition of Division

Allah said,

(And be not as those who divided and differed among themselves after the clear proofs had come to them) (3:105).

In this Ayah, Allah forbids this Ummah from imitating the division and discord of the nations that came before them. These nations also abandoned enjoining righteousness and forbidding evil, although they had proof of its necessity.

Imam Ahmad recorded that Abu `Amir `Abdullah bin Luhay said, "We performed Hajj with Mu`awiyah bin Abi Sufyan. When we arrived at Makkah, he stood up after praying Zuhr and said, `The Messenger of Allah said,

«إِنَّ أَهْلَ الْكِتَابَيْنِ افْتَرَقُوا فِي دِينِهِمْ عَلَى ثِنْتَيْنِ وَسَبْعِينَ مِلَّةً، وَإِنَّ هَذِهِ الْأُمَّةَ سَتَفْتَرِقُ عَلَى ثَلَاثٍ وَسَبْعِينَ مِلَّةً يَعْنِي الْأَهْوَاءَ كُلُّهَا فِي النَّارِ إِلَّا وَاحِدَةً وَهِيَ

الْجَمَاعَةُ وَإِنَّهُ سَيَخْرُجُ فِي أُمَّتِي أَقْوَامٌ تَجَارَى بِهِمْ تِلْكَ الْأَهْوَاءُ كَمَا يَتَجَارَى الْكَلَبُ بِصَاحِبِهِ، لَا يَبْقَى مِنْهُ عِرْقٌ وَلَا مَفْصِلٌ إِلَّا دَخَلَهُ»

(The People of the Two Scriptures divided into seventy-two sects. This Ummah will divide into seventy-three sects, all in the Fire except one, that is, the Jama`ah. Some of my Ummah will be guided by desire, like one who is infected by rabies; no vein or joint will be saved from these desires.)

(Mu`awiyah said next:) By Allah, O Arabs! If you do not adhere to what came to you from your Prophet then other people are even more prone not to adhere to it." Similar was recorded by Abu Dawud from Ahmad bin Hanbal and Muhammad bin Yahya.

The Benefits of Brotherly Ties and Unity and the Consequence of Division on the Day of the Gathering

Allah said next,

(On the Day when some faces will become white and some faces will become black;) (3:106) on the Day of Resurrection. This is when the faces of followers of the Sunnah and the Jama`ah will radiate with whiteness, and the faces of followers of Bid`ah (innovation) and division will be darkened, as has been reported from Ibn `Abbas. Allah said,

(As for those whose faces will become black (to them will be said): "Did you reject faith after accepting it")

Al-Hasan Al-Basri said, "They are the hypocrites."

(Then taste the torment (in Hell) for rejecting faith,) and this description befits every disbeliever.

(And for those whose faces will become white, they will be in Allah's mercy (Paradise), therein they shall dwell forever.) in Paradise, where they will reside for eternity and shall never desire to be removed. Abu `Isa At-Tirmidhi recorded that Abu Ghalib said, "Abu Umamah saw heads (of the Khawarij sect) hanging on the streets of Damascus. He commented, `The Dogs of the Fire and the worst dead people under the cover of the sky. The best dead men are those whom these have killed.' He then recited,

(On the Day (i.e. the Day of Resurrection) when some faces will become white and some faces will become black;) until the end of the Ayah. I said to Abu Umamah, `Did you hear this from the Messenger of Allah' He said, `If I only heard it from the Messenger of Allah once, twice, thrice, four times, or seven times, I would not have narrated it to you.' " At-Tirmidhi said, "This Hadith is Hasan." Ibn Majah and Ahmad recorded similarly.

Allah said,

(These are the Ayat of Allah. We recite them to you) meaning, `These are the verses of Allah, His proofs and signs that We reveal to you, O Muhammad,'

(in truth) making known the true reality of this world and the Hereafter.

(and Allah wills no injustice to the `Alamin.) for He never treats them with injustice. Rather, He is the Just Ruler Who is able to do everything and has knowledge of everything. Therefore, He does not need to treat any of His creatures with injustice, and this is why He said next,

(and to Allah belongs all that is in the heavens and all that is in the Earth.),

they are all His servants and His property,

(And all matters go back to Allah,) for His is the decision concerning the affairs of this life and the Hereafter, and His is the Supreme Authority in this life and the Hereafter.

Surah: 3 Ayah: 110, Ayah: 111 & Ayah: 112

﴿ كُنتُمْ خَيْرَ أُمَّةٍ أُخْرِجَتْ لِلنَّاسِ تَأْمُرُونَ بِٱلْمَعْرُوفِ وَتَنْهَوْنَ عَنِ ٱلْمُنكَرِ وَتُؤْمِنُونَ بِٱللَّهِ ۗ وَلَوْ ءَامَنَ أَهْلُ ٱلْكِتَٰبِ لَكَانَ خَيْرًا لَّهُم ۚ مِّنْهُمُ ٱلْمُؤْمِنُونَ وَأَكْثَرُهُمُ ٱلْفَٰسِقُونَ ﴾

110. You (true believers in Islâmic Monotheism, and real followers of Prophet Muhammad (peace be upon him) and his Sunnah) are the best of peoples ever raised up for mankind; you enjoin Al-Ma'rûf (i.e. Islâmic Monotheism and all that Islâm has ordained) and forbid Al-Munkar (polytheism, disbelief and all that Islâm has forbidden), and you believe in Allâh. And had the people of the Scripture (Jews and Christians) believed, it would have been better for them; among them are some who have faith, but most of them are Al-Fâsiqûn (disobedient to Allâh - and rebellious against Allâh's Command).

﴿ لَن يَضُرُّوكُمْ إِلَّآ أَذًى ۖ وَإِن يُقَٰتِلُوكُمْ يُوَلُّوكُمُ ٱلْأَدْبَارَ ثُمَّ لَا يُنصَرُونَ ﴾

111. They will do you no harm, barring a trifling annoyance; and if they fight against you, they will show you their backs, and they will not be helped.

﴿ ضُرِبَتْ عَلَيْهِمُ ٱلذِّلَّةُ أَيْنَ مَا ثُقِفُوٓاْ إِلَّا بِحَبْلٍ مِّنَ ٱللَّهِ وَحَبْلٍ مِّنَ ٱلنَّاسِ وَبَآءُو بِغَضَبٍ مِّنَ ٱللَّهِ وَضُرِبَتْ عَلَيْهِمُ ٱلْمَسْكَنَةُ ۚ ذَٰلِكَ بِأَنَّهُمْ كَانُواْ يَكْفُرُونَ بِـَٔايَٰتِ ٱللَّهِ وَيَقْتُلُونَ ٱلْأَنۢبِيَآءَ بِغَيْرِ حَقٍّ ۚ ذَٰلِكَ بِمَا عَصَواْ وَّكَانُواْ يَعْتَدُونَ ﴾

112. Indignity is put over them wherever they may be, except when under a covenant (of protection) from Allâh, and from men; they have drawn on themselves the Wrath of Allâh, and destruction is put over them. This is because they disbelieved in the Ayât (proofs, evidences, verses, lessons, signs, revelations, etc.) of Allâh and killed the Prophets without right. This is because they disobeyed (Allâh) and used to transgress beyond bounds (in Allâh's disobedience, crimes and sins).

Transliteration

110. Kuntum khayra ommatin okhrijat lilnnasi ta/muroona bialmaAAroofi watanhawna AAani almunkari watu/minoona biAllahi walaw amana ahlu alkitabi lakana khayran lahum minhumu almu/minoona waaktharuhumu alfasiqoona   111. Lan yadurrookum illa athan wa-in yuqatilookum yuwallookumu al-adbara thumma la yunsaroona   112. Duribat AAalayhimu alththillatu ayna ma thuqifoo illa bihablin mina Allahi wahablin mina alnnasi wabaoo bighadabin mina Allahi waduribat AAalayhimu almaskanatu thalika bi-annahum kanoo yakfuroona bi-ayati Allahi wayaqtuloona al-anbiyaa bighayri haqqin thalika bima AAasaw wakanoo yaAAtadoona

Tafsir Ibn Kathir

Virtues of the Ummah of Muhammad (peace and blessings of Allah be upon him) - the Best Nation Ever

Allah states that the Ummah of Muhammad is the best nation ever,

(You are the best of peoples ever raised up for mankind) (3:110).

Al-Bukhari recorded that Abu Hurayrah commented on this Ayah, "(You, Muslims, are) the best nation of people for the people, you bring them tied in chains on their necks (capture them in war) and they later embrace Islam." Similar was said by Ibn `Abbas, Mujahid, `Atiyah Al-`Awfi, `Ikrimah, `Ata' and Ar-Rabi` bin Anas that,

(You are the best of peoples ever raised up for mankind;) means, the best of peoples for the people.

The meaning of the Ayah is that the Ummah of Muhammad is the most righteous and beneficial nation for mankind. Hence Allah's description of them,

(you enjoin Al-Ma`ruf and forbid Al-Munkar and believe in Allah) (3:110).

Ahmad, At-Tirmidhi, Ibn Majah, and Al-Hakim recorded that Hakim bin Mu`awiyah bin Haydah narrated that his father said that the Messenger of Allah said,

«أَنْتُمْ تُوَفُّونَ سَبْعِينَ أُمَّةً، أَنْتُمْ خَيْرُهَا، وَأَنْتُمْ أَكْرَمُ عَلَى اللهِ عَزَّ وَجَلَّ»

(You are the final of seventy nations, you are the best and most honored among them to Allah.)

Chapter 3: Al-i-'Imran (The Family of Imran), Verses 093-200

This is a well-known Hadith about which At-Tirmidhi said, "Hasan", and which is also narrated from Mu`adh bin Jabal and Abu Sa`id. The Ummah of Muhammad achieved this virtue because of its Prophet, Muhammad, peace be upon him, the most regarded of Allah's creation and the most honored Messenger with Allah. Allah sent Muhammad with the perfect and complete Law that was never given to any Prophet or Messenger before him. In Muhammad's Law, few deeds take the place of the many deeds that other nations performed. For instance, Imam Ahmad recorded that `Ali bin Abi Talib said, "The Messenger of Allah said,

«أُعْطِيتُ مَا لَمْ يُعْطَ أَحَدٌ مِنَ الْأَنْبِيَاءِ»

(I was given what no other Prophet before me was given.)

We said, `O Messenger of Allah! What is it' He said,

«نُصِرْتُ بِالرُّعْبِ، وَأُعْطِيتُ مَفَاتِيحَ الْأَرْضِ، وَسُمِّيتُ أَحْمَدَ، وَجُعِلَ التُّرَابُ لِي طَهُورًا، وَجُعِلَتْ أُمَّتِي خَيْرَ الْأُمَمِ»

(I was given victory by fear, I was given the keys of the earth, I was called Ahmad, the earth was made a clean place for me (to pray and perform Tayammum with it) and my Ummah was made the best Ummah.)."

The chain of narration for this Hadith is Hasan. There are several Hadiths that we should mention here.

The Two Sahihs recorded that Az-Zuhri said that, Sa`id bin Al-Musayyib said that Abu Hurayrah narrated to him, "I heard the Messenger of Allah saying,

«يَدْخُلُ الْجَنَّةَ مِنْ أُمَّتِي زُمْرَةٌ وَهُمْ سَبْعُونَ أَلْفًا، تُضِيءُ وُجُوهُهُمْ إِضَاءَةَ الْقَمَرِ لَيْلَةَ الْبَدْرِ»

(A group of seventy thousand from my Ummah will enter Paradise, while their faces are radiating, just like the moon when it is full.'`Ukkashah bin Mihsan Al-Asadi stood up, saying, `O Messenger of Allah! Supplicate to Allah that I am one of them.' The Messenger of Allah said,

«اللَّهُمَّ اجْعَلْهُ مِنْهُمْ»

`O Allah! Make him one of them.' A man from the Ansar also stood and said, `O Messenger of Allah! Supplicate to Allah that I am one of them.' The Messenger said,

«سَبَقَكَ بِهَا عُكَّاشَةُ»

`Ukkashah has beaten you to it.')

Another Hadith that Establishes the Virtues of the Ummah of Muhammad in this Life and the Hereafter.

Imam Ahmad recorded that Jabir said, "I heard the Messenger of Allah saying,

«إِنِّي لَأَرْجُو أَنْ يَكُونَ مَنْ يَتَّبِعُنِي مِنْ أُمَّتِي يَوْمَ الْقِيَامَةِ رُبُعَ الْجَنَّةِ»

(`I hope that those who follow me will be one-fourth of the residents of Paradise on the Day of Resurrection.' We said, `Allahu Akbar'. He then said,

«أَرْجُو أَنْ يَكُونُوا ثُلُثَ النَّاسِ»

`I hope that they will be one-third of the people.' We said, `Allahu Akbar'. He then said,

«أَرْجُو أَنْ تَكُونُوا الشَّطْرَ»

`I hope that you will be one-half.')"

Imam Ahmad recorded the same Hadith with another chain of narration, and this Hadith meets the criteria of Muslim in his Sahih. In the Two Sahihs, it is recorded that `Abdullah bin Mas`ud said, "The Messenger of Allah said to us,

«أَمَا تَرْضَوْنَ أَنْ تَكُونُوا رُبُعَ أَهْلِ الْجَنَّةِ؟»

(Does it please you that you will be one-fourth of the people of Paradise)

We said, `Allahu Akbar!' He added,

«أَمَا تَرْضَوْنَ أَنْ تَكُونُوا ثُلُثَ أَهْلِ الْجَنَّةِ؟»

(Does it please you that you will be one-third of the people of Paradise) We said, `Allahu Akbar!' He said,

«إِنِّي لَأَرْجُو أَنْ تَكُونُوا شَطْرَ أَهْلِ الْجَنَّةِ؟»

(I hope that you will be half of the people of Paradise.)" Another Hadith

Chapter 3: Al-i-'Imran (The Family of Imran), Verses 093-200

Imam Ahmad recorded that Buraydah said that the Prophet said,

«أَهْلُ الْجَنَّةِ عِشْرُونَ وَمِائَةُ صَفَ، هذِهِ الْأُمَّةُ مِنْ ذلِكَ ثَمَانُونَ صَفًّا»

(The people of Paradise are one hundred and twenty rows, this Ummah takes up eighty of them.)

Imam Ahmad also collected this Hadith through another chain of narration. At-Tirmidhi and Ibn Majah also collected this Hadith, and At-Tirmidhi said, `This Hadith is Hasan.` `Abdur-Razzaq recorded that Abu Hurayrah said that, the Prophet said,

«نَحْنُ الْآخِرُونَ الْأَوَّلُونَ يَوْمَ الْقِيَامَةِ، نَحْنُ أَوَّلُ النَّاسِ دُخُولًا الْجَنَّةَ، بَيْدَ أَنَّهُمْ أُوتُوا الْكِتَابَ مِنْ قَبْلِنَا وَأُوتِينَاهُ مِنْ بَعْدِهِمْ، فَهَدَانَا اللهُ لِمَا اخْتَلَفُوا فِيهِ مِنَ الْحَقِّ، فَهَذَا الْيَوْمُ الَّذِي اخْتَلَفُوا فِيهِ، النَّاسُ لَنَا فِيهِ تَبَعٌ، غَدًا لِلْيَهُودِ، وَلِلنَّصَارَى بَعْدَ غَدٍ»

(We (Muslims) are the last to come, but the foremost on the Day of Resurrection, and the first people to enter Paradise, although the former nations were given the Scriptures before us and we after them. Allah gave us the guidance of truth that they have been disputing about. This (Friday) is the Day that they have been disputing about, and all the other people are behind us in this matter: the Jews' (day of congregation is) tomorrow (Saturday) and the Christians' is the day after tomorrow (Sunday).)

Al-Bukhari and Muslim collected this Hadith. Muslim recorded Abu Hurayrah saying that the Messenger of Allah said,

«نَحْنُ الْآخِرُونَ الْأَوَّلُونَ يَوْمَ الْقِيَامَةِ، نَحْنُ أَوَّلُ مَنْ يَدْخُلُ الْجَنَّةَ»

(We (Muslims) are the last (to come), but (will be) the foremost on the Day of Resurrection, and will be the first people to enter Paradise...) until the end of the Hadith.

These and other Hadiths conform to the meaning of the Ayah,

(You are the best of peoples ever raised up for mankind; you enjoin Al-Ma`ruf (all that Islam has ordained) and forbid Al-Munkar (all that Islam has forbidden), and you believe in Allah).

Therefore, whoever among this Ummah acquires these qualities, will have a share in this praise. Qatadah said, "We were told that `Umar bin Al-Khattab recited this Ayah

(3:110) during a Hajj that he performed, when he saw that the people were rushing. He then said, `Whoever likes to be among this (praised) Ummah, let him fulfill the condition that Allah set in this Ayah.''' Ibn Jarir recorded this. Those from this Ummah who do not acquire these qualities will be just like the People of the Scriptures whom Allah criticized, when He said,

(They did not forbid one another from the Munkar which they committed...) (5:79).

This is the reason why, after Allah praised the Muslim Ummah with the qualities that He mentioned, He criticized the People of the Scriptures and chastised them, saying,

(And had the People of the Scripture (Jews and Christians) believed) (3:110),

in what was sent down to Muhammad ,

(it would have been better for them; among them are some who have faith, but most of them are Fasiqun (rebellious).)

Therefore only a few of them believe in Allah and in what was sent down to you and to them. The majority of them follow deviation, disbelief, sin and rebellion.

The Good News that Muslims will Dominate the People of the Book

While delivering the good news to His believing servants that victory and dominance will be theirs against the disbelieving, atheistic People of the Scriptures, Allah then said,

(They will do you no harm, barring a trifling annoyance; and if they fight against you, they will show you their backs, and they will not be helped.) (3:111)

This is what occurred, for at the battle of Khaybar, Allah brought humiliation and disgrace to the Jews. Before that, the Jews in Al-Madinah, the tribes of Qaynuqa`, Nadir and Qurayzah, were also humiliated by Allah. Such was the case with the Christians in the area of Ash-Sham later on, when the Companions defeated them in many battles and took over the leadership of Ash-Sham forever. There shall always be a group of Muslims in Ash-Sham area until `Isa, son of Maryam, descends while they are like this (on the truth, apparent and victorious). `Isa will at that time rule according to the Law of Muhammad , break the cross, kill the swine, banish the Jizyah and only accept Islam from the people.

Allah said next,

(Indignity is put over them wherever they may be, except when under a covenant (of protection) from Allah, and a covenant from men;) meaning, Allah has placed humiliation and disgrace on them wherever they may be, and they will never be safe,

(except when under a covenant from Allah,) under the Dhimmah (covenant of protection) from Allah that requires them to pay the Jizyah (tax, to Muslims,) and makes them subservient to Islamic Law.

Chapter 3: Al-i-'Imran (The Family of Imran), Verses 093-200

(and a covenant from men;) meaning, covenant from men, such as pledges of protection and safety offered to them by Muslim men and women, and even a slave, according to one of the sayings of the scholars. Ibn `Abbas said that,

(except when under a covenant from Allah, and a covenant from men;) refers to a covenant of protection from Allah and a pledge of safety from people. Similar was said by Mujahid, `Ikrimah, `Ata', Ad-Dahhak, Al-Hasan, Qatadah, As-Suddi and Ar-Rabi` bin Anas. Allah's statement,

(they have drawn on themselves the wrath of Allah,) means, they earned Allah's anger, which they deserved,

(and destitution is put over them), meaning they deserve it by decree and legislatively.

Allah said next,

(This is because they disbelieved in the Ayat of Allah and killed the Prophets without right.) meaning, what drove them to this was their arrogance, transgression and envy, earning them humiliation, degradation and disgrace throughout this life and the Hereafter. Allah said,

(This is because they disobeyed and used to transgress (the limits set by Allah).) meaning, what lured them to disbelieve in Allah's Ayat and kill His Messengers, is the fact that they often disobeyed Allah's commands, committed His prohibitions and transgressed His set limits. We seek refuge from this behavior, and Allah Alone is sought for each and every type of help.

Surah: 3 Ayah: 113, Ayah: 114, Ayah: 115, Ayah: 116 & Ayah: 117

﴿ ۞ لَيْسُواْ سَوَآءً مِّنْ أَهْلِ ٱلْكِتَٰبِ أُمَّةٌ قَآئِمَةٌ يَتْلُونَ ءَايَٰتِ ٱللَّهِ ءَانَآءَ ٱلَّيْلِ وَهُمْ يَسْجُدُونَ ﴿١١٣﴾ ﴾

113. Not all of them are alike; a party of the people of the Scripture stand for the right, they recite the Verses of Allâh during the hours of the night, prostrating themselves in prayer.

﴿ يُؤْمِنُونَ بِٱللَّهِ وَٱلْيَوْمِ ٱلْأَخِرِ وَيَأْمُرُونَ بِٱلْمَعْرُوفِ وَيَنْهَوْنَ عَنِ ٱلْمُنكَرِ وَيُسَٰرِعُونَ فِى ٱلْخَيْرَٰتِ وَأُوْلَٰٓئِكَ مِنَ ٱلصَّٰلِحِينَ ﴿١١٤﴾ ﴾

114. They believe in Allâh and the Last Day; they enjoin Al-Ma'rûf (Islâmic Monotheism, and following Prophet Muhammad (peace be upon him)) and forbid Al-Munkar (polytheism, disbelief and opposing Prophet Muhammad (peace be upon him)) and they hasten in (all) good works; and they are among the righteous.

$$\left\{ \text{وَمَا يَفْعَلُوا۟ مِنْ خَيْرٍ فَلَن يُكْفَرُوهُ ۗ وَٱللَّهُ عَلِيمٌۢ بِٱلْمُتَّقِينَ} \right\}$$

115. And whatever good they do, nothing will be rejected of them; for Allâh knows well those who are Al-Muttaqûn (the pious - see V.2:2).

$$\left\{ \text{إِنَّ ٱلَّذِينَ كَفَرُوا۟ لَن تُغْنِىَ عَنْهُمْ أَمْوَٰلُهُمْ وَلَآ أَوْلَٰدُهُم مِّنَ ٱللَّهِ شَيْـًٔا ۖ وَأُو۟لَٰٓئِكَ أَصْحَٰبُ ٱلنَّارِ ۚ هُمْ فِيهَا خَٰلِدُونَ} \right\}$$

116. Surely, those who reject Faith (disbelieve in Muhammad (peace be upon him) as being Allâh's Prophet and in all that which he has brought from Allâh), neither their properties, nor their offspring will avail them aught against Allâh. They are the dwellers of the Fire, therein they will abide. (Tafsir At-Tabarî).

$$\left\{ \text{مَثَلُ مَا يُنفِقُونَ فِى هَٰذِهِ ٱلْحَيَوٰةِ ٱلدُّنْيَا كَمَثَلِ رِيحٍ فِيهَا صِرٌّ أَصَابَتْ حَرْثَ قَوْمٍ ظَلَمُوٓا۟ أَنفُسَهُمْ فَأَهْلَكَتْهُ ۚ وَمَا ظَلَمَهُمُ ٱللَّهُ وَلَٰكِنْ أَنفُسَهُمْ يَظْلِمُونَ} \right\}$$

117. The likeness of what they spend in this world is the likeness of a wind which is extremely cold; it struck the harvest of a people who did wrong against themselves and destroyed it, (i.e. the good deed of a person is only accepted if he is a monotheist and believes in all the Prophets of Allâh, including the Christ (peace be upon him) and Muhammad (peace be upon him)) Allâh wronged them not, but they wronged themselves.

Transliteration

113. Laysoo sawaan min ahli alkitabi ommatun qa-imatun yatloona ayati Allahi anaa allayli wahum yasjudoona 114. Yu/minoona biAllahi waalyawmi al-akhiri waya/muroona bialmaAAroofi wayanhawna AAani almunkari wayusariAAoona fee alkhayrati waola-ika mina alssaliheena 115. Wama yafAAaloo min khayrin falan yukfaroohu waAllahu AAaleemun bialmuttaqeena 116. Inna allatheena kafaroo lan tughniya AAanhum amwaluhum wala awladuhum mina Allahi shayan waola-ika as-habu alnnari hum feeha khalidoona 117. Mathalu ma yunfiqoona fee hathihi alhayati alddunya kamathali reehin feeha sirrun asabat hartha qawmin thalamoo anfusahum faahlakat-hu wama thalamahumu Allahu walakin anfusahum yathlimoona

Tafsir Ibn Kathir

Virtues of the People of the Scriptures Who Embrace Islam

Muhammad bin Ishaq and others, including Al-`Awfi who reported it from Ibn `Abbas, said; "These Ayat were revealed about the clergy of the People of the Scriptures who embraced the faith. For instance, there is `Abdullah bin Salam, Asad bin `Ubayd, Tha`labah bin Sa`yah, Usayd bin Sa`yah, and so forth. This Ayah means that those among the People of the Book whom Allah rebuked earlier are not at all the same as those among them who embraced Islam. Hence Allah's statement,

(Not all of them are alike) (3:113)."

Therefore, these two types of people are not equal, and indeed, there are believers and also criminals among the People of the Book, just as Allah said,

(a party of the People of the Scripture stand for the right) for they implement the Book of Allah, adhere to His Law and follow His Prophet Muhammad . Therefore, this type is on the straight path,

(they recite the verses of Allah during the hours of the night, prostrating themselves in prayer.)

They often stand in prayer at night for Tahajjud, and recite the Qur'an in their prayer,

(They believe in Allah and the Last Day; they enjoin Al-Ma`ruf and forbid Al-Munkar; and they hasten in (all) good works; and they are among the righteous) (3: 114).

This is the same type of people mentioned at the end of the Surah;

(And there are, certainly, among the People of the Scripture (Jews and Christians), those who believe in Allah and in that which has been revealed to you, and in that which has been revealed to them, humbling themselves before Allah.) (3:199).

Allah said here,

(And whatever good they do, nothing will be rejected of them;) (3:115) meaning, their good deeds will not be lost with Allah. Rather, He will award them the best rewards,

(for Allah knows well the Muttaqin (the pious).) for no deed performed by any person ever escapes His knowledge, nor is any reward for those who do good deeds ever lost with Him. Allah mentions the disbelieving polytheists:

(neither their properties nor their offspring will avail them against Allah) (3:116). meaning, nothing can avert Allah's torment and punishment from striking them,

(They are the dwellers of the Fire, therein they will abide.)

The Parable of What the Disbelievers Spend in This Life

Allah gave a parable for what the disbelievers spend in this life, as Mujahid, Al-Hasan and As-Suddi said.

(The likeness of what they spend in this world is the likeness of a wind of Sir;) a frigid wind, as Ibn `Abbas, `Ikrimah, Sa`id bin Jubayr, Al-Hasan, Qatadah, Ad-Dahhak, Ar-Rabi` bin Anas and others have said. `Ata' said that Sir, means, `cold and snow.' Ibn `Abbas and Mujahid are also reported to have said that Sir means, `fire'. This latter meaning does not contradict the meanings we mentioned above, because extreme cold weather, especially when accompanied by snow, burns plants and produce, and has the same effect fire has on such growth.

(It struck the harvest of a people who did wrong against themselves and destroyed it) (3:117), by burning. This Ayah mentions a calamity that strikes produce that is ready to harvest, destroying it by burning and depriving its owner of it when he needs it the most. Such is the case with the disbelievers, for Allah destroys the rewards for their good deeds in this life, just as He destroyed the produce of the sinner because of his sins. Both types did not build their work on firm foundations,

(And Allah wronged them not, but they wronged themselves.)

Surah: 3 Ayah: 118, Ayah: 119 & Ayah: 120

﴿ يَٰٓأَيُّهَا ٱلَّذِينَ ءَامَنُوا۟ لَا تَتَّخِذُوا۟ بِطَانَةً مِّن دُونِكُمْ لَا يَأْلُونَكُمْ خَبَالًا وَدُّوا۟ مَا عَنِتُّمْ قَدْ بَدَتِ ٱلْبَغْضَآءُ مِنْ أَفْوَٰهِهِمْ وَمَا تُخْفِى صُدُورُهُمْ أَكْبَرُ ۚ قَدْ بَيَّنَّا لَكُمُ ٱلْءَايَٰتِ ۖ إِن كُنتُمْ تَعْقِلُونَ ﴾

118. O you who believe! Take not as (your) Bitânah (advisors, consultants, protectors, helpers, friends) those outside your religion (pagans, Jews, Christians, and hypocrites) since they will not fail to do their best to corrupt you. They desire to harm you severely. Hatred has already appeared from their mouths, but what their breasts conceal is far worse. Indeed We have made plain to you the Ayât (proofs, evidences, verses) if you understand.

﴿ هَٰٓأَنتُمْ أُو۟لَآءِ تُحِبُّونَهُمْ وَلَا يُحِبُّونَكُمْ وَتُؤْمِنُونَ بِٱلْكِتَٰبِ كُلِّهِۦ وَإِذَا لَقُوكُمْ قَالُوٓا۟ ءَامَنَّا وَإِذَا خَلَوْا۟ عَضُّوا۟ عَلَيْكُمُ ٱلْأَنَامِلَ مِنَ ٱلْغَيْظِ ۚ قُلْ مُوتُوا۟ بِغَيْظِكُمْ ۗ إِنَّ ٱللَّهَ عَلِيمٌۢ بِذَاتِ ٱلصُّدُورِ ﴾

119. Lo! You are the ones who love them but they love you not, and you believe in all the Scriptures (i.e. you believe in the Taurât (Torah) and the Injeel (Gospel), while they disbelieve in your Book, the Qur'ân). And when they meet you, they say, "We believe". But when they are alone, they bite the tips of their fingers at you in rage. Say: "Perish in your rage. Certainly, Allâh knows what is in the breasts (all the secrets)."

﴿ إِن تَمْسَسْكُمْ حَسَنَةٌ تَسُؤْهُمْ وَإِن تُصِبْكُمْ سَيِّئَةٌ يَفْرَحُوا۟ بِهَا ۖ وَإِن تَصْبِرُوا۟ وَتَتَّقُوا۟ لَا يَضُرُّكُمْ كَيْدُهُمْ شَيْـًٔا ۗ إِنَّ ٱللَّهَ بِمَا يَعْمَلُونَ مُحِيطٌ ﴾

120. If a good befalls you, it grieves them, but if some evil overtakes you, they rejoice at it. But if you remain patient and become Al-Muttaqûn (the pious - see V.2:2), not the least harm will their cunning do to you. Surely, Allâh surrounds all that they do.

Transliteration

118. Ya ayyuha allatheena amanoo la tattakhithoo bitanatan min doonikum la ya/loonakum khabalan waddoo ma AAanittum qad badati albaghdao min afwahihim

wama tukhfee sudooruhum akbaru qad bayyanna lakumu al-ayati in kuntum taAAqiloona 119. Ha antum ola-i tuhibboonahum wala yuhibboonakum watu/minoona bialkitabi kullihi wa-itha laqookum qaloo amanna wa-itha khalaw AAaddoo AAalaykumu al-anamila mina alghaythi qul mootoo bighaythikum inna Allaha AAaleemun bithati alssudoori 120. In tamsaskum hasanatun tasu/hum wa-in tusibkum sayyi-atun yafrahoo biha wa-in tasbiroo watattaqoo la yadurrukum kayduhum shay-an inna Allaha bima yaAAmaloona muheetun

Tafsir Ibn Kathir

The Prohibition of Taking Advisors From Among the Disbelievers

Allah forbids His believing servants from taking the hypocrites as advisors, so that the hypocrites do not have the opportunity to expose the secrets of the believers and their plans against their enemies. The hypocrites try their very best to confuse, oppose and harm the believers any way they can, and by using any wicked, evil means at their disposal. They wish the very worst and difficult conditions for the believers. Allah said,

(Take not as (your) Bitanah those other than your own) (3:118), in reference to taking followers of other religions as consultants and advisors, for advisors of a certain person have access to his most secret affairs. Al-Bukhari and An-Nasa'i recorded that, Abu Sa`id said that the Messenger of Allah said,

«مَا بَعَثَ اللهُ مِنْ نَبِيٍّ وَلَا اسْتَخْلَفَ مِنْ خَلِيفَةٍ إِلَّا كَانَتْ لَهُ بِطَانَتَانِ: بِطَانَةٌ تَأْمُرُهُ بِالْخَيْرِ وَتَحُضُّهُ عَلَيْهِ، وَبِطَانَةٌ تَأْمُرُهُ بِالسُّوءِ وَتَحُضُّهُ عَلَيْهِ، وَالْمَعْصُومُ مَنْ عَصَمَ اللهُ»

(Allah has not sent any Prophet nor was there any Khalifah but they have two types of advisors, one that commands him with righteousness and advises it, and another that commands him with evil and advises him with it. Only those whom Allah gives immunity are immune.)

Ibn Abi Hatim reported that Ibn Abi Ad-Dahqanah said, "`Umar bin Al-Khattab was told, `There is young man here from the people of Hirah (in Iraq, who were Christians) who is a proficient scribe. Why do you not appoint him as a scribe' `Umar said, `I would then be taking advisors from among the disbelievers.'" This Ayah and the story about `Umar testify to the fact that Muslims are not allowed to use Ahl Adh-Dhimmah to be scribes in matters that affect the affairs of Muslims and expose their secrets, for they might convey these secrets to combatant disbelievers. This is why Allah said,

(since they will not fail to do their best to corrupt you. They desire to harm you severely.)

Allah then said,

(Hatred has already appeared from their mouths, but what their breasts conceal is far worse.) meaning, enmity appears on their faces and in what they sometimes utter, as well as, the enmity they have against Islam and its people in their hearts. Since this fact is apparent to every person who has sound comprehension, therefore,

(Indeed We have made plain to you the Ayat if you understand.)

Allah said next,

(O! You are the ones who love them but they love you not), meaning, O believers! You like the hypocrites because you think they are believers, for they pretend to be so, but they do not like you publicly or secretly.

(And you believe in all the Scriptures) meaning, you have no doubt in any part of Allah's Book, while the hypocrites have deep doubts, confusion and reservations about it.

Muhammad bin Ishaq reported that Ibn `Abbas said that,

(and you believe in all the Scriptures,) means, you believe in your Book, their Book, and the previous Books, while the hypocrites disbelieve in your Book, and this is why they deserve that you dislike them instead of them disliking you. Ibn Jarir collected this statement.

(And when they meet you, they say, "We believe." But when they are alone, they bite their Anamil at you in rage.)

The word Anamil, means the tips of the fingers, as Qatadah stated. This is the behavior of the hypocrites who pretend to be believers and kind when they are with the believers, all the while concealing the opposite in their hearts in every respect. This is the exact situation that Allah describes,

(But when they are alone, they bite their Anamil at you in rage) and rage is extreme anger and fury. Allah said to them,

(Say: "Perish in your rage. Certainly, Allah knows what is in the breasts (all the secrets).") for no matter how much you envy the believers and feel rage towards them, know that Allah shall perfect His favor on His believing servants, complete His religion, raise high His Word and give dominance to His religion. Therefore, O hypocrites, die in rage,

(Allah knows what is in the breasts.)

Allah has perfect knowledge of what you conceal in your hearts and chests and in the rage, envy and hatred you have against the believers. Allah will punish you for all this in this life, and they will have the good that you dislike for them. In the Hereafter, you will suffer severe torment in the Fire where you will remain for eternity.

Chapter 3: Al-i-'Imran (The Family of Imran), Verses 093-200

Thereafter, Allah said,

(If a good befalls you, it grieves them, but if some evil overtakes you, they rejoice at it) (3:120). This only emphasizes the severity of the enmity that the hypocrites feel against the believers. If the believers enjoy fertile years, victories, support and their numbers and following increase, the hypocrites become displeased. When the Muslims suffer a drought or their enemies gain the upper hand against them, by Allah's decree, just as occurred during the battle of Uhud, the hypocrites become pleased. Allah said to His believing servants,

(But if you remain patient and have Taqwa, not the least harm will their cunning do to you.)

Allah directs the believers to safety from the wickedness of evil people and the plots of the sinners, by recommending them to revert to patience and by having fear of Allah and trusting Him. Allah encompasses the enemies of the believers, all the while the believers have no power or strength except from Him. Whatever Allah wills, occurs, and whatever He does not will, does not occur. Nothing happens in His Kingdom except with His decision and according to His decrees. Verily, whoever relies on Allah, Allah shall suffice for him.

Allah then mentions the story of Uhud, the defeat that He tested the believers with, His distinguishing the believers from the hypocrites and their patience.

Surah: 3 Ayah: 121, Ayah: 122 & Ayah: 123

﴿ وَإِذْ غَدَوْتَ مِنْ أَهْلِكَ تُبَوِّئُ ٱلْمُؤْمِنِينَ مَقَٰعِدَ لِلْقِتَالِ ۗ وَٱللَّهُ سَمِيعٌ عَلِيمٌ ﴾

121. And (remember) when you (Muhammad (peace be upon him)) left your household in the morning to post the believers at their stations for the battle (of Uhud). And Allâh is All-Hearer, All-Knower.

﴿ إِذْ هَمَّت طَّآئِفَتَانِ مِنكُمْ أَن تَفْشَلَا وَٱللَّهُ وَلِيُّهُمَا ۗ وَعَلَى ٱللَّهِ فَلْيَتَوَكَّلِ ٱلْمُؤْمِنُونَ ﴾

122. When two parties from among you were about to lose heart, but Allâh was their Walî (Supporter and Protector). And in Allâh should the believers put their trust.

﴿ وَلَقَدْ نَصَرَكُمُ ٱللَّهُ بِبَدْرٍ وَأَنتُمْ أَذِلَّةٌ ۖ فَٱتَّقُوا۟ ٱللَّهَ لَعَلَّكُمْ تَشْكُرُونَ ﴾

123. And Allâh has already made you victorious at Badr, when you were a weak little force. So fear Allâh much that you may be grateful.

Transliteration

121. Wa-ith ghadawta min ahlika tubawwi-o almu/mineena maqaAAida lilqitali waAllahu sameeAAun AAaleemun 122. Ith hammat ta-ifatani minkum an tafshala waAllahu waliyyuhuma waAAala Allahi falyatawakkali almu/minoona 123. Walaqad

nasarakumu Allahu bibadrin waantum athillatun faittaqoo Allaha laAAallakum tashkuroona

Tafsir Ibn Kathir

The Battle of Uhud

According to the majority of scholars, these Ayat are describing the battle of Uhud, as Ibn `Abbas, Al-Hasan, Qatadah, As-Suddi and others said. The battle of Uhud occurred on a Saturday, in the month of Shawwal on the third year of Hijrah. `Ikrimah said that Uhud occurred in the middle of the month of Shawwal, and Allah knows best.

The Reason Behind the Battle of Uhud

The idolators suffered many casualties among their noble men at the battle of Badr. The caravan that Abu Sufyan led (before Badr) returned safely to Makkah, prompting the remaining Makkan leaders and the children of those who were killed at Badr to demand from Abu Sufyan to, "Spend this money on fighting Muhammad!" Consequently, they spent the money from the caravan on warfare expenses and mobilized their forces including the Ahabish tribes (tribes living around the city). They gathered three thousand soldiers and marched until they camped near Uhud facing Al-Madinah. The Messenger of Allah led the Friday prayer and when he finished with it, he performed the funeral prayer for a man from Bani An-Najjar called Malik bin `Amr. The Prophet then asked the Muslims for advice, if they should march to meet the disbelievers, or fortify themselves in Al-Madinah. `Abdullah bin Ubayy (the chief hypocrite) advised that they should remain in Al-Madinah, saying that if the disbelievers lay siege to Al-Madinah, the siege would be greatly disadvantageous to them. He added that if they decide to attack Al-Madinah, its men would face off with them, while women and children could throw rocks at them from above their heads; and if they decide to return to Makkah, they would return with failure. However, some companions who did not attend the battle of Badr advised that the Muslims should go out to Uhud to meet the disbelievers.

The Messenger of Allah went to his home, put on his shield and came out. The companions were weary then and said to each other, "Did we compel the Messenger of Allah to go out" They said, "O Messenger of Allah! If you wish, we will remain in Al-Madinah. " The Messenger of Allah said,

«مَا يَنْبَغِي لِنَبِيٍّ إِذَا لَبِسَ لَأْمَتَهُ أَنْ يَرْجِعَ حَتَّى يَحْكُمَ اللهُ لَه»

(It is not for a Prophet to wear his shield for war then lay down his arms before Allah decides in his favor.)

The Messenger of Allah marched with a thousand of his Companions. When they reached the Shawt area, `Abdullah bin Ubayy went back to Al-Madinah with a third of the army, claiming he was angry the Prophet did not listen to his advice. He and his supporters said, "If we knew that you would fight today, we would have accompanied you. However, we do not think that you will fight today." The Messenger of Allah marched until he reached the hillside in the area of Uhud, where they camped in the valley with Mount Uhud behind them. The Messenger of Allah said,

«لَا يُقَاتِلَنَّ أَحَدٌ حَتَّى نَأْمُرَهُ بِالْقِتَالِ»

(No one starts fighting until I issue the command to fight.)

The Messenger prepared his forces for battle, and his army was seven hundred men. He appointed `Abdullah bin Jubayr, from Bani `Amr bin `Awf, to lead the archers who were fifty men. The Prophet said to them,

«انْضَحُوا الْخَيْلَ عَنَّا، وَلَا نُؤْتَيَنَّ مِنْ قِبَلِكُمْ، وَالْزَمُوا مَكَانَكُمْ، إِنْ كَانَتِ النَّوْبَةُ لَنَا أَوْ عَلَيْنَا، وَإِنْ رَأَيْتُمُونَا تَخْطَفُنَا الطَّيْرُ فَلَا تَبْرَحُوا مَكَانَكُمْ»

(Keep the horsemen away from us, and be aware that we might be attacked from your direction. If victory was for or against us, remain in your positions. And even if you see us being picked up by birds, do not abandon your positions.)

The Prophet wore two protective shields and gave the flag to Mus`ab bin `Umayr of Bani `Abd Ad-Dar. The Prophet also allowed some young men to participate in fighting, but not others, whom he allowed to participate in the battle of Al-Khandaq two years later. The Quraysh mobilized their forces of three thousand men with two hundred horsemen on each flank. They appointed Khalid bin Al-Walid to lead the right side of the horsemen and `Ikrimah Ibn Abi Jahl on the left side. They also gave their grand flag to the tribe of Bani `Abd Ad-Dar. Allah willing, we will mention the details of this battle later on, if Allah wills. Allah said here,

(And (remember) when you left your household in the morning to post the believers at their stations for the battle) (3:121), designating them to various positions, dividing the army to the left and right sides and placing them wherever you command them.

(And Allah is All-Hearer, All-Knower), He hears what you say and knows what you conceal in your hearts. Allah said next,

(When two parties from among you were about to lose heart,) (3:122).

Al-Bukhari recorded that Jabir bin `Abdullah said, "The Ayah,

(When two parties from among you were about to lose heart) was revealed about us, (the two Muslim tribes of) Bani Harithah and Bani Salamah. I (or we) would not be pleased if it was not revealed, because Allah said in it,

(but Allah was their Wali (Supporter and Protector)) (3:122)."

Muslim recorded this Hadith from Sufyan bin `Uyaynah.

Reminding the Believers of Their Victory at Badr

Allah said,

(And Allah has already made you victorious at Badr,)(3:123) meaning, during the battle of Badr, which occurred on a Friday, the seventeenth of Ramadan, in the second year of Hijrah.

The day of Badr is known as Yawm Al-Furqan (the Day of the Clarification), by which Allah gave victory and dominance to Islam and its people and disgraced and destroyed Shirk, even though the Muslims were few. The Muslims numbered three hundred and thirteen men, with two horses and seventy camels. The rest were foot soldiers without enough supplies for the battle. The enemy army consisted of nine hundred to a thousand men, having enough shields and supplies, battle-ready horses and even various adornments.

However, Allah gave victory to His Messenger , supported His revelation, and illuminated success on the faces of the Prophet and his following. Allah also brought disgrace to Shayatan and his army. This is why Allah reminded His believing servants and pious party of this favor,

(And Allah has already made you victorious at Badr, when you were a weak little force), cwhen you were few then. This Ayah reminds them that victory is only from Allah, not because of a large army and adequate supplies. This is why Allah said in another Ayah,

(. .and on the day of Hunayn (battle) when you rejoiced at your great number, but it availed you naught) (9:25), until,

(And Allah is Oft-Forgiving, Most Merciful) (9:27).

Badr is an area between Makkah and Al-Madinah and is known by the well that bears its name, which in turn was so named after Badr bin An-Narayn, the person who dug the well.

(So have Taqwa of Allah that you may be grateful.) (3:123), means, fulfill the obligations of His obedience.

Surah: 3 Ayah: 124, Ayah: 125, Ayah: 126, Ayah: 127, Ayah: 128 & Ayah: 129

﴿ إِذْ تَقُولُ لِلْمُؤْمِنِينَ أَلَن يَكْفِيَكُمْ أَن يُمِدَّكُمْ رَبُّكُم بِثَلَٰثَةِ ءَالَٰفٍ مِّنَ ٱلْمَلَٰٓئِكَةِ مُنزَلِينَ ۞ ﴾

124. (Remember) when you (Muhammad (peace be upon him)) said to the believers, "Is it not enough for you that your Lord (Allâh) should help you with three thousand angels sent down?"

﴿ بَلَىٰ ۚ إِن تَصْبِرُوا۟ وَتَتَّقُوا۟ وَيَأْتُوكُم مِّن فَوْرِهِمْ هَـٰذَا يُمْدِدْكُمْ رَبُّكُم بِخَمْسَةِ ءَالَـٰفٍ مِّنَ ٱلْمَلَـٰٓئِكَةِ مُسَوِّمِينَ ﴾ ﴿١٢٥﴾

125. "Yes, if you hold on to patience and piety, and the enemy comes rushing at you; your Lord will help you with five thousand angels having marks (of distinction)."

﴿ وَمَا جَعَلَهُ ٱللَّهُ إِلَّا بُشْرَىٰ لَكُمْ وَلِتَطْمَئِنَّ قُلُوبُكُم بِهِ ۗ وَمَا ٱلنَّصْرُ إِلَّا مِنْ عِندِ ٱللَّهِ ٱلْعَزِيزِ ٱلْحَكِيمِ ﴾ ﴿١٢٦﴾

126. Allâh made it not but as a message of good news for you and as an assurance to your hearts. And there is no victory except from Allâh, the All-Mighty, the All-Wise.

﴿ لِيَقْطَعَ طَرَفًا مِّنَ ٱلَّذِينَ كَفَرُوٓا۟ أَوْ يَكْبِتَهُمْ فَيَنقَلِبُوا۟ خَآئِبِينَ ﴾ ﴿١٢٧﴾

127. That He might cut off a part of those who disbelieve, or expose them to infamy, so that they retire frustrated.

﴿ لَيْسَ لَكَ مِنَ ٱلْأَمْرِ شَىْءٌ أَوْ يَتُوبَ عَلَيْهِمْ أَوْ يُعَذِّبَهُمْ فَإِنَّهُمْ ظَـٰلِمُونَ ﴾ ﴿١٢٨﴾

128. Not for you (O Muhammad (peace be upon him) but for Allâh) is the decision; whether He turns in mercy to (pardons) them or punishes them; verily, they are the Zâlimûn (polytheists, disobedients, and wrong-doers).

﴿ وَلِلَّهِ مَا فِى ٱلسَّمَـٰوَٰتِ وَمَا فِى ٱلْأَرْضِ ۚ يَغْفِرُ لِمَن يَشَآءُ وَيُعَذِّبُ مَن يَشَآءُ ۚ وَٱللَّهُ غَفُورٌ رَّحِيمٌ ﴾ ﴿١٢٩﴾

129. And to Allâh belongs all that is in the heavens and all that is in the earth. He forgives whom He wills, and punishes whom He wills. And Allâh is Oft-Forgiving, Most Merciful.

Transliteration

124. Ith taqoolu lilmu/mineena alan yakfiyakum an yumiddakum rabbukum bithalathati alafin mina almala-ikati munzaleena 125. Bala in tasbiroo watattaqoo waya/tookum min fawrihim hatha yumdidkum rabbukum bikhamsati alafin mina almala-ikati musawwimeena 126. Wama jaAAalahu Allahu illa bushra lakum walitatma-inna quloobukum bihi wama alnnasru illa min AAindi Allahi alAAazeezi alhakeemi 127. LiyaqtaAAa tarafan mina allatheena kafaroo aw yakbitahum fayanqaliboo kha-ibeena 128. Laysa laka mina al-amri shay-on aw yatooba AAalayhim aw yuAAaththibahum fa-innahum thalimoona 129. Walillahi ma fee alssamawati wama fee al-ardi yaghfiru liman yashao wayuAAaththibu man yashao waAllahu ghafoorun raheemun

Tafsir Ibn Kathir

The Support of the Angels

The scholars of Tafsir differ over whether the promise contained in these Ayat referred to the battle of Badr or Uhud. The First View

There are two opinions about this, one of them saying that Allah's statement,

((Remember) when you said to the believers) (3:124), is related to His statement,

(And Allah has already made you victorious at Badr) (3:123).

This was reported from Al-Hasan Al-Basri, `Amr Ash-Sha`bi, Ar-Rabi` bin Anas and several others, Ibn Jarir also agreed with this opinion. `Abbad bin Mansur said that Al-Hasan said that Allah's statement,

((Remember) when you said to the believers, "Is it not enough for you that your Lord should help you with three thousand angels") (3:124), is about the battle of Badr; Ibn Abi Hatim also recorded this statement.

Ibn Abi Hatim then reported that `Amr Ash-Sha`bi said, "On the day of Badr, the Muslims received information that Kurz bin Jabir (a prominent tribe chief) was aiding the idolators, and this news was hard on them, so Allah revealed;

("Is it not enough for you that your Lord (Allah) should help you with three thousand angels sent down"), until,

(having marks (of distinction)) (3:124,125).

The news of the defeat of the idolators (at Badr) reached Kurz and he did not reinforce them, and thus, Allah did not reinforce the Muslims with the five (thousands of angels)."

As for Ar-Rabi` bin Anas, he said, "Allah supported the Muslims with one thousand (angels), then the number reached three thousand, then five thousand." If one asks, according to this opinion, how can we combine between this Ayah and Allah's statement about Badr,

((Remember) when you sought help of your Lord and He answered you (saying): "I will help you with a thousand angels, each behind the other (following one another) in succession.") (8:9), until,

(Verily! Allah is All-Mighty, All-Wise) We say that the one thousand mentioned here does not contradict the three thousand mentioned in the above Ayah (3:124). The word "in succession" means they follow each other and thus indicates that thousands more will follow them. The two Ayat above (8:9 and 3:124) are similar in meaning and it appears that they both were about the battle of Badr, because the angels did fight in the battle of Badr, as the evidence indicates. Allah knows best. Allah's statement,

(But if you hold on to patience and have Taqwa,) (3:125) means, if you observe patience while fighting the enemy, all the while fearing Me and obeying My command. Al-Hasan, Qatadah, Ar-Rabi` and As-Suddi said that Allah's statement,

(and they will come rushing) means, they (angels) will rush to you instantaneously. Al-`Awfi said that Ibn `Abbas said that the Ayah means, "All at once". It is also said that it means, before their anger subsides (against the disbelievers). The Second View

The second opinion stipulates that the promise mentioned here (concerning the angels participating in battle) is related to Allah's statement,

(And (remember) when you left your household in the morning to post the believers at their stations for the battle) of Uhud. However, we should add, the angels did not come to the aid of Muslims at Uhud, because Allah made it conditional,

(But if you hold on to patience and have Taqwa) (3: 125).

The Muslims were not patient at Uhud. Rather, they ran away and, consequently, did not receive the support of even one angel.

Allah's statement,

(your Lord will help you with five thousand angels having marks), of distinction.

Abu Ishaq As-Subay`i said; from Harithah bin Mudarrib said that `Ali bin Abi Talib said, "The angels were distinguished by wearing white wool at Badr." The angels also had special markings distinguishing their horses.

Allah said,

(Allah made it not but as a message of good news for you and as an assurance to your hearts) (3:126).

This Ayah means, "Allah sent down angels and told you about their descent to encourage you and to comfort and reassure your hearts. You should know that victory only comes from Allah and that if He willed, He would have defeated your enemy without you having to fight them." For instance, Allah said after commanding the believers to fight,

(But if it had been Allah's will, He Himself could certainly have punished them (without you). But (He lets you fight) in order to test some of you with others. But those who are killed in the way of Allah, He will never let their deeds be lost. He will guide them and set right their state. And admit them to Paradise which He has made known to them) (47:4-6).

This is why Allah said here,

(Allah made it not but as a message of good news for you and as an assurance to your hearts. And there is no victory except from Allah, the All-Mighty, the All-Wise) (3:126).

This Ayah means, "Allah is the Almighty Whose power can never be undermined, and He has the perfect wisdom in His decrees and in all His decisions." Allah said,

(That He might cut off a part of those who disbelieve,) (3:127) meaning, out of His wisdom, He commands you to perform Jihad and to fight.

Allah then mentions the various consequences of performing Jihad against the disbelievers. For instance, Allah said,

(That He might cut off a part...) meaning, to cause a part of a nation to perish,

(of those who disbelieve, or expose them to infamy,) by disgracing them and forcing them to return with only their rage, having failed in their aim to harm you. This is why Allah said next,

(or expose them to infamy, so that they retire) to go back to their land,

(frustrated) without achieving their aims.

Allah then mentions a statement that testifies that the decision in this life and the Hereafter is for Him Alone without partners,

(Not for you is the decision) (3:128)

meaning, "The matter is all in My Hand." Allah also said,

(your duty is only to convey (the Message) and on Us is the reckoning.) (13:40), and,

(Not upon you is their guidance, but Allah guides whom He wills.) (2:272), and,

(Verily, you guide not whom you like, but Allah guides whom He wills) (28: 56).

Muhammad bin Ishaq said that Allah's statement,

(Not for you is the decision;), means, "No part of the decision regarding My servants is yours, except what I command you." Allah then mentions the rest of the consequences of Jihad,

(whether He pardons them) concerning the acts of disbelief that they commit, thus delivering them from misguidance to the guidance.

(or punishes them;) in this life and the Hereafter because of their disbelief and errors,

(verily, they are the wrongdoers), and thus, they deserve such a fate.

Al-Bukhari recorded that, Salim bin `Abdullah said that his father said that he heard the Messenger of Allah saying -- when he raised his head from bowing in the second unit of the Fajr prayer -- "O Allah! Curse so-and-so," after saying; Sami` Allahu Liman Hamidah, Rabbana wa lakal-Hamd. Thereafter, Allah revealed this Ayah,

Chapter 3: Al-i-'Imran (The Family of Imran), Verses 093-200

(Not for you is the decision;) This was also recorded by An-Nasa'i. Imam Ahmad recorded that Salim bin `Abdullah said that his father said that he heard the Messenger of Allah saying,

«اللَّهُمَّ الْعَنْ فُلَانًا، اللَّهُمَّ الْعَنِ الْحَارِثَ بْنَ هِشَامٍ، اللَّهُمَّ الْعَنْ سُهَيْلَ بْنَ عَمْرٍو، اللَّهُمَّ الْعَنْ صَفْوَانَ بْنَ أُمَيَّة»

(O Allah! Curse so-and-so. O Allah! Curse Al-Harith bin Hisham. O Allah! Curse Suhayl bin `Amr. O Allah! Curse Safwan bin Umayyah.)

Thereafter, this Ayah was revealed;

(Not for you is the decision; whether He turns in mercy to (pardon) them or punishes them; verily, they are the wrongdoers) (3:128).

All these persons were pardoned (after they embraced Islam later on).

Al-Bukhari recorded that Abu Hurayrah said that when Allah's Messenger would supplicate against or for someone, he would do so when he was finished bowing and saying; Sami` Allahu Liman Hamidah, Rabbana wa lakal-Hamd. He would then say, (the Qunut)

«اللَّهُمَّ أَنْجِ الْوَلِيدَ بْنَ الْوَلِيدِ، وَسَلَمَةَ بْنَ هِشَامٍ وَعَيَّاشَ بْنَ أَبِي رَبِيعَةَ، وَالْمُسْتَضْعَفِينَ مِنَ الْمُؤْمِنِينَ، اللَّهُمَّ اشْدُدْ وَطْأَتَكَ عَلَى مُضَرَ، وَاجْعَلْهَا عَلَيْهِمْ سِنِينَ كَسِنِي يُوسُف»

(O Allah! Save Al-Walid bin Al-Walid, Salamah bin Hisham, `Ayyash bin Abi Rabi`ah and the weak and the helpless people among the faithful believers. O Allah! Be hard on the tribe of Mudar and let them suffer from years of famine like that of the time of Yusuf.)

He would say this supplication aloud. He sometimes would supplicate during the Dawn prayer, "O Allah! Curse so-and-so (persons)," mentioning some Arab tribes. Thereafter, Allah revealed,

(Not for you is the decision.)

Al-Bukhari recorded that Hamid and Thabit said that, Anas bin Malik said that the Prophet was injured during the battle of Uhud and said,

«كَيْفَ يُفْلِحُ قَوْمٌ شَجُّوا نَبِيَّهُمْ؟»

(How can a people achieve success after having injured their Prophet)

Thereafter,

(Not for you is the decision,) was revealed.

Imam Ahmad recorded that Anas said that, the Prophet's front tooth was broken during the battle of Uhud and he also sustained injuries on his forehead until blood dripped on his face. The Prophet said,

«كَيْفَ يُفْلِحُ قَوْمٌ فَعَلُوا هذَا بِنَبِيِّهِمْ، وَهُوَ يَدْعُوهُمْ إِلَى رَبِّهِمْ عَزَّ وَجَلَّ؟»

(How can a people achieve success after having done this to their Prophet who is calling them to their Lord, the Exalted and Most Honored) Allah revealed,

(Not for you is the decision; whether He turns in mercy to (pardons) them or punishes them; verily, they are the wrongdoers.) Muslim also collected this Hadith.

Allah then said,

(And to Allah belongs all that is in the heavens and all that is in the Earth.) (3:129), everything is indeed the property of Allah and all are servants in His Hand.

(He forgives whom He wills, and punishes whom He wills.) for His is the decision and none can resist His decision. Allah is never asked about what He does, while they will be asked,

(and Allah is Oft-Forgiving, Most Merciful.)

Surah: 3 Ayah: 130, Ayah: 131, Ayah: 132, Ayah: 133, Ayah: 134, Ayah: 135 & Ayah: 136

﴿ يَا أَيُّهَا الَّذِينَ ءَامَنُوا لَا تَأْكُلُوا الرِّبَوا أَضْعَافًا مُضَاعَفَةً وَاتَّقُوا اللَّهَ لَعَلَّكُمْ تُفْلِحُونَ ﴿١٣٠﴾ ﴾

130. O you who believe! Eat not Ribâ (usury) doubled and multiplied, but fear Allâh that you may be successful.

﴿ وَاتَّقُوا النَّارَ الَّتِي أُعِدَّتْ لِلْكَافِرِينَ ﴿١٣١﴾ ﴾

131. And fear the Fire, which is prepared for the disbelievers.

﴿ وَأَطِيعُوا اللَّهَ وَالرَّسُولَ لَعَلَّكُمْ تُرْحَمُونَ ﴿١٣٢﴾ ﴾

132. And obey Allâh and the Messenger (Muhammad (peace be upon him)) that you may obtain mercy.

Chapter 3: Al-i-'Imran (The Family of Imran), Verses 093-200

﴿ ۞ وَسَارِعُوٓا۟ إِلَىٰ مَغْفِرَةٍ مِّن رَّبِّكُمْ وَجَنَّةٍ عَرْضُهَا ٱلسَّمَـٰوَٰتُ وَٱلْأَرْضُ أُعِدَّتْ لِلْمُتَّقِينَ ۝ ﴾

133. And march forth in the way (which leads to) forgiveness from your Lord, and for Paradise as wide as the heavens and the earth, prepared for Al-Muttaqûn (the pious - see V.2:2).

﴿ ٱلَّذِينَ يُنفِقُونَ فِى ٱلسَّرَّآءِ وَٱلضَّرَّآءِ وَٱلْكَـٰظِمِينَ ٱلْغَيْظَ وَٱلْعَافِينَ عَنِ ٱلنَّاسِ وَٱللَّهُ يُحِبُّ ٱلْمُحْسِنِينَ ۝ ﴾

134. Those who spend (in Allâh's Cause) in prosperity and in adversity, who repress anger, and who pardon men; verily, Allâh loves Al-Muhsinûn (the good-doers).

﴿ وَٱلَّذِينَ إِذَا فَعَلُوا۟ فَـٰحِشَةً أَوْ ظَلَمُوٓا۟ أَنفُسَهُمْ ذَكَرُوا۟ ٱللَّهَ فَٱسْتَغْفَرُوا۟ لِذُنُوبِهِمْ وَمَن يَغْفِرُ ٱلذُّنُوبَ إِلَّا ٱللَّهُ وَلَمْ يُصِرُّوا۟ عَلَىٰ مَا فَعَلُوا۟ وَهُمْ يَعْلَمُونَ ۝ ﴾

135. And those who, when they have committed Fahishah (illegal sexual intercourse) or wronged themselves with evil, remember Allâh and ask forgiveness for their sins; - and none can forgive sins but Allâh - And do not persist in what (wrong) they have done, while they know.

﴿ أُو۟لَـٰٓئِكَ جَزَآؤُهُم مَّغْفِرَةٌ مِّن رَّبِّهِمْ وَجَنَّـٰتٌ تَجْرِى مِن تَحْتِهَا ٱلْأَنْهَـٰرُ خَـٰلِدِينَ فِيهَا وَنِعْمَ أَجْرُ ٱلْعَـٰمِلِينَ ۝ ﴾

136. For such, the reward is Forgiveness from their Lord, and Gardens with rivers flowing underneath (Paradise), wherein they shall abide forever. How excellent is this reward for the doers (who do righteous deeds according to Allâh's Orders).

Transliteration

130. Ya ayyuha allatheena amanoo la ta/kuloo alrriba adAAafan mudaAAafatan waittaqoo Allaha laAAallakum tuflihoona   131. Waittaqoo alnnara allatee oAAiddat lilkafireena   132. WaateeAAoo Allaha waalrrasoola laAAallakum turhamoona   133. WasariAAoo ila maghfiratin min rabbikum wajannatin AAarduha alssamawatu waalardu oAAiddat lilmuttaqeena 134. Allatheena yunfiqoona fee alssarra-i waalddarra-i waalkathimeena alghaytha waalAAafeena AAani alnnasi waAllahu yuhibbu almuhsineena 135. Waallatheena itha faAAaloo fahishatan aw thalamoo anfusahum thakaroo Allaha faistaghfaroo lithunoobihim waman yaghfiru alththunooba illa Allahu walam yusirroo AAala ma faAAaloo wahum yaAAlamoona   136. Ola-ika jazaohum maghfiratun min rabbihim wajannatun tajree min tahtiha al-anharu khalideena feeha waniAAma ajru alAAamileena

Tafsir Ibn Kathir

Interest (Riba) is Prohibited

Allah prohibits His believing servants from dealing in Riba and from requiring interest on their capital, just as they used to do during the time of Jahiliyyah. For instance, when the time to pay a loan comes, the creditor would say to the debtor, "Either pay now, or the loan will incur interest." If the debtor asks for deferment of the loan, the creditor would require interest and this would occur year after year until the little capital becomes multiplied many times. Allah also commands His servants to have Taqwa of Him so that they may achieve success in this life and the Hereafter. Allah also threatens them with the Fire and warns them against it, saying,

(And fear the Fire, which is prepared for the disbelievers. And obey Allah and the Messenger that you may obtain mercy.) (3:131,132).

The Encouragment to Do Good for which Paradise is the Result

Allah encourages His servants to perform righteous deeds and to rush to accomplish the acts of obedience. Allah said,

(And march forth in the way (which leads to) forgiveness from your Lord, and for Paradise as wide as the heavens and the earth, prepared for the Muttaqin (the pious)) (3:133).

Just as the Fire was prepared for the disbelievers. It was reported that the meaning of Allah's statement,

(as wide as the heavens and the earth) draws the attention to the spaciousness of Paradise. For instance, Allah said in another Ayah, while describing the couches of Paradise,

(lined with silk brocade) (55:54), so what about their outer covering It was also said that Paradise is as wide as its length, because it is a dome under the Throne. The width and length of a dome or a circle are the same in distance. This is supported by what is found in the Sahih;

«إِذَا سَأَلْتُمُ اللهَ الْجَنَّةَ فَاسْأَلُوهُ الْفِرْدَوْسَ، فَإِنَّهُ أَعْلَى الْجَنَّةِ، وَأَوْسَطُ الْجَنَّةِ، وَمِنْهُ تَفَجَّرُ أَنْهَارُ الْجَنَّةِ، وَسَقْفُهَا عَرْشُ الرَّحْمَنِ»

(When you ask Allah for Paradise, ask Him for Al-Firdaws which is the highest and best part of Paradise. From it originate the rivers of Paradise, and above it is the Throne of the Most Beneficent (Allah).)

This Ayah (3:133 above) is similar to Allah's statement in Surat Al-Hadid,

(Race with one another in hastening towards forgiveness from your Lord (Allah), and Paradise the width whereof is as the width of the heaven and the Earth) (57:21).

Chapter 3: Al-i-'Imran (The Family of Imran), Verses 093-200

Al-Bazzar recorded that Abu Hurayrah said that a man came to the Messenger of Allah and asked him, about Allah's statement,

(Paradise as wide as the heavens and the Earth) (3:133); "Where is the Fire then" The Prophet said,

«أَرَأَيْتَ اللَّيْلَ إِذَا جَاءَ لَبِسَ كُلَّ شَيْءٍ، فَأَيْنَ النَّهَارُ؟»

(When the night comes, it overtakes everything, so where is the day) The man said, "Where Allah wants it to be." The Prophet said,

«وَكَذلِكَ النَّارُ تَكُونُ حَيْثُ شَاءَ اللهُ عَزَّ وَجَل»

(Similarly, the Fire is where Allah wants it to be.) This Hadith has two possible meanings. First, when we do not see the night during the day, this does not mean that the night is not somewhere else, even though we cannot see it. Such is the case with Hell-fire, for it is where Allah wants it to be. The second meaning is that when the day overcomes this part of the world, the night overtakes the other part. Such is the case with Paradise, for it is in the utmost heights above the heavens and under the Throne. The width of Paradise is, as Allah stated,

(whereof is as the width of the heaven and the Earth) (57:21).

The Fire, on the other hand, is in the lowest of lows. Therefore, Paradise being as wide as the heavens and Earth does not contradict the fact that the Fire exists wherever Allah wills it to be.

Allah said, while describing the people of Paradise,

(Those who spend (in Allah's cause) in prosperity and in adversity) (3:134), in hard times and easy times, while active (or enthusiastic) and otherwise, healthy or ill, and in all conditions, just as Allah said in another Ayah,

(Those who spend their wealth (in Allah's cause) by night and day, in secret and in public) (2:274) These believers are never distracted from obeying Allah, spending on what pleases Him, being kind to His servants and their relatives, and other acts of righteousness. Allah said,

(who repress anger, and who pardon men;) (3:134) for when they are angry, they control their anger and do act upon it. Rather, they even forgive those who hurt them. Imam Ahmad recorded that Abu Hurayrah said that the Prophet said,

«لَيْسَ الشَّدِيدُ بِالصُّرَعَةِ، وَلكِنَّ الشَّدِيدَ الَّذِي يَمْلِكُ نَفْسَهُ عِنْدَ الْغَضَبِ»

(The strong person is not he who is able to physically overcome people. The strong person is he who overcomes his rage when he is angry.)

This Hadith is also recorded in the Two Sahihs. Imam Ahmad recorded that Ibn `Abbas said that the Messenger of Allah said,

«مَنْ أَنْظَرَ مُعْسِرًا أَوْ وَضَعَ لَهُ، وَقَاهُ اللهُ مِنْ فَيْحِ جَهَنَّمَ، أَلَا إِنَّ عَمَلَ الْجَنَّةِ حَزْنٌ بِرَبْوَةٍ ثَلَاثًا أَلَا إِنَّ عَمَلَ النَّارِ سَهْلٌ بِسَهْوَةٍ. وَالسَّعِيدُ مَنْ وُقِيَ الْفِتَنَ، وَمَا مِنْ جَرْعَةٍ أَحَبُّ إِلَى اللهِ مِنْ جَرْعَةِ غَيْظٍ يَكْظِمُهَا عَبْدٌ، مَا كَظَمَهَا عَبْدٌ للهِ إِلَّا مَلَأَ جَوْفَهُ إِيمَانًا»

(He who gives time to a debtor or forgives him, then Allah will save him from the heat of Jahannam (Hell-fire). Behold! The deeds of Paradise are difficult to reach, for they are on top of a hill, while the deeds of the Fire are easy to find in the lowlands. The happy person is he who is saved from the tests. Verily, there is no dose of anything better to Allah than a dose of rage that the servant controls, and whenever the servant of Allah controls it, he will be internally filled with faith.)

This Hadith was recorded by Imam Ahmad, its chain of narration is good, it does not contain any disparraged narrators, and the meaning is good.

Imam Ahmad recorded that Sahl bin Mu`adh bin Anas said that his father said that the Messenger of Allah said,

«مَنْ كَظَمَ غَيْظًا وَهُوَ قَادِرٌ عَلَى أَنْ يُنْفِذَهُ دَعَاهُ اللهُ عَلَى رُؤُوسِ الْخَلَائِقِ حَتَّى يُخَيِّرَهُ مِنْ أَيِّ الْحُورِ شَاءَ»

(Whoever controlled rage while able to act upon it, then Allah will call him while all creation is a witness, until He gives him the choice of any of the Huris (fair females with wide, lovely eyes - as mates for the pious) he wishes.)

Abu Dawud, At-Tirmidhi and Ibn Majah collected this Hadith, which At-Tirmidhi said was "Hasan Gharib".

Ibn Marduwyah recorded that Ibn `Umar said that the Messenger of Allah said,

«مَا تَجَرَّعَ عَبْدٌ مِنْ جَرْعَةٍ أَفْضَلَ أَجْرًا مِنْ جَرْعَةِ غَيْظٍ كَظَمَهَا ابْتِغَاءَ وَجْهِ اللهِ»

(There is not a dose of anything that the servant takes which is better than a dose of control of rage that he feels, when he does it seeking Allah's Face.) Ibn Jarir and Ibn Majah also collected this Hadith.

Chapter 3: Al-i-'Imran (The Family of Imran), Verses 093-200   57

Allah said,

(who repress anger) meaning, they do not satisfy their rage upon people. Rather, they refrain from harming them and await their rewards with Allah, the Exalted and Most Honored. Allah then said,

(and who pardon men;) They forgive those who treat them with injustice. Therefore, they do not hold any ill feelings about anyone in their hearts, and this is the most excellent conduct in this regard. This is why Allah said,

(verily, Allah loves the Muhsinin (the good-doers)).

This good conduct is a type of Ihsan (excellence in the religion). There is a Hadith that reads,

«ثَلَاثٌ أُقْسِمُ عَلَيْهِنَّ: مَا نَقَصَ مَالٌ مِنْ صَدَقَةٍ، وَمَا زَادَ اللهُ عَبْدًا بِعَفْوٍ إِلَّا عِزًّا، وَمَنْ تَوَاضَعَ لِلهِ رَفَعَهُ اللهُ»

(I swear regarding three matters: no charity shall ever decrease the wealth; whenever one forgives people, then Allah will magnify his honor; and he who is humble for Allah, then Allah will raise his rank.)

Allah said,

(And those who, when they have committed Fahishah or wronged themselves with evil, remember Allah and ask forgiveness for their sins) (3:135).

Therefore, if they commit an error they follow it with repentance and ask forgiveness. Imam Ahmad recorded that Abu Hurayrah said that the Prophet said,

«إِنَّ رَجُلًا أَذْنَبَ ذَنْبًا فَقَالَ: رَبِّ إِنِّي أَذْنَبْتُ ذَنْبًا فَاغْفِرْهُ، فَقَالَ اللهُ عَزَّ وَجَلَّ: عَبْدِي عَمِلَ ذَنْبًا فَعَلِمَ أَنَّ لَهُ رَبًّا يَغْفِرُ الذَّنْبَ وَيَأْخُذُ بِهِ، قَدْ غَفَرْتُ لِعَبْدِي، ثُمَّ عَمِلَ ذَنْبًا آخَرَ فَقَالَ: رَبِّ إِنِّي عَمِلْتُ ذَنْبًا فَاغْفِرْهُ، فَقَالَ تَبَارَكَ وَتَعَالَى: عَلِمَ عَبْدِي أَنَّ لَهُ رَبًّا يَغْفِرُ الذَّنْبَ وَيَأْخُذُ بِهِ، قَدْ غَفَرْتُ لِعَبْدِي، ثُمَّ عَمِلَ ذَنْبًا آخَرَ فَقَالَ: رَبِّ إِنِّي عَمِلْتُ ذَنْبًا فَاغْفِرْهُ لِي، فَقَالَ اللهُ عَزَّ وَجَلَّ: عَلِمَ عَبْدِي أَنَّ لَهُ رَبًّا يَغْفِرُ الذَّنْبَ وَيَأْخُذُ بِهِ، قَدْ غَفَرْتُ لِعَبْدِي، ثُمَّ عَمِلَ

ذَنْبًا آخَرَ فَقَالَ: رَبِّ إِنِّي عَمِلْتُ ذَنْبًا فَاغْفِرْهُ لِي، فَقَالَ اللهُ عَزَّ وَجَلَّ: عَلِمَ عَبْدِي أَنَّ لَهُ رَبًّا يَغْفِرُ الذَّنْبَ وَيَأْخُذُ بِهِ، أُشْهِدُكُمْ أَنِّي قَدْ غَفَرْتُ لِعَبْدِي فَلْيَعْمَلْ مَا شَاءَ»

(A man once committed an error and said, `O Lord! I committed an error, so forgive me.' Allah said, `My servant committed an error and knew that he has a Lord Who forgives or punishes for the error. I have forgiven My servant.' The man committed another error and said, `O Lord! I committed an error, so forgive me.' Allah said, `My servant knew that he has a Lord Who forgives or punishes for the sin. I have forgiven My servant.' The man committed another error and said, `O Lord! I committed an error, so forgive me.' Allah said, `My servant knew that he has a Lord Who forgives or punishes for the error. I have forgiven my servant.' He then committed another error and said, `O Lord! I committed an error, so forgive me.' Allah said, `My servant knew that he has a Lord Who forgives or punishes for the error. Bear witness that I have forgiven My servant, so let him do whatever he likes.') A similar narration was collected in the Sahih.

`Abdur-Razzaq recorded that Anas bin Malik said, "I was told that when the Ayah,

(And those who, when they have committed Fahishah or wronged themselves with evil, remember Allah and ask forgiveness for their sins,) was revealed, Iblis (Shayatan) cried." Allah's statement,

(and none can forgive sins but Allah), means that none except Allah forgives sins. tAllah said,

(And do not persist in what (wrong) they have done, while they know), for they repent from their error, return to Allah before death, do not insist on error, and if they err again, they repent from it. Allah said here,

(while they know) Mujahid and `Abdullah bin `Ubayd bin `Umayr commented, "Whoever repents, then Allah will forgive him." Similarly, Allah said,

(Know they not that Allah accepts repentance from His servants) (9:104), and,

(And whoever does evil or wrongs himself but afterwards seeks Allah's forgiveness, he will find Allah Oft-Forgiving, Most Merciful.) (4: 110) and there are several examples similar to this Ayah.

Next, Allah said after this description,

(For such, the reward is forgiveness from their Lord) (3:136), as a reward for these qualities, (forgiveness from their Lord, and Gardens with rivers flowing underneath (Paradise)) carrying all kinds of drinks,

(wherein they shall abide forever) and ever,

(How excellent is this reward for the doers) Allah praises Paradise in this part of the Ayah.

Surah: 3 Ayah: 137, Ayah: 138, Ayah: 139, Ayah: 140, Ayah: 141, Ayah: 142 & Ayah: 143

﴿ قَدْ خَلَتْ مِن قَبْلِكُمْ سُنَنٌ فَسِيرُوا۟ فِى ٱلْأَرْضِ فَٱنظُرُوا۟ كَيْفَ كَانَ عَـٰقِبَةُ ٱلْمُكَذِّبِينَ ۝ ﴾

137. Many similar ways (and mishaps of life) were faced by nations (believers and disbelievers) that have passed away before you (as you have faced in the battle of Uhud), so travel through the earth, and see what was the end of those who disbelieved (in the Oneness of Allâh, and disobeyed Him and His Messengers).

﴿ هَـٰذَا بَيَانٌ لِّلنَّاسِ وَهُدًى وَمَوْعِظَةٌ لِّلْمُتَّقِينَ ۝ ﴾

138. This (the Qur'ân) is a plain statement for mankind, a guidance and instruction to those who are Al-Muttaqûn (the pious - see V.2:2).

﴿ وَلَا تَهِنُوا۟ وَلَا تَحْزَنُوا۟ وَأَنتُمُ ٱلْأَعْلَوْنَ إِن كُنتُم مُّؤْمِنِينَ ۝ ﴾

139. So do not become weak (against your enemy), nor be sad, and you will be superior (in victory) if you are indeed (true) believers.

﴿ إِن يَمْسَسْكُمْ قَرْحٌ فَقَدْ مَسَّ ٱلْقَوْمَ قَرْحٌ مِّثْلُهُۥ ۚ وَتِلْكَ ٱلْأَيَّامُ نُدَاوِلُهَا بَيْنَ ٱلنَّاسِ وَلِيَعْلَمَ ٱللَّهُ ٱلَّذِينَ ءَامَنُوا۟ وَيَتَّخِذَ مِنكُمْ شُهَدَآءَ ۗ وَٱللَّهُ لَا يُحِبُّ ٱلظَّـٰلِمِينَ ۝ ﴾

140. If a wound (and killing) has touched you, be sure a similar wound (and killing) has touched the others. And so are the days (good and not so good), We give to men by turns, that Allâh may test those who believe, and that He may take martyrs from among you. And Allâh likes not the Zâlimûn (polytheists and wrong-doers).

﴿ وَلِيُمَحِّصَ ٱللَّهُ ٱلَّذِينَ ءَامَنُوا۟ وَيَمْحَقَ ٱلْكَـٰفِرِينَ ۝ ﴾

141. And that Allâh may test (or purify) the believers (from sins) and destroy the disbelievers.

$$\bm{\{} \text{أَمْ حَسِبْتُمْ أَن تَدْخُلُوا۟ ٱلْجَنَّةَ وَلَمَّا يَعْلَمِ ٱللَّهُ ٱلَّذِينَ جَـٰهَدُوا۟ مِنكُمْ وَيَعْلَمَ ٱلصَّـٰبِرِينَ} \; ﴿١٤٢﴾ \; \bm{\}}$$

142. Do you think that you will enter Paradise before Allâh tests those of you who fought (in His Cause) and (also) tests those who are As-Sâbirin (the patient)?

$$\bm{\{} \text{وَلَقَدْ كُنتُمْ تَمَنَّوْنَ ٱلْمَوْتَ مِن قَبْلِ أَن تَلْقَوْهُ فَقَدْ رَأَيْتُمُوهُ وَأَنتُمْ تَنظُرُونَ} \; ﴿١٤٣﴾ \; \bm{\}}$$

143. You did indeed wish for death (Ash-Shahâdah - martyrdom) before you met it. Now you have seen it openly with your own eyes.

Transliteration

137. Qad khalat min qablikum sunanun faseeroo fee al-ardi faonthuroo kayfa kana AAaqibatu almukaththibeena 138. Hatha bayanun lilnnasi wahudan wamawAAithatun lilmuttaqeena 139. Wala tahinoo wala tahzanoo waantumu al-aAAlawna in kuntum mu/mineena 140. In yamsaskum qarhun faqad massa alqawma qarhun mithluhu watilka al-ayyamu nudawiluha bayna alnnasi waliyaAAlama Allahu allatheena amanoo wayattakhitha minkum shuhadaa waAllahu la yuhibbu alththalimeena 141. Waliyumahhisa Allahu allatheena amanoo wayamhaqa alkafireena 142. Am hasibtum an tadkhuloo aljannata walamma yaAAlami Allahu allatheena jahadoo minkum wayaAAlama alssabireena 143. Walaqad kuntum tamannawna almawta min qabli an talqawhu faqad raaytumoohu waantum tanthuroona

Tafsir Ibn Kathir

The Wisdom Behind the Losses Muslims Suffered During Uhud

Allah states to His believing servants who suffered losses in the battle of Uhud, including seventy dead,

(Many similar ways (and mishaps of life) were faced before you), for the previous nations who followed their Prophets before you, they too suffered losses. However, the good end was theirs, and the ultimate defeat was for the disbelievers. This is why Allah said,

(so travel through the earth, and see what was the end of those who denied). Allah said next,

(This is a plain statement for mankind), meaning, the Qur'an explains the true reality of things and narrates how the previous nations suffered by the hands of their enemies.

(And a guidance and instruction) for the Qur'an contains the news of the past, and,

(guidance) for your hearts,

(and instruction for the Muttaqin) to discourage committing the prohibited and forbidden matters. Allah comforts the believers by saying,

(So do not become weak), because of what you suffered,

(nor be sad, and you will be triumphant if you are indeed believers), for surely, the ultimate victory and triumph will be yours, O believers.

(If a wound has touched you, be sure a similar wound has touched the others) (3:140).

Therefore, the Ayah says, if you suffered injuries and some of you were killed, then your enemies also suffered injuries and fatalities.

(And so are the days, that We give to men by turns), and at times -- out of wisdom -- We allow the enemy to overcome you, although the final good end will be yours.

(and that Allah may know (test) those who believe,) meaning, "So that We find out who would be patient while fighting the enemies," according to Ibn `Abbas.

(and that He may take martyrs from among you) those who would be killed in Allah's cause and gladly offer their lives seeking His pleasure.

(And Allah likes not the wrongdoers. And that Allah may test those who believe) (3:140,141), by forgiving them their sins if they have any. Otherwise, Allah will raise their grades according to the losses they suffered. Allah's statement,

(and destroy the disbelievers), for it is their conduct that if they gain the upper hand, they transgress and commit aggression. However, this conduct only leads to ultimate destruction, extermination, perishing and dying out.

Allah then said,

(Do you think that you will enter Paradise before Allah knows (tests) those of you who will perform Jihad and (also) knows (tests) those who are the patient) (3:142).

The Ayah asks, do you think that you will enter Paradise without being tested with warfare and hardships Allah said in Surat Al-Baqarah,

(Or think you that you will enter Paradise without such (trials) as came to those who passed away before you They were afflicted with severe poverty and ailments and were so shaken. ..) (2:214). Allah said,

(Alif Lam Mim. Do people think that they will be left alone because they say: "We believe," and will not be tested) (29:1,2), This is why He said here,

(Do you think that you will enter Paradise before Allah knows (tests) those of you who will perform Jihad and (also) knows (tests) those who are the patient) (3:142) meaning, you will not earn Paradise until you are tested and thus Allah knows who among you are the ones who struggle and fight in His cause and are patient in the face of the enemy. Allah said,

(You did indeed wish for death (martyrdom) before you met it. Now you have seen it openly with your own eyes) (3:143).

The Ayah proclaims, O believers! Before today, you wished that you could meet the enemy and were eager to fight them. What you wished has occurred, so fight them and be patient.

In the Two Sahihs it is recorded that the Messenger of Allah said,

«لَا تَتَمَنَّوْا لِقَاءَ الْعَدُوِّ، وَسَلُوا اللهَ الْعَافِيَةَ، فَإِذَا لَقِيتُمُوهُمْ فَاصْبِرُوا، وَاعْلَمُوا أَنَّ الْجَنَّةَ تَحْتَ ظِلَالِ السُّيُوفِ»

(Do not wish to encounter the enemy, and ask Allah for your well-being. However, if you do encounter them, then observe patience and know that Paradise is under the shade of swords.)

This is why Allah said here,

(Now you have seen it): death, you saw it when the swords appeared, the blades were sharpened, the spears crisscrossed and men stood in lines for battle. This part of the Ayah contains a figure of speech that mentions imagining what can be felt but not seen.

Surah: 3 Ayah: 144, Ayah: 145, Ayah: 146, Ayah: 147 & Ayah: 148

﴿ وَمَا مُحَمَّدٌ إِلَّا رَسُولٌ قَدْ خَلَتْ مِن قَبْلِهِ ٱلرُّسُلُ أَفَإِيْن مَّاتَ أَوْ قُتِلَ ٱنقَلَبْتُمْ عَلَىٰٓ أَعْقَٰبِكُمْ وَمَن يَنقَلِبْ عَلَىٰ عَقِبَيْهِ فَلَن يَضُرَّ ٱللَّهَ شَيْـًٔا وَسَيَجْزِى ٱللَّهُ ٱلشَّٰكِرِينَ ﴾

144. Muhammad (peace be upon him) is no more than a Messenger, and indeed (many) Messengers have passed away before him. If he dies or is killed, will you then turn back on your heels (as disbelievers)? And he who turns back on his heels, not the least harm will he do to Allâh; and Allâh will give reward to those who are grateful.

﴿ وَمَا كَانَ لِنَفْسٍ أَن تَمُوتَ إِلَّا بِإِذْنِ ٱللَّهِ كِتَٰبًا مُّؤَجَّلًا وَمَن يُرِدْ ثَوَابَ ٱلدُّنْيَا نُؤْتِهِ مِنْهَا وَمَن يُرِدْ ثَوَابَ ٱلْأَخِرَةِ نُؤْتِهِ مِنْهَا وَسَنَجْزِى ٱلشَّٰكِرِينَ ﴾

145. And no person can ever die except by Allâh's Leave and at an appointed term. And whoever desires a reward in (this) world, We shall give him of it; and whoever desires a reward in the Hereafter, We shall give him thereof. And We shall reward the grateful.

Chapter 3: Al-i-'Imran (The Family of Imran), Verses 093-200

﴿ وَكَأَيِّن مِّن نَّبِيٍّ قَـٰتَلَ مَعَهُ رِبِّيُّونَ كَثِيرٌ فَمَا وَهَنُواْ لِمَآ أَصَابَهُمْ فِى سَبِيلِ ٱللَّهِ وَمَا ضَعُفُواْ وَمَا ٱسْتَكَانُواْ ۗ وَٱللَّهُ يُحِبُّ ٱلصَّـٰبِرِينَ ﴿١٤٦﴾ ﴾

146. And many a Prophet (i.e. many from amongst the Prophets) fought (in Allâh's Cause) and along with him (fought) large bands of religious learned men. But they never lost heart for that which did befall them in Allâh's Way, nor did they weaken nor degrade themselves. And Allâh loves As-Sâbirin (the patient).

﴿ وَمَا كَانَ قَوْلَهُمْ إِلَّآ أَن قَالُواْ رَبَّنَا ٱغْفِرْ لَنَا ذُنُوبَنَا وَإِسْرَافَنَا فِىٓ أَمْرِنَا وَثَبِّتْ أَقْدَامَنَا وَٱنصُرْنَا عَلَى ٱلْقَوْمِ ٱلْكَـٰفِرِينَ ﴿١٤٧﴾ ﴾

147. And they said nothing but: "Our Lord! Forgive us our sins and our transgressions (in keeping our duties to You), establish our feet firmly, and give us victory over the disbelieving folk."

﴿ فَـَٔاتَىٰهُمُ ٱللَّهُ ثَوَابَ ٱلدُّنْيَا وَحُسْنَ ثَوَابِ ٱلْـَٔاخِرَةِ ۗ وَٱللَّهُ يُحِبُّ ٱلْمُحْسِنِينَ ﴿١٤٨﴾ ﴾

148. So Allâh gave them the reward of this world, and the excellent reward of the Hereafter. And Allâh loves Al-Muhsinûn (the good-doers).

Transliteration

144. Wama muhammadun illa rasoolun qad khalat min qablihi alrrusulu afa-in mata aw qutila inqalabtum AAala aAAqabikum waman yanqalib AAala AAaqibayhi falan yadurra Allaha shay-an wasayajzee Allahu alshshakireena 145. Wama kana linafsin an tamoota illa bi-ithni Allahi kitaban mu-ajjalan waman yurid thawaba alddunya nu/tihi minha waman yurid thawaba al-akhirati nu/tihi minha wasanajzee alshshakireena 146. Wakaayyin min nabiyyin qatala maAAahu ribbiyyoona katheerun fama wahanoo lima asabahum fee sabeeli Allahi wama daAAufoo wama istakanoo waAllahu yuhibbu alssabireena 147. Wama kana qawlahum illa an qaloo rabbana ighfir lana thunoobana wa-israfana fee amrina wathabbit aqdamana waonsurna AAala alqawmi alkafireena 148. Faatahumu Allahu thawaba alddunya wahusna thawabi al-akhirati waAllahu yuhibbu almuhsineena

Tafsir Ibn Kathir

The Rumor that the Prophet was Killed at Uhud

When Muslims suffered defeat in battle at Uhud and some of them were killed, Shaytan shouted, "Muhammad has been killed." Ibn Qami'ah went back to the idolators and claimed, "I have killed Muhammad." Some Muslims believed this rumor and thought that the Messenger of Allah had been killed, claiming that this could happen, for Allah narrated that this occurred to many Prophets before. Therefore, the Muslims' resolve was weakened and they did not actively participate in battle. This is why Allah sent down to His Messenger His statement,

(Muhammad is no more than a Messenger, and indeed Messengers have passed away before him.) he is to deliver Allah's Message and may be killed in the process, just as what happened to many Prophets before. Ibn Abi Najih said that his father said that a man from the Muhajirin passed by an Ansari man who was bleeding (during Uhud) and said to him, "O fellow! Did you know that Muhammad was killed" The Ansari man said, "Even if Muhammad was killed, he has indeed conveyed the Message. Therefore, defend your religion." The Ayah,

(Muhammad is no more than a Messenger, and indeed (many) Messengers have passed away before him), was revealed. This story was collected by Al-Hafiz Abu Bakr Al-Bayhaqi in Dala'il An-Nubuwwah.

Allah said next, while chastising those who became weak,

(If he dies or is killed, will you then turn back on your heels), become disbelievers,

(And he who turns back on his heels, not the least harm will he do to Allah; and Allah will give reward to those who are grateful), those who obeyed Allah, defended His religion and followed His Messenger whether he was alive or dead. The Sahih, Musnad and Sunan collections gathered various chains of narration stating that Abu Bakr recited this Ayah when the Messenger of Allah died. Al-Bukhari recorded that `A'ishah said that Abu Bakr came riding his horse from his dwelling in As-Sunh. He dismounted, entered the Masjid and did not speak to anyone until he came to her (in her room) and went directly to the Prophet, who was covered with a marked blanket. Abu Bakr uncovered his face, knelt down and kissed him, then started weeping and proclaimed, "My father and my mother be sacrificed for you! Allah will not combine two deaths on you. You have died the death, which was written for you."

Ibn `Abbas narrated that Abu Bakr then came out, while `Umar was addressing the people, and Abu Bakr told him to sit down but `Umar refused, and the people attended to Abu Bakr and left `Umar. Abu Bakr said, "To proceed; whoever among you worshipped Muhammad, then Muhammad is dead, but whoever worshipped Allah, Allah is alive and will never die. Allah said,

(Muhammad is no more than a Messenger and indeed (many) Messengers have passed away before him. If he dies or is killed, will you then turn back on your heels And he who turns back on his heels, not the least harm will he do to Allah; and Allah will reward the grateful.)"

The narrator added, "By Allah, it was as if the people never knew that Allah had revealed this verse before until Abu Bakr recited it, and then whoever heard it, started reciting it." Sa`id bin Al-Musayyib said that `Umar said, "By Allah! When I heard Abu Bakr recite this Ayah, my feet could not hold me, and I fell to the ground."

Allah said,

(And no person can ever die except by Allah's leave and at an appointed term.) (3:145) meaning, no one dies except by Allah's decision, after he has finished the term that Allah has destined for him. This is why Allah said, (at an appointed term) which is similar to His statements,

(And no aged man is granted a length of life nor is a part cut off from his life, but it is in a Book) (35:11), and,

(He it is Who has created you from clay, and then has decreed a (stated) term (for you to die). And there is with Him another determined term (for you to be resurrected)) (6:2).

This Ayah (3:145) encourages cowards to participate in battle; for doing so, or avoiding battle neither decreases, nor increases the life term. Ibn Abi Hatim narrated that, Habib bin Suhban said that a Muslim man, Hujr bin `Adi, said in a battle, "What prevents you from crossing this river (the Euphrates) to the enemy

(And no person can ever die except by Allah's leave and at an appointed term)" He then crossed the river riding his horse, and when he did, the Muslims followed him. When the enemy saw them, they started shouting, "Diwan (Persian; crazy)," and they ran away.

Allah said next,

(And whoever desires a reward in the world, We shall give him of it; and whoever desires a reward in the Hereafter, We shall give him thereof).

Therefore, the Ayah proclaims, whoever works for the sake of this life, will only earn what Allah decides he will earn. However, he will not have a share in the Hereafter. Whoever works for the sake of the Hereafter, Allah will give him a share in the Hereafter, along with what He decides for him in this life. In similar statements, Allah said,

(Whosoever desires (by his deeds) the reward of the Hereafter, We give him increase in his reward, and whosoever desires the reward of this world (by his deeds), We give him thereof (what is decreed for him), and he has no portion in the Hereafter.) (42:20), and,

(Whoever desires the quick-passing (transitory enjoyment of this world), We readily grant him what We will for whom We like. Then, afterwards, We have appointed for him Hell; he will burn therein disgraced and despised. And whoever desires the Hereafter and strives for it, with the necessary effort due for it while he is a believer, then such are the ones whose striving shall be appreciated) (17:18-19).

In this Ayah (3:145), Allah said,

(And We shall reward the grateful.) meaning, We shall award them with Our favor and mercy in this life and the Hereafter, according to the degree of their appreciation (of Allah) and their good deeds.

Allah then comforts the believers because of what they suffered in Uhud,

(And many a Prophet fought and along with him many Ribbiyyun.)

It was said that this Ayah means that many Prophets and their companions were killed in earlier times, as is the view chosen by Ibn Jarir. It was also said that the Ayah means that many Prophets witnessed their companions' death before their eyes. However, Ibn Ishaq mentioned another explanation in his Sirah, saying that this Ayah means, "Many a Prophet was killed, and he had many companions whose resolve did not weaken after their Prophet died, and they did not become feeble in the face of the enemy. What they suffered in Jihad in Allah's cause and for the sake of their religion did not make them lose heart. This is patience,

(and Allah loves the patient.)" As-Suhayli agreed with this explanation and defended it vigorously. This view is supported by Allah saying;

(And along with him many Ribbiyyun).

In his book about the battles, Al-Amawi mentioned only this explanation for the Ayah. Sufyan Ath-Thawri reported that, Ibn Mas`ud said that,

(many Ribbiyyun) means, thousands. Ibn `Abbas, Mujahid, Sa`id bin Jubayr, `Ikrimah, Al-Hasan, Qatadah, As-Suddi, Ar-Rabi` and `Ata' Al-Khurasani said that the word Ribbiyyun means, `large bands'. `Abdur-Razzaq narrated that Ma`mmar said that Al-Hasan said that,

(many Ribbiyyun) means, many scholars. He also said that it means patient and pious scholars.

(But they never lost heart for that which befell them in Allah's way, nor did they weaken nor degrade themselves.)

Qatadah and Ar-Rabi` bin Anas said that,

(nor did they weaken), means, after their Prophet was killed.

(nor degrade themselves), by reverting from the true guidance and religion. Rather, they fought on the path that Allah's Prophet fought on until they met Allah. Ibn `Abbas said that,

(nor degrade themselves) means, nor became humiliated, while As-Suddi and Ibn Zayd said that it means, they did not give in to the enemy.

(And Allah loves the patient. And they said nothing but: "Our Lord! Forgive us our sins and our transgressions, establish our feet firmly, and give us victory over the disbelieving folk.") (3:146-147), and this was the statement that they kept repeating. Therefore,

(So Allah gave them the reward of this world) victory, triumph and the good end,

(and the excellent reward of the Hereafter) added to the gains in this life,

(And Allah loves the good-doers).

Surah: 3 Ayah: 149, Ayah: 150, Ayah: 151, Ayah: 152 & Ayah: 153

﴿ يَٰٓأَيُّهَا ٱلَّذِينَ ءَامَنُوٓاْ إِن تُطِيعُواْ ٱلَّذِينَ كَفَرُواْ يَرُدُّوكُمْ عَلَىٰٓ أَعْقَٰبِكُمْ فَتَنقَلِبُواْ خَٰسِرِينَ ۝ ﴾

149. O you who believe! If you obey those who disbelieve, they will send you back on your heels, and you will turn back (from Faith) as losers.

﴿ بَلِ ٱللَّهُ مَوْلَىٰكُمْ ۖ وَهُوَ خَيْرُ ٱلنَّٰصِرِينَ ۝ ﴾

150. Nay, Allâh is your Maulâ (Patron, Lord, Helper, Protector), and He is the Best of helpers.

﴿ سَنُلْقِى فِى قُلُوبِ ٱلَّذِينَ كَفَرُواْ ٱلرُّعْبَ بِمَآ أَشْرَكُواْ بِٱللَّهِ مَا لَمْ يُنَزِّلْ بِهِۦ سُلْطَٰنًا ۖ وَمَأْوَىٰهُمُ ٱلنَّارُ ۚ وَبِئْسَ مَثْوَى ٱلظَّٰلِمِينَ ۝ ﴾

151. We shall cast terror into the hearts of those who disbelieve, because they joined others in worship with Allâh, for which He had sent no authority; their abode will be the Fire and how evil is the abode of the Zâlimûn (polytheists and wrong-doers).

﴿ وَلَقَدْ صَدَقَكُمُ ٱللَّهُ وَعْدَهُۥٓ إِذْ تَحُسُّونَهُم بِإِذْنِهِۦ ۖ حَتَّىٰٓ إِذَا فَشِلْتُمْ وَتَنَٰزَعْتُمْ فِى ٱلْأَمْرِ وَعَصَيْتُم مِّنۢ بَعْدِ مَآ أَرَىٰكُم مَّا تُحِبُّونَ ۚ مِنكُم مَّن يُرِيدُ ٱلدُّنْيَا وَمِنكُم مَّن يُرِيدُ ٱلْءَاخِرَةَ ۚ ثُمَّ صَرَفَكُمْ عَنْهُمْ لِيَبْتَلِيَكُمْ ۖ وَلَقَدْ عَفَا عَنكُمْ ۗ وَٱللَّهُ ذُو فَضْلٍ عَلَى ٱلْمُؤْمِنِينَ ۝ ﴾

152. And Allâh did indeed fulfil His Promise to you when you were killing them (your enemy) with His Permission; until (the moment) you lost your courage and fell to disputing about the order, and disobeyed after He showed you (of the booty) which you love. Among you are some that desire this world and some that desire the Hereafter. Then He made you flee from them (your enemy), that He might test you. But surely, He forgave you, and Allâh is Most Gracious to the believers.

﴿ ۞ إِذْ تُصْعِدُونَ وَلَا تَلْوُۥنَ عَلَىٰٓ أَحَدٍ وَٱلرَّسُولُ يَدْعُوكُمْ فِىٓ أُخْرَىٰكُمْ فَأَثَٰبَكُمْ غَمًّۢا بِغَمٍّ لِّكَيْلَا تَحْزَنُواْ عَلَىٰ مَا فَاتَكُمْ وَلَا مَآ أَصَٰبَكُمْ ۗ وَٱللَّهُ خَبِيرٌۢ بِمَا تَعْمَلُونَ ۝ ﴾

153. (And remember) when you ran away (dreadfully) without even casting a side glance at anyone, and the Messenger (Muhammad (peace be upon him)) was in

your rear calling you back. There did Allâh give you one distress after another by way of requital to teach you not to grieve for that which had escaped you, nor for that which had befallen you. And Allâh is Well-Aware of all that you do.

Transliteration

149. Ya ayyuha allatheena amanoo in tuteeAAoo allatheena kafaroo yaruddookum AAala aAAqabikum fatanqaliboo khasireena   150. Bali Allahu mawlakum wahuwa khayru alnnasireena   151. Sanulqee fee quloobi allatheena kafaroo alrruAAba bima ashrakoo biAllahi ma lam yunazzil bihi sultanan wama/wahumu alnnaru wabi/sa mathwa alththalimeena   152. Walaqad sadaqakumu Allahu waAAdahu ith tahussoonahum bi-ithnihi hatta itha fashiltum watanazaAAtum fee al-amri waAAasaytum min baAAdi ma arakum ma tuhibboona minkum man yureedu alddunya waminkum man yureedu al-akhirata thumma sarafakum AAanhum liyabtaliyakum walaqad AAafa AAankum waAllahu thoo fadlin AAala almu/mineena   153. Ith tusAAidoona wala talwoona AAala ahadin waalrrasoolu yadAAookum fee okhrakum faathabakum ghamman bighammin likay la tahzanoo AAala ma fatakum wala ma asabakum waAllahu khabeerun bima taAAmaloona

Tafsir Ibn Kathir

The Prohibition of Obeying the Disbelievers; the Cause of Defeat at Uhud

Allah warns His believing servants against obeying the disbelievers and hypocrites, because such obedience leads to utter destruction in this life and the Hereafter. This is why Allah said,

(If you obey those who disbelieve, they will send you back on your heels, and you will turn back (from faith) as losers) (3:149).

Allah also commands the believers to obey Him, take Him as their protector, seek His aid and trust in Him. Allah said,

(Nay, Allah is your protector, and He is the best of helpers).

Allah next conveys the good news that He will put fear of the Muslims, and feelings of subordination to the Muslims in the hearts of their disbelieving enemies, because of their Kufr and Shirk. And Allah has prepared torment and punishment for them in the Hereafter. Allah said,

(We shall cast terror into the hearts of those who disbelieve, because they joined others in worship with Allah, for which He sent no authority; their abode will be the Fire and how evil is the abode of the wrongdoers). In addition, the Two Sahihs recorded that Jabir bin `Abdullah said that the Messenger of Allah said,

Chapter 3: Al-i-'Imran (The Family of Imran), Verses 093-200

«أُعْطِيتُ خَمْسًا لَمْ يُعْطَهُنَّ أَحَدٌ مِنَ الْأَنْبِيَاءِ قَبْلِي: نُصِرْتُ بِالرُّعْبِ مَسِيرَةَ شَهْرٍ، وَجُعِلَتْ لِيَ الْأَرْضُ مَسْجِدًا وَطَهُورًا، وَأُحِلَّتْ لِيَ الْغَنَائِمُ، وَأُعْطِيتُ الشَّفَاعَةَ، وَكَانَ النَّبِيُّ يُبْعَثُ إِلَى قَوْمِهِ خَاصَّةً وَبُعِثْتُ إِلَى النَّاسِ عَامَّةً»

(I was given five things that no other Prophet before me was given. I was aided with fear the distance of one month, the earth was made a Masjid and clean place for me, I was allowed war booty, I was given the Intercession, and Prophets used to be sent to their people, but I was sent to all mankind particularly.)

Allah said,

(And Allah did indeed fulfill His promise to you) (3:152),

in the beginning of the day of Uhud,

(when you were killing them), slaying your enemies,

(with His permission), for He allowed you to do that against them,

(until when you Fashiltum). Ibn Jurayj said that Ibn `Abbas said that Fashiltum means, `lost courage'.

(and fell to disputing about the order, and disobeyed) such as the mistake made by the archers,

(after He showed you what you love), that is, victory over the disbelievers,

(Among you are some that desire this world) referring to those who sought to collect the booty when they saw the enemy being defeated,

(and some that desire the Hereafter. Then He made you flee from them, that He might test you).

This Ayah means, Allah gave them the upper hand to try and test you, O believers,

(but surely, He forgave you),

He forgave the error you committed, because, and Allah knows best, the idolators were many and well supplied, while Muslims had few men and few supplies.

Al-Bukhari recorded that Al-Bara' said, "We met the idolators on that day (Uhud) and the Prophet appointed `Abdullah bin Jubayr as the commander of the archers. He instructed them, `Retain your position, and if you see that we have defeated them, do not abandon your positions. If you see that they defeated us, do not rush to help us.' The disbelievers gave flight when we met them, and we saw their women fleeing up the mountain while lifting up their clothes revealing their anklets and their legs. So, the companions (of `Abdullah bin Jubayr) said, `The booty, the booty!' `Abdullah bin Jubayr said, `Allah's Messenger commanded me not to allow you to abandon your position.' They refused to listen, and when they left their position, Muslims were defeated and seventy of them were killed. Abu Sufyan shouted, `Is Muhammad present among these people' The Prophet said, `Do not answer him.' Then he asked, `Is the son of Abu Quhafah (Abu Bakr) present among these people' The Prophet said, `Do not answer him.' He asked again, `Is the son of Al-Khattab (`Umar) present among these people As for these (men), they have been killed, for had they been alive, they would have answered me.' `Umar could not control himself and said (to Abu Sufyan), `You lie, O enemy of Allah! The cause of your misery is still present.' Abu Sufyan said, `O Hubal, be high!' On that the Prophet said (to his Companions), `Answer him back.' They said, `What shall we say' He said, `Say, Allah is Higher and more Sublime.' Abu Sufyan said, `We have the (idol) Al-`Uzza, and you have no `Uzza.' The Prophet said, `Answer him back.' They asked, `What shall we say' He said, `Say, Allah is our protector and you have no protector.' Abu Sufyan said, `Our victory today is vengeance for yours in the battle of Badr, and in war (the victory) is always undecided and is shared in turns by the belligerents. You will find some of your killed men mutilated, but I did not urge my men to do so, yet I do not feel sorry for their deed.''' Only Al-Bukhari collected this Hadith using this chain of narration. cMuhammad bin Ishaq said that, `Abdullah bin Az-Zubayr narrated that Az-Zubayr bin Al-`Awwam said, "By Allah! I saw the female servants and female companions of Hind (Abu Sufyan's wife) when they uncovered their legs and gave flight. At that time, there was no big or small effort separating us from capturing them. However, the archers went down the mount when the enemy gave flight from the battlefield, seeking to collect the booty. They uncovered our back lines to the horsemen of the disbelievers, who took the chance and attacked us from behind. Then a person shouted, `Muhammad has been killed.' So we pulled back, and the disbelievers followed us, after we had killed those who carried their flag, and none of them dared to come close the flag, until then.''' Muhammad bin Ishaq said next, "The flag of the disbelievers was left on the ground until `Amrah bint `Alqamah Al-Harithiyyah picked it up and gave it to the Quraysh who held it."

Allah said,

(Then He made you flee from them, that He might test you) (3:152).

Al-Bukhari recorded that Anas bin Malik said, "My uncle Anas bin An-Nadr was absent from the battle of Badr. He said, `I was absent from the first battle the Prophet fought (against the pagans). (By Allah) if Allah gives me a chance to fight along with the Messenger of Allah, then Allah will see how (bravely) I will fight.' On the day of Uhud when the Muslims turned their backs and fled, he said, `O Allah! I apologize to You for what these (meaning the Muslims) have done, and I denounce what these pagans have done.' Then he advanced lifting his sword, and when Sa`d bin Mu`adh met him, he said to him, `O Sa`d bin Mu`adh! Where are you! Paradise! I am smelling its aroma coming from before (Mount) Uhud,' and he went forth, fought and was killed. We found more than eighty stab wounds, sword blows or arrow holes on his body, which was mutilated so badly that none except his sister could recognize him, and she could only do so by his fingers or by a mole." This is the narration reported by Al-Bukhari, Muslim also collected a similar narration from Thabit from Anas.

The Defeat that the Muslims Suffered During the Battle of Uhud

Allah said,

((And remember) when you (Tus`iduna) ran away dreadfully without casting even a side glance at anyone), and Allah made the disbelievers leave you after you went up the mount, escaping your enemy. Al-Hasan and Qatadah said that, Tus`iduna, means, `go up the mountain'.

(without even casting a side glance at anyone) meaning, you did not glance at anyone else due to shock, fear and fright.

(and the Messenger was in your rear calling you back), for you left him behind you, while he was calling you to stop fleeing from the enemy and to return and fight.

As-Suddi said, "When the disbelievers attacked Muslim lines during the battle of Uhud and defeated them, some Muslims ran away to Al-Madinah, while some of them went up Mount Uhud, to a rock and stood on it. On that, the Messenger of Allah kept heralding, `Come to me, O servants of Allah! Come to me, O servants of Allah!' Allah mentioned that the Muslims went up the Mount and that the Prophet called them to come back, and said,

((And remember) when you ran away without even casting a side glance at anyone, and the Messenger was in your rear calling you back)." Similar was said by Ibn `Abbas, Qatadah, Ar-Rabi` and Ibn Zayd.

The Ansar and Muhajirin Defended the Messenger

Al-Bukhari recorded that Qays bin Abi Hazim said, "I saw Talhah's hand, it was paralyzed, because he shielded the Prophet with it." meaning on the day of Uhud. It is recorded in the Two Sahihs that Abu `Uthman An-Nahdi said, "On that day (Uhud) during which the Prophet fought, only Talhah bin `Ubaydullah and Sa`d remained with the Prophet."

Sa`id bin Al-Musayyib said, "I heard Sa`d bin Abi Waqqas saying, `The Messenger of Allah gave me arrows from his quiver on the day of Uhud and said, `Shoot, may I sacrifice my father and mother for you.'" Al-Bukhari also collected this Hadith. The Two Sahihs recorded that Sa`d bin Abi Waqqas said, "On the day of Uhud, I saw two men wearing white clothes, one to the right of the Prophet and one to his left, who were defending the Prophet fiercely. I have never seen these men before or after that day." Meaning angels Jibril and Mika'il, peace be upon them.

Abu Al-Aswad said that, `Urwah bin Az-Zubayr said, "Ubayy bin Khalaf of Bani Jumah swore in Makkah that he would kill the Messenger of Allah . When the Messenger was told of his vow, he said, `Rather, I shall kill him, Allah willing.' On the day of Uhud, Ubayy came while wearing iron shields and proclaiming, `May I not be saved, if Muhammad is saved.' He then headed to the direction of the Messenger of Allah intending to kill him, but Mus`ab bin `Umayr, from Bani Abd Ad-Dar, intercepted him and shielded the Prophet with his body, and Mus`ab bin `Umayr was killed. The Messenger of Allah saw Ubayy's neck exposed between the shields and helmet, stabbed him with his spear, and Ubayy fell from his horse to the ground. However, no blood spilled from his wound. His people came and carried him away while he was moaning like an ox. They said to him, `Why are you so anxious, it is only a flesh wound' Ubayy mentioned to them the Prophet's vow, `Rather, I shall kill Ubayy', then commented, `By He in Whose Hand is my soul! If what hit me hits the people of Dhul-Majaz (a popular pre-Islamic marketplace), they would all have perished.' He then died and went to the Fire,

(So, away with the dwellers of the blazing Fire!) (67:11)."

This was collected by Musa bin `Uqbah from Az-Zuhri from Sa`id bin Al-Musayyib.

It is recorded in the Two Sahih that when he was asked about the injuries the Messenger sustained (in Uhud), Sahl bin Sa`d said, "The face of Allah's Messenger was injured, his front tooth was broken and his helmet was smashed on his head. Therefore, Fatimah, the daughter of Allah's Messenger washed off the blood while `Ali was pouring water on her hand. When Fatimah saw that the bleeding increased more by the water, she took a mat, burnt it, and placed the ashes in the wound of the Prophet and the blood stopped oozing out." Allah said next,

(There did Allah give you one distress after another) (3:153),

He gave you grief over your grief. Ibn `Abbas said, `The first grief was because of the defeat, especially when it was rumored that Muhammad was killed. The second grief was when the idolators went up the mount and The Messenger of Allah said, `O Allah! It is not for them to rise above us.'"

`Abdur-Rahman bin `Awf said, "The first distress was because of the defeat and the second when a rumor started that Muhammad was killed, which to them, was worse than defeat." Ibn Marduwyah recorded both of these. Mujahid and Qatadah said, "The first distress was when they heard that Muhammad was killed and the second when they suffered casualties and injury." It has also been reported that Qatadah and Ar-Rabi` bin Anas said that it was the opposite (order). As-Suddi said that the first distress was because of the victory and booty that they missed and the second because of the enemy rising above them (on the mount). Allah said,

(by way of requital to teach you not to grieve for that which had escaped you), for that you missed the booty and triumph over your enemy.

(nor for what struck you), of injury and fatalities, as Ibn `Abbas, `Abdur-Rahman bin `Awf, Al-Hasan, Qatadah and As-Suddi stated. Allah said next,

(And Allah is Well-Aware of all that you do.) all praise is due to Him, and thanks, there is no deity worthy of worship except Him, the Most High, Most Honored.

Surah: 3 Ayah: 154 & Ayah: 155

﴿ ثُمَّ أَنزَلَ عَلَيْكُم مِّنۢ بَعْدِ ٱلْغَمِّ أَمَنَةً نُّعَاسًا يَغْشَىٰ طَآئِفَةً مِّنكُمْ ۖ وَطَآئِفَةٌ قَدْ أَهَمَّتْهُمْ أَنفُسُهُمْ يَظُنُّونَ بِٱللَّهِ غَيْرَ ٱلْحَقِّ ظَنَّ ٱلْجَٰهِلِيَّةِ ۖ يَقُولُونَ هَل لَّنَا مِنَ ٱلْأَمْرِ مِن شَىْءٍ ۗ قُلْ إِنَّ ٱلْأَمْرَ كُلَّهُۥ لِلَّهِ ۗ يُخْفُونَ فِىٓ أَنفُسِهِم مَّا لَا يُبْدُونَ لَكَ ۖ يَقُولُونَ لَوْ كَانَ لَنَا مِنَ ٱلْأَمْرِ شَىْءٌ مَّا قُتِلْنَا هَٰهُنَا ۗ قُل لَّوْ كُنتُمْ فِى بُيُوتِكُمْ لَبَرَزَ ٱلَّذِينَ كُتِبَ عَلَيْهِمُ ٱلْقَتْلُ إِلَىٰ مَضَاجِعِهِمْ ۖ وَلِيَبْتَلِىَ ٱللَّهُ مَا فِى صُدُورِكُمْ وَلِيُمَحِّصَ مَا فِى قُلُوبِكُمْ ۗ وَٱللَّهُ عَلِيمٌۢ بِذَاتِ ٱلصُّدُورِ ۝ ﴾

154. Then after the distress, He sent down security for you. Slumber overtook a party of you, while another party was thinking about themselves (as how to save their own selves, ignoring the others and the Prophet (peace be upon him)) and thought wrongly of Allâh - the thought of ignorance. They said, "Have we any part in the affair?" Say you (O Muhammad (peace be upon him)) "Indeed the affair belongs wholly to Allâh." They hide within themselves what they dare not reveal to you, saying: "If we had anything to do with the affair, none of us would have been killed here." Say: "Even if you had remained in your homes, those for whom death was decreed would certainly have gone forth to the place of their death," but that Allâh might test what is in your breasts; and to purify that which was in your hearts (sins), and Allâh is All-Knower of what is in (your) breasts.

﴿ إِنَّ ٱلَّذِينَ تَوَلَّوْا۟ مِنكُمْ يَوْمَ ٱلْتَقَى ٱلْجَمْعَانِ إِنَّمَا ٱسْتَزَلَّهُمُ ٱلشَّيْطَٰنُ بِبَعْضِ مَا كَسَبُوا۟ ۖ وَلَقَدْ عَفَا ٱللَّهُ عَنْهُمْ ۗ إِنَّ ٱللَّهَ غَفُورٌ حَلِيمٌ ۝ ﴾

155. Those of you who turned back on the day the two hosts met (i.e. the battle of Uhud), it was Shaitân (Satan) who caused them to backslide (run away from the battlefield) because of some (sins) they had earned. But Allâh, indeed, has forgiven them. Surely, Allâh is Oft-Forgiving, Most Forbearing.

Transliteration

154. Thumma anzala AAalaykum min baAAdi alghammi amanatan nuAAasan yaghsha ta-ifatan minkum wata-ifatun qad ahammat-hum anfusuhum yathunnoona biAllahi ghayra alhaqqi thanna aljahiliyyati yaqooloona hal lana mina al-amri min shay-in qul inna al-amra kullahu lillahi yukhfoona fee anfusihim ma la yubdoona laka yaqooloona law kana lana mina al-amri shay-on ma qutilna hahuna qul law kuntum fee buyootikum labaraza allatheena kutiba AAalayhimu alqatlu ila madajiAAihim waliyabtaliya Allahu ma fee sudoorikum waliyumahhisa ma fee quloobikum waAllahu AAaleemun bithati alssudoori 155. Inna allatheena tawallaw minkum yawma iltaqa aljamAAani innama istazallahumu alshshaytanu bibaAAdi ma kasaboo walaqad AAafa Allahu AAanhum inna Allaha ghafoorun haleemun

Tafsir Ibn Kathir

Slumber Overcame the Believers; the Fear that the Hypocrites Suffered

Allah reminds His servants of His favor when He sent down on them tranquillity and slumber that overcame them while they were carrying their weapons and feeling distress and grief. In this case, slumber is a favor and carries meanings of calmness and safety. For instance, Allah said in Surat Al-Anfal about the battle of Badr,

((Remember) when He covered you with a slumber as a security from Him) (8:11).

Al-Bukhari recorded that Anas said that, Abu Talhah said, "I was among those who were overcome by slumber during the battle of Uhud. My sword fell from my hand several times and I would pick it up, then it would fall and I would pick it up again." Al-Bukhari collected this Hadith in the stories of the battles without a chain of narration, and in the book of Tafsir with a chain of narrators. At-Tirmidhi, An-Nasa'i and Al-Hakim recorded from Anas that Abu Talhah said, "On the day of Uhud, I raised my head and looked around and found that everyone's head was nodding from slumber." This is the wording of At-Tirmidhi, who said, "Hasan Sahih". An-Nasa'i also recorded this Hadith from Anas who said that Abu Talhah said, "I was among those who were overcome by slumber."

The second group mentioned in the Ayah were the hypocrites who only thought about themselves, for they are the most cowardly people and those least likely to support the truth,

(and thought wrongly of Allah - the thought of ignorance) (3:154), for they are liars and people who have doubts and evil thoughts about Allah, the Exalted and Most Honored. Allah said,

(Then after the distress, He sent down security for you. Slumber overtook a party of you), the people of faith, certainty, firmness and reliance (on Allah) who are certain that Allah shall give victory to His Messenger and fulfill his objective.

(While another party was thinking about themselves), and they were not overcome by slumber because of their worry, fright and fear,

(and thought wrongly of Allah --- the thought of ignorance).

Similarly, Allah said in another statement,

(Nay, but you thought that the Messenger and the believers would never return to their families) (48:12).

This group thought that the idolators achieved ultimate victory, when their forces took the upper hand in battle, and that Islam and its people would perish. This is typical of people of doubt and hesitation, in the event of a hardship, they fall into such evil thoughts. Allah then described them that,

(they said) in this situation,

Chapter 3: Al-i-'Imran (The Family of Imran), Verses 093-200

("Have we any part in the affair") Allah replied,

(Say: "Indeed the affair belongs wholly to Allah." They hide within themselves what they dare not reveal to you.) wAllah exposed their secrets, that is,

(saying: "If we had anything to do with the affair, none of us would have been killed here.") although they tried to conceal this thought from the Messenger of Allah.

Ibn Ishaq recorded that `Abdullah bin Az-Zubayr said that Az-Zubayr said, "I was with the Messenger of Allah when fear intensified and Allah sent sleep to us (during the battle of Uhud). At that time, every man among us (except the hypocrites) was nodding off. By Allah! As if in a dream, I heard the words of Mu`attib bin Qushayr, `If we had anything to do with the affair, none of us would have been killed here.' I memorized these words of his, which Allah mentioned later on,

(saying: "If we had anything to do with the affair, none of us would have been killed here.)"

Ibn Abi Hatim collected this Hadith.

Allah the Exalted said,

(Say: "Even if you had remained in your homes, those for whom death was decreed would certainly have gone forth to the place of their death,") meaning, this is Allah's appointed destiny and a decision that will certainly come to pass, and there is no escaping it. Allah's statement,

(that Allah might test what is in your breasts; and to purify that which was in your hearts,) means, so that He tests you with whatever befell you, to distinguish good from evil and the deeds and statements of the believers from those of the hypocrites,

(and Allah is All-Knower of what is in the breasts), and what the hearts conceal.

Some of the Believers Give Flight on the Day of Uhud

Allah then said, (Those of you who turned back on the day the two hosts met, Shaytan only caused them to err because of some of what they had earned) (3:155),

because of some of their previous errors. Indeed, some of the Salaf said, "The reward of the good deed includes being directed to another good deed that follows it, while the retribution of sin includes committing another sin that follows it." Allah then said,

(but Allah, indeed, has forgiven them), their giving flight,

(surely, Allah is Oft-Forgiving, Most Forbearing)

He forgives sins, pardons and exonerates His creatures. Imam Ahmad recorded that Shaqiq said, " `Abdur-Rahman bin `Awf met Al-Walid bin `Uqbah, who said to him, `Why did you desert `Uthman, the Leader of the Faithful' `Abdur-Rahman said, `Tell him that I did not run away during Uhud, remain behind during Badr, nor abandon the Sunnah of `Umar.' Al-Walid told `Uthman what `Abdur-Rahman said. `Uthman replied, 'As for his statement, 'I did not run away during Uhud,' how can he blame me for an error that Allah has already forgiven. Allah said,

(Those of you who turned back on the day the two hosts met, Shaytan only caused them to err because of some of what they had earned. But Allah, indeed, has forgiven them).

As for his statement that I remained behind from participating in Badr, I was nursing Ruqayyah, the daughter of the Messenger of Allah , until she passed away. The Messenger of Allah gave me a share in the booty of Badr, and whoever gets a share in the booty from the Messenger of Allah will have participated in battle. As for his statement that I abandoned the Sunnah of `Umar, neither I nor he are able to endure it. Go and convey this answer to him.'"

Surah: 3 Ayah: 156, Ayah: 157 & Ayah: 158

﴿ يَـٰٓأَيُّهَا ٱلَّذِينَ ءَامَنُواْ لَا تَكُونُواْ كَٱلَّذِينَ كَفَرُواْ وَقَالُواْ لِإِخْوَٰنِهِمْ إِذَا ضَرَبُواْ فِى ٱلْأَرْضِ أَوْ كَانُواْ غُزًّى لَّوْ كَانُواْ عِندَنَا مَا مَاتُواْ وَمَا قُتِلُواْ لِيَجْعَلَ ٱللَّهُ ذَٰلِكَ حَسْرَةً فِى قُلُوبِهِمْ ۗ وَٱللَّهُ يُحْىِۦ وَيُمِيتُ ۗ وَٱللَّهُ بِمَا تَعْمَلُونَ بَصِيرٌ ﴾

156. O you who believe! Be not like those who disbelieve (hypocrites) and who say to their brethren when they travel through the earth or go out to fight: "If they had stayed with us, they would not have died or been killed," so that Allâh may make it a cause of regret in their hearts. It is Allâh that gives life and causes death. And Allâh is All-Seer of what you do.

﴿ وَلَئِن قُتِلْتُمْ فِى سَبِيلِ ٱللَّهِ أَوْ مُتُّمْ لَمَغْفِرَةٌ مِّنَ ٱللَّهِ وَرَحْمَةٌ خَيْرٌ مِّمَّا يَجْمَعُونَ ﴾

157. And if you are killed or die in the Way of Allâh, forgiveness and mercy from Allâh are far better than all that they amass (of worldly wealths).

﴿ وَلَئِن مُّتُّمْ أَوْ قُتِلْتُمْ لَإِلَى ٱللَّهِ تُحْشَرُونَ ﴾

158. And whether you die, or are killed, verily, unto Allâh you shall be gathered.

Transliteration

156. Ya ayyuha allatheena amanoo la takoonoo kaallatheena kafaroo waqaloo li-ikhwanihim itha daraboo fee al-ardi aw kanoo ghuzzan law kanoo AAindana ma matoo wama qutiloo liyajAAala Allahu thalika hasratan fee quloobihim waAllahu yuhyee wayumeetu waAllahu bima taAAmaloona baseerun 157. Wala-in qutiltum fee sabeeli Allahi aw muttum lamaghfiratun mina Allahi warahmatun khayrun mimma yajmaAAoona 158. Wala-in muttum aw qutiltum la-ila Allahi tuhsharoona

Tafsir Ibn Kathir

Prohibiting the Ideas of the Disbeleivers about Death and Predestination

Allah forbids His believing servants from the disbelievers' false creed, seen in their statement about those who died in battle and during travel; "Had they abandoned these trips, they would not have met their demise." Allah said,

(O you who believe! Be not like those who disbelieve (hypocrites) and who say to their brethren), about their dead brethren,

(when they travel through the earth) for the purpose of trading and otherwise,

(or go out to fight), participating in battles,

("If they had stayed with us,") in our area,

("they would not have died or been killed,") they would not have died while traveling or been killed in battle. Allah's statement,

(so that Allah may make it a cause of regret in their hearts.) means, Allah creates this evil thought in their hearts so that their sadness and the grief they feel for their loss would increase. Allah refuted them by saying,

(It is Allah that gives life and causes death.) for the creation is under Allah's power, and the decision is His Alone. No one lives or dies except by Allah's leave, and no one's life is increased or decreased except by His decree.

(And Allah is All-Seer of what you do,) for His knowledge and vision encompasses all His creation and none of their affairs ever escapes Him. Allah's statement,

(And if you are killed or die in the way of Allah, forgiveness and mercy from Allah are far better than all that they amass.) (3:157), indicating that death and martyrdom in Allah's cause are a means of earning Allah's mercy, forgiveness and pleasure. This, indeed, is better than remaining in this life with its short lived delights. Furthermore, whoever dies or is killed will return to Allah, the Exalted and Most Honored, and He will reward him if he has done good deeds, or will punish him for his evil deeds. Allah said,

(And whether you die or are killed, verily, unto Allah you shall be gathered.) (3:158).

Surah: 3 Ayah: 159, Ayah: 160, Ayah: 161, Ayah: 162, Ayah: 163 & Ayah: 164

﴿ فَبِمَا رَحْمَةٍ مِّنَ ٱللَّهِ لِنتَ لَهُمْ ۖ وَلَوْ كُنتَ فَظًّا غَلِيظَ ٱلْقَلْبِ لَٱنفَضُّواْ مِنْ حَوْلِكَ ۖ فَٱعْفُ عَنْهُمْ وَٱسْتَغْفِرْ لَهُمْ وَشَاوِرْهُمْ فِى ٱلْأَمْرِ ۖ فَإِذَا عَزَمْتَ فَتَوَكَّلْ عَلَى ٱللَّهِ ۚ إِنَّ ٱللَّهَ يُحِبُّ ٱلْمُتَوَكِّلِينَ ﴾

159. And by the Mercy of Allâh, you dealt with them gently. And had you been severe and harsh-hearted, they would have broken away from about you; so pass over (their faults), and ask (Allâh's) Forgiveness for them; and consult them in the affairs. Then when you have taken a decision, put your trust in Allâh, certainly, Allâh loves those who put their trust (in Him).

﴿ إِن يَنصُرْكُمُ ٱللَّهُ فَلَا غَالِبَ لَكُمْ ۖ وَإِن يَخْذُلْكُمْ فَمَن ذَا ٱلَّذِى يَنصُرُكُم مِّنۢ بَعْدِهِۦ ۗ وَعَلَى ٱللَّهِ فَلْيَتَوَكَّلِ ٱلْمُؤْمِنُونَ ﴾ ﴿١٦٠﴾

160. If Allâh helps you, none can overcome you; and if He forsakes you, who is there after Him that can help you? And in Allâh (Alone) let believers put their trust.

﴿ وَمَا كَانَ لِنَبِىٍّ أَن يَغُلَّ ۚ وَمَن يَغْلُلْ يَأْتِ بِمَا غَلَّ يَوْمَ ٱلْقِيَـٰمَةِ ۚ ثُمَّ تُوَفَّىٰ كُلُّ نَفْسٍ مَّا كَسَبَتْ وَهُمْ لَا يُظْلَمُونَ ﴾ ﴿١٦١﴾

161. It is not for any Prophet to take illegally a part of booty (Ghulul), and whosoever deceives his companions as regards the booty, he shall bring forth on the Day of Resurrection that which he took (illegally). Then every person shall be paid in full what he has earned, and they shall not be dealt with unjustly.

﴿ أَفَمَنِ ٱتَّبَعَ رِضْوَٰنَ ٱللَّهِ كَمَنۢ بَآءَ بِسَخَطٍ مِّنَ ٱللَّهِ وَمَأْوَىٰهُ جَهَنَّمُ ۚ وَبِئْسَ ٱلْمَصِيرُ ﴾ ﴿١٦٢﴾

162. Is then one who follows (seeks) the good Pleasure of Allâh (by not taking illegally a part of the booty) like the one who draws on himself the Wrath of Allâh (by taking a part of the booty illegally - Ghulul)? - his abode is Hell, and worst, indeed is that destination!

﴿ هُمْ دَرَجَـٰتٌ عِندَ ٱللَّهِ ۗ وَٱللَّهُ بَصِيرٌۢ بِمَا يَعْمَلُونَ ﴾ ﴿١٦٣﴾

163. They are in varying grades with Allâh, and Allâh is All-Seer of what they do.

﴿ لَقَدْ مَنَّ ٱللَّهُ عَلَى ٱلْمُؤْمِنِينَ إِذْ بَعَثَ فِيهِمْ رَسُولًا مِّنْ أَنفُسِهِمْ يَتْلُوا۟ عَلَيْهِمْ ءَايَـٰتِهِۦ وَيُزَكِّيهِمْ وَيُعَلِّمُهُمُ ٱلْكِتَـٰبَ وَٱلْحِكْمَةَ وَإِن كَانُوا۟ مِن قَبْلُ لَفِى ضَلَـٰلٍ مُّبِينٍ ﴾ ﴿١٦٤﴾

164. Indeed Allâh conferred a great favor on the believers when He sent among them a Messenger (Muhammad (peace be upon him)) from among themselves, reciting unto them His Verses (the Qur'ân), and purifying them (from sins by their following him), and instructing them (in) the Book (the Qur'ân) and Al-Hikmah (the wisdom and the Sunnah of the Prophet (peace be upon him) (i.e. his legal

ways, statements, acts of worship)) while before that they had been in manifest error.

Transliteration

159. Fabima rahmatin mina Allahi linta lahum walaw kunta faththan ghaleetha alqalbi lainfaddoo min hawlika faoAAfu AAanhum waistaghfir lahum washawirhum fee al-amri fa-itha AAazamta fatawakkal AAala Allahi inna Allaha yuhibbu almutawakkileena 160. In yansurkumu Allahu fala ghaliba lakum wa-in yakhthulkum faman tha allathee yansurukum min baAAdihi waAAala Allahi falyatawakkali almu/minoona 161. Wama kana linabiyyin an yaghulla waman yaghlul ya/ti bima ghalla yawma alqiyamati thumma tuwaffa kullu nafsin ma kasabat wahum la yuthlamoona 162. Afamani ittabaAAa ridwana Allahi kaman baa bisakhatin mina Allahi wama/wahu jahannamu wabi/sa almaseeru   163. Hum darajatun AAinda Allahi waAllahu baseerun bima yaAAmaloona   164. Laqad manna Allahu AAala almu/mineena ith baAAatha feehim rasoolan min anfusihim yatloo AAalayhim ayatihi wayuzakkeehim wayuAAallimuhumu alkitaba waalhikmata wa-in kanoo min qablu lafee dalalin mubeenin

Tafsir Ibn Kathir

Among the Qualities of Our Prophet Muhammad are Mercy and Kindness

Allah addresses His Messenger and reminds him and the believers of the favor that He has made his heart and words soft for his Ummah, those who follow his command and refrain from what he prohibits.

(And by the mercy of Allah, you dealt with them gently) (3:159). meaning, who would have made you this kind, if it was not Allah's mercy for you and them. Qatadah said that,

(And by the mercy of Allah, you dealt with them gently) means, "With Allah's mercy you became this kind." Al-Hasan Al-Basri said that this, indeed, is the description of the behavior that Allah sent Muhammad with. This Ayah is similar to Allah's statement,

(Verily, there has come unto you a Messenger from among yourselves. It grieves him that you should receive any injury or difficulty. He is anxious over you (to be rightly guided, to repent to Allah); for the believers (he is) full of pity, kind, and merciful) (9:128). Allah said next,

(And had you been severe and harsh-hearted, they would have broken away from about you;)

The severe person is he who utters harsh words, and,

(harsh-hearted) is the person whose heart is hard. Had this been the Prophet's behavior, "They would have scattered from around you. However, Allah gathered them and made you kind and soft with them, so that their hearts congregate around you." `Abdullah bin `Amr said that he read the description of the Messenger of Allah in previous Books, "He is not severe, harsh, obscene in the marketplace or dealing evil for evil. Rather, he forgives and pardons."

The Order for Consultation and to Abide by it

Allah said,

(So pardon them, and ask (Allah's) forgiveness for them; and consult them in the affairs.)

The Messenger of Allah used to ask his Companions for advice about various matters, to comfort their hearts, and so they actively implement the decision they reach. For instance, before the battle of Badr, the Prophet asked his Companions for if Muslims should intercept the caravan (led by Abu Sufyan). They said, "O Messenger of Allah! If you wish to cross the sea, we would follow you in it, and if you march forth to Barkul-Ghimad we would march with you. We would never say what the Children of Israel said to Musa, `So go, you and your Lord, and fight you two, we are sitting right here.' Rather, we say march forth and we shall march forth with you; and before you, and to your right and left shall we fight." The Prophet also asked them for their opinion about where they should set up camp at Badr. Al-Mundhir bin `Amr suggested to camp close to the enemy, for he wished to acquire martyrdom.

Concerning the battle of Uhud, the Messenger asked the Companions if they should fortify themselves in Al-Madinah or go out to meet the enemy, and the majority of them requested that they go out to meet the enemy, and he did. He also took their advice on the day of Khandaq (the Trench) about conducting a peace treaty with some of the tribes of Al-Ahzab (the Confederates), in return for giving them one-third of the fruits of Al-Madinah. However, Sa`d bin `Ubadah and Sa`d bin Mu`adh rejected this offer and the Prophet went ahead with their advice. The Prophet also asked them if they should attack the idolators on the Day of Hudaybiyyah, and Abu Bakr disagreed, saying, "We did not come here to fight anyone. Rather, we came to perform `Umrah." The Prophet agreed.

On the day of Ifk, (i.e. the false accusation), the Messenger of Allah said to them, "O Muslims! Give me your advice about some men who falsely accused my wife (`A'ishah). By Allah! I never knew of any evil to come from my wife. And they accused whom They accused he from whom I only knew righteous conduct, by Allah!" The Prophet asked `Ali and Usamah about divorcing `A'ishah. In summary, the Prophet used to take his Companions' advice for battles and other important events.

Ibn Majah recorded that Abu Hurayrah said that the Prophet said;

«الْمُسْتَشَارُ مُؤْتَمَنٌ»

(The one whom advice is sought from is to be entrusted) tThis was recorded by Abu Dawud, At-Tirmidhi, and An-Nasa'i who graded it Hasan.

Trust in Allah After Taking the Dec

Allah's statement,

(Then when you have taken a decision, put your trust in Allah,) means, if you conduct the required consultation and you then make a decision, trust in Allah over your decision,

(certainly, Allah loves those who put their trust (in Him)).

Allah's statement,

(If Allah helps you, none can overcome you; and if He forsakes you, who is there after Him that can help you And in Allah (Alone) let believers put their trust), is similar to His statement that we mentioned earlier,

(And there is no victory except from Allah the Almighty, the All-Wise) (3:126).

Allah next commands the believers to trust in Him,

(And in Allah (Alone) let believers put their trust).

Treachery with the Spoils of War was not a Trait of the Prophet

Allah said,

(It is not for any Prophet to illegally take a part of the booty,)

Ibn `Abbas, Mujahid and Al-Hasan said that the Ayah means, "It is not for a Prophet to breach the trust." Ibn Jarir recorded that, Ibn `Abbas said that, this Ayah,

(It is not for any Prophet to illegally take a part of the booty,) was revealed in connection with a red robe that was missing from the spoils of war of Badr. Some people said that the Messenger of Allah might have taken it. When this rumor circulated, Allah sent down,

(It is not for any Prophet to illegally take a part of the booty, and whosoever is deceitful with the booty, he shall bring forth on the Day of Resurrection that which he took.)

This was also recorded by Abu Dawud and At-Tirmidhi, who said "Hasan Gharib". This Ayah exonerates the Messenger of Allah of all types of deceit and treachery, be it returning what was entrusted with him, dividing the spoils of war, etc.

Allah then said,

(and whosoever is deceitful with the booty, he shall bring forth on the Day of Resurrection that which he took. Then every person shall be paid in full what he has earned, and they shall not be dealt with unjustly.)

This Ayah contains a stern warning and threat against Ghulul (stealing from the booty), and there are also Hadiths, that prohibit such practice. Imam Ahmad recorded that Abu Malik Al-Ashja`i said that the Prophet said,

«أَعْظَمُ الْغُلُولِ عِنْدَ اللهِ ذِرَاعٌ مِنَ الْأَرْضِ، تَجِدُونَ الرَّجُلَيْنِ جَارَيْنِ فِي الْأَرْضِ أَوْ فِي الدَّارِ فَيَقْطَعُ أَحَدُهُمَا مِنْ حَظِّ صَاحِبِهِ ذِرَاعًا، فَإِذَا اقْتَطَعَهُ، طُوِّقَهُ مِنْ سَبْعِ أَرَضِينَ إِلَى يَوْمِ الْقِيَامَةِ»

(The worst Ghulul (i.e. stealing) with Allah is a yard of land, that is, when you find two neighbors in a land or home and one of them illegally acquires a yard of his neighbor's land. When he does, he will be tied with it from the seven earths until the Day of Resurrection.)

Imam Ahmad recorded that Abu Humayd As-Sa`idi said, "The Prophet appointed a man from the tribe of Al-Azd, called Ibn Al-Lutbiyyah, to collect the Zakah. When he returned he said, `This (portion) is for you and this has been given to me as a gift.' The Prophet stood on the Minbar and said,

«مَا بَالُ الْعَامِلِ نَبْعَثُهُ فَيَجِيءُ فَيَقُولُ: هَذَا لَكُمْ، وَهَذَا أُهْدِيَ لِي، أَفَلَا جَلَسَ فِي بَيْتِ أَبِيهِ وَأُمِّهِ فَيَنْظُرُ أَيُهْدَى إِلَيْهِ أَمْ لَا؟ وَالَّذِي نَفْسُ مُحَمَّدٍ بِيَدِهِ، لَا يَأْتِي أَحَدٌ مِنْكُمْ مِنْهَا بِشَيْءٍ إِلَّا جَاءَ بِهِ يَوْمَ الْقِيَامَةِ عَلَى رَقَبَتِهِ، إِنْ كَانَ بَعِيرًا لَهُ رُغَاءٌ، أَوْ بَقَرَةً لَهَا خُوَارٌ، أَوْ شَاةً تَيْعَرُ»

(What is the matter with a man whom we appoint to collect Zakah, when he returns he said, `This is for you and this has been given to me as a gift.' Why hadn't he stayed in his father's or mother's house to see whether he would be given presents or not By Him in Whose Hand my life is, whoever takes anything from the resources of the Zakah (unlawfully), he will carry it on his neck on the Day of Resurrection; if it be a camel, it will be grunting; if a cow, it will be mooing; and if a sheep, it will be bleating. The Prophet then raised his hands till we saw the whiteness of his armpits, and he said thrice,

«اللَّهُمَّ هَلْ بَلَّغْتُ»

`O Allah! Haven't I conveyed Your Message.')"

Chapter 3: Al-i-'Imran (The Family of Imran), Verses 093-200

Hisham bin `Urwah added that Abu Humayd said, "I have seen him with my eyes and heard him with my ears, and ask Zayd bin Thabit." This is recorded in the Two Sahihs.

In the book of Ahkam of his Sunan, Abu `Isa At-Tirmidhi recorded that Mu`adh bin Jabal said, "The Messenger of Allah sent me to Yemen, but when I started on the journey, he sent for me to come back and said,

«أَتَدْرِي لِمَ بَعَثْتُ إِلَيْكَ؟ لَا تُصِيبَنَّ شَيْئًا بِغَيْرِ إِذْنِي، فَإِنَّهُ غُلُولٌ»

(Do you know why I summoned you back Do not take anything without my permission, for if you do, it will be Ghulul.)

(and whosoever deceives his companions over the booty, he shall bring forth on the Day of Resurrection that which he took).

(This is why I summoned you, so now go and fulfill your mission.)" At-Tirmidhi said, "This Hadith is Hasan Gharib."

In addition, Imam Ahmad recorded that Abu Hurayrah said, "The Prophet got up among us and mentioned Ghulul and emphasized its magnitude. He then said,

«لَا أُلْفِيَنَّ أَحَدَكُمْ يَجِيءُ يَوْمَ الْقِيَامَةِ عَلَى رَقَبَتِهِ بَعِيرٌ لَهُ رُغَاءٌ، فَيَقُولُ: يَا رَسُولَ اللهِ أَغِثْنِي، فَأَقُولُ: لَا أَمْلِكُ لَكَ مِنَ اللهِ شَيْئًا، قَدْ أَبْلَغْتُكَ، لَا أُلْفِيَنَّ أَحَدَكُمْ يَجِيءُ يَوْمَ الْقِيَامَةِ عَلَى رَقَبَتِهِ فَرَسٌ لَهَا حَمْحَمَةٌ، فَيَقُولُ: يَا رَسُولَ اللهِ أَغِثْنِي، فَأَقُولُ: لَا أَمْلِكُ لَكَ مِنَ اللهِ شَيْئًا، قَدْ أَبْلَغْتُكَ، لَا أُلْفِيَنَّ أَحَدَكُمْ يَجِي يَوْمَ الْقِيَامَةِ عَلَى رَقَبَتِهِ رِقَاعٌ تَخْفِقُ فَيَقُولُ: يَا رَسُولَ اللهِ أَغِثْنِي، فَأَقُولُ: لَا أَمْلِكُ لَكَ مِنَ اللهِ شَيْئًا، قَدْ أَبْلَغْتُكَ، لَا أُلْفِيَنَّ أَحَدَكُمْ يَجِي يَوْمَ الْقِيَامَةِ عَلَى رَقَبَتِهِ صَامِتٌ، فَيَقُولُ: يَا رَسُولَ اللهِ أَغِثْنِي، فَأَقُولُ: لَا أَمْلِكُ لَكَ مِنَ اللهِ شَيْئًا، قَدْ أَبْلَغْتُكَ»

(I will not like to see anyone among you on the Day of Resurrection, carrying a grunting camel over his neck. Such a man will say, 'O Allah's Messenger! Intercede on my behalf,' and I will say, 'I can't intercede for you with Allah, for I have conveyed (Allah's Message) to you.' I will not like to see any of you coming on the Day of Resurrection while carrying a neighing horse over his neck. Such a man will be saying,

`O Allah's Messenger! Intercede on my behalf,' and I will reply, 'I can't intercede for you with Allah, for I have conveyed (Allah's Message) to you.' I will not like to see any of you coming on the Day of Resurrection while carrying clothes that will be fluttering, and the man will say, 'O Allah's Messenger! Intercede (with Allah) for me, ' and I will say, 'I can't help you with Allah, for I have conveyed (Allah's Message) to you.' I will not like to see any of you coming on the Day of Resurrection while carrying gold and silver on his neck. This person will say, 'O Allah's Messenger! Intercede (with Allah) for me.' And I will say, 'I can't help you with Allah, for I have conveyed (Allah's Message) to you.')" This Hadith was recorded in the Two Sahihs .

Imam Ahmad recorded that `Umar bin Al-Khattab said, "During the day (battle) of Khaybar, several Companions of the Messenger of Allah came to him and said, `So-and-so died as a martyr, so-and-so died as a martyr.' When they mentioned a certain man that died as a martyr, the Messenger of Allah said,

《كَلَّا إِنِّي رَأَيْتُهُ فِي النَّارِ فِي بُرْدَةٍ غَلَّهَا أَوْ عَبَاءَةٍ》

(No. I have seen him in the Fire because of a robe that he stole (from the booty).)

The Messenger of Allah then said,

《يَا ابْنَ الْخَطَّابِ، اذْهَبْ فَنَادِ فِي النَّاسِ: إِنَّهُ لَا يَدْخُلُ الْجَنَّةَ إِلَّا الْمُؤْمِنُونَ》

(O Ibn Al-Khattab! Go and announce to the people that only the faithful shall enter Paradise.)

So I went out and proclaimed that none except the faithful shall enter Paradise." This was recorded by Muslim and At-Tirmidhi, who said "Hasan Sahih".

The Honest and Dishonest are Not Similar

Allah said,

(Is then one who follows (seeks) the pleasure of Allah like the one who draws on himself the wrath of Allah His abode is Hell, and worse indeed is that destination!) (3:162),

This refers to those seeking what pleases Allah by obeying His legislation, thus earning His pleasure and tremendous rewards, while being saved from His severe torment. This type of person is not similar to one who earns Allah's anger, has no means of escaping it and who will reside in Jahannam on the Day of Resurrection, and what an evil destination it is.

There are many similar statements in the Qur'an, such as,

(Shall he then who knows that what has been revealed unto you (O Muhammad) from your Lord is the truth be like him who is blind) (13:19), and,

(Is he whom We have promised an excellent promise (Paradise) which he will find true, like him whom We have made to enjoy the luxuries of the life of (this) world) (28:61).

Allah then said,

(They are in varying grades with Allah,) (3:163) meaning, the people of righteousness and the people of evil are in grades, as Al-Hasan Al-Basri and Muhammad bin Ishaq said. Abu `Ubaydah and Al-Kisa'i said that this Ayah refers to degrees, meaning there are various degrees and dwellings in Paradise, as well as, various degrees and dwellings in the Fire. In another Ayah, Allah said,

(For all there will be degrees (or ranks) according to what they did) (6:132). Next, Allah said,

(and Allah is All-Seer of what they do), and He will compensate or punish them, and will never rid them of a good deed, or increase their evil deeds. Rather, each will be treated according to his deeds.

The Magnificent Blessing in the Advent of Our Prophet Muhammad

Allah the Most High said:

(Indeed Allah conferred a great favor on the believers when He sent among them a Messenger from among themselves,)

Meaning, from their own kind, so that it is possible for them to speak with him, ask him questions, associate with him, and benefit from him. Just as Allah said:

(And among His signs is that he created for them mates, that they may find rest in.)

Meaning; of their own kind. And Allah said;

(Say: "I am only a man like you. It has been revealed to me that your God is One God") (18:110).

(And We never sent before you any of the Messengers but verily, they ate food and walked in the markets) (25:20).

(And We sent not before you any but men unto whom We revealed, from among the people of townships) (12:109), and,

(O you assembly of Jinn and mankind! "Did not there come to you Messengers from among you...") (6:130).

Allah's favor is perfected when His Messenger to the people is from their own kind, so that they are able to talk to him and inquire about the meanings of Allah's Word. This is why Allah said, (reciting unto them His verses) (3:164), the Qur'an, (and purifying them), commanding them to do righteous works and forbidding them from committing evil. This is how their hearts will be purified and cleansed of the sin and evil that used to fill them when they were disbelievers and ignorant.

(and instructing them (in) the Book and the Hikmah,) the Qur'an and the Sunnah,

(while before that they had been), before sending this Prophet, Muhammad ,

(in manifest error.) indulging in plain and unequivocal error and ignorance that are clear to everyone.

Surah: 3 Ayah: 165, Ayah: 166, Ayah: 167 & Ayah: 168

﴿ أَوَلَمَّا أَصَـٰبَتْكُم مُّصِيبَةٌ قَدْ أَصَبْتُم مِّثْلَيْهَا قُلْتُمْ أَنَّىٰ هَـٰذَا ۖ قُلْ هُوَ مِنْ عِندِ أَنفُسِكُمْ ۗ إِنَّ ٱللَّهَ عَلَىٰ كُلِّ شَىْءٍ قَدِيرٌ ﴾

165. (What is the matter with you?) When a single disaster smites you, although you smote (your enemies) with one twice as great, you say: "From where does this come to us?" Say (to them), "It is from yourselves (because of your evil deeds)." And Allâh has power over all things.

﴿ وَمَآ أَصَـٰبَكُمْ يَوْمَ ٱلْتَقَى ٱلْجَمْعَانِ فَبِإِذْنِ ٱللَّهِ وَلِيَعْلَمَ ٱلْمُؤْمِنِينَ ﴾

166. And what you suffered (of the disaster) on the day (of the battle of Uhud when) the two armies met, was by the leave of Allâh, in order that He might test the believers.

﴿ وَلِيَعْلَمَ ٱلَّذِينَ نَافَقُواْ ۚ وَقِيلَ لَهُمْ تَعَالَوْاْ قَـٰتِلُواْ فِى سَبِيلِ ٱللَّهِ أَوِ ٱدْفَعُواْ ۖ قَالُواْ لَوْ نَعْلَمُ قِتَالًا لَّٱتَّبَعْنَـٰكُمْ ۗ هُمْ لِلْكُفْرِ يَوْمَئِذٍ أَقْرَبُ مِنْهُمْ لِلْإِيمَـٰنِ ۚ يَقُولُونَ بِأَفْوَٰهِهِم مَّا لَيْسَ فِى قُلُوبِهِمْ ۗ وَٱللَّهُ أَعْلَمُ بِمَا يَكْتُمُونَ ﴾

167. And that He might test the hypocrites, it was said to them: "Come, fight in the Way of Allâh or (at least) defend yourselves." They said: "Had we known that fighting will take place, we would certainly have followed you." They were that day, nearer to disbelief than to Faith, saying with their mouths what was not in their hearts. And Allâh has full knowledge of what they conceal.

﴿ ٱلَّذِينَ قَالُواْ لِإِخْوَٰنِهِمْ وَقَعَدُواْ لَوْ أَطَاعُونَا مَا قُتِلُواْ ۗ قُلْ فَٱدْرَءُواْ عَنْ أَنفُسِكُمُ ٱلْمَوْتَ إِن كُنتُمْ صَـٰدِقِينَ ﴾

168. (They are) the ones who said about their killed brethren while they themselves sat (at home): "If only they had listened to us, they would not have been killed." Say: "Avert death from your own selves, if you speak the truth."

Chapter 3: Al-i-'Imran (The Family oF Imran), Verses 093-200   87

Transliteration

165. Awa lamma asabatkum museebatun qad asabtum mithlayha qultum anna hatha qul huwa min AAindi anfusikum inna Allaha AAala kulli shay-in qadeerun 166. Wama asabakum yawma iltaqa aljamAAani fabi-ithni Allahi waliyaAAlama almu/mineena 167. WaliyaAAlama allatheena nafaqoo waqeela lahum taAAalaw qatiloo fee sabeeli Allahi awi idfaAAoo qaloo law naAAlamu qitalan laittabaAAnakum hum lilkufri yawma-ithin aqrabu minhum lileemani yaqooloona bi-afwahihim ma laysa fee quloobihim waAllahu aAAlamu bima yaktumoona   168. Allatheena qaloo li-ikhwanihim waqaAAadoo law ataAAoona ma qutiloo qul faidraoo AAan anfusikumu almawta in kuntum sadiqeena

Tafsir Ibn Kathir

The Reason and Wisdom Behind the Defeat at Uhud

Allah said,

(When a single disaster smites you), in reference to when the Muslims suffered seventy fatalities during the battle of Uhud,

(although you smote (your enemies) with one twice as great,) during Badr, when the Muslims killed seventy Mushriks and captured seventy others,

(you say: "From where does this come to us") why did this defeat happen to us

(Say, "It is from yourselves.") Ibn Abi Hatim recorded that `Umar bin Al-Khattab said, "When Uhud occurred, a year after Badr, Muslims were punished for taking ransom from the disbelievers at Badr (in return for releasing the Mushriks whom they captured in that battle). Thus, they suffered the loss of seventy fatalities and the Companions of the Messenger of Allah gave flight and abandoned him. The Messenger suffered a broken tooth, the helmet was smashed on his head and blood flowed onto his face. Allah then revealed,

(When a single disaster smites you, although you smote (your enemies) with one twice as great, you say: "From where does this come to us" Say, "It is from yourselves".), because you took the ransom." Furthermore, Muhammad bin Ishaq, Ibn Jurayj, Ar-Rabi` bin Anas and As-Suddi said that the Ayah,

(Say, "It is from yourselves.") means, because you, the archers, disobeyed the Messenger's command to not abandon your positions.

(And Allah has power over all things.) and He does what He wills and decides what He wills, and there is none who can resist His decision.

Allah then said,

(And what you suffered on the day the two armies met, was by the leave of Allah), for when you ran away from your enemy, who killed many of you and injured many others, all this occurred by Allah's will and decree out of His perfect wisdom, (in order that He might test the believers.) who were patient, firm and were not shaken,

(And that He might test the hypocrites, it was said to them: "Come, fight in the way of Allah or defend yourselves." They said: "Had we known that fighting will take place, we would certainly have followed you.") (3:167),

This refers to the Companions of `Abdullah bin Ubayy bin Salul who went back (to Al-Madinah) with him before the battle. Some believers followed them and encouraged them to come back and fight, saying,

(or defend), so that the number of Muslims increases, as Ibn `Abbas, `Ikrimah, Sa`id bin Jubayr, Ad-Dahhak, Abu Salih, Al-Hasan and As-Suddi stated. Al-Hasan bin Salih said that this part of the Ayah means, help by supplicating for us, while others said it means, man the posts. However, they refused, saying,

("Had we known that fighting will take place, we would certainly have followed you.") meaning, according to Mujahid, if we knew that you would fight today, we would join you, but we think you will not fight. Allah said,

(They were that day, nearer to disbelief than to faith,)

This Ayah indicates that a person passes through various stages, sometimes being closer to Kufr and sometimes closer to faith, as evident by,

(They were that day, nearer to disbelief than to faith,)

Allah then said,

(saying with their mouths what was not in their hearts.) for they utter what they do not truly believe in, such as,

("Had we known that fighting will take place, we would certainly have followed you.")

They knew that there was an army of idolators that came from a far land raging against the Muslims, to avenge their noble men whom the Muslims killed in Badr. These idolators came in larger numbers than the Muslims, so it was clear that a battle will certainly occur. Allah said;

(And Allah has full knowledge of what they conceal.)

((They are) the ones who said about their killed brethren while they themselves sat (at home): "If only they had listened to us, they would not have been killed.") had they listened to our advice and not gone out, they would not have met their demise. Allah said,

(Say: "Avert death from your own selves, if you speak the truth.") meaning, if staying at home saves one from being killed or from death, then you should not die. However death will come to you even if you were hiding in fortified castles. Therefore, fend death off of yourselves, if you are right.

Mujahid said that Jabir bin `Abdullah said, "This Ayah (3:168) was revealed about `Abdullah bin Ubayy bin Salul (the chief hypocrite)."

Surah: 3 Ayah: 169, Ayah: 170, Ayah: 171, Ayah: 172, Ayah: 173, Ayah: 174 & Ayah: 175

﴿ وَلَا تَحْسَبَنَّ ٱلَّذِينَ قُتِلُوا۟ فِى سَبِيلِ ٱللَّهِ أَمْوَٰتًۢا ۚ بَلْ أَحْيَآءٌ عِندَ رَبِّهِمْ يُرْزَقُونَ ﴾

169. Think not of those who are killed in the Way of Allâh as dead. Nay, they are alive, with their Lord, and they have provision.

﴿ فَرِحِينَ بِمَآ ءَاتَىٰهُمُ ٱللَّهُ مِن فَضْلِهِۦ وَيَسْتَبْشِرُونَ بِٱلَّذِينَ لَمْ يَلْحَقُوا۟ بِهِم مِّنْ خَلْفِهِمْ أَلَّا خَوْفٌ عَلَيْهِمْ وَلَا هُمْ يَحْزَنُونَ ﴾

170. They rejoice in what Allâh has bestowed upon them of His Bounty and rejoice for the sake of those who have not yet joined them, but are left behind (not yet martyred) that on them no fear shall come, nor shall they grieve.

﴿ يَسْتَبْشِرُونَ بِنِعْمَةٍ مِّنَ ٱللَّهِ وَفَضْلٍ وَأَنَّ ٱللَّهَ لَا يُضِيعُ أَجْرَ ٱلْمُؤْمِنِينَ ﴾

171. They rejoice in a Grace and a Bounty from Allâh, and that Allâh will not waste the reward of the believers.

﴿ ٱلَّذِينَ ٱسْتَجَابُوا۟ لِلَّهِ وَٱلرَّسُولِ مِنۢ بَعْدِ مَآ أَصَابَهُمُ ٱلْقَرْحُ ۚ لِلَّذِينَ أَحْسَنُوا۟ مِنْهُمْ وَٱتَّقَوْا۟ أَجْرٌ عَظِيمٌ ﴾

172. Those who answered (the Call of) Allâh and the Messenger (Muhammad (peace be upon him)) after being wounded; for those of them who did good deeds and feared Allâh, there is a great reward.

﴿ ٱلَّذِينَ قَالَ لَهُمُ ٱلنَّاسُ إِنَّ ٱلنَّاسَ قَدْ جَمَعُوا۟ لَكُمْ فَٱخْشَوْهُمْ فَزَادَهُمْ إِيمَـٰنًا وَقَالُوا۟ حَسْبُنَا ٱللَّهُ وَنِعْمَ ٱلْوَكِيلُ ﴾

173. Those (i.e. believers) unto whom the people (hypocrites) said, "Verily, the people (pagans) have gathered against you (a great army), therefore, fear them." But it (only) increased them in Faith, and they said: "Allâh (Alone) is Sufficient for us, and He is the Best Disposer of affairs (for us)."

﴿ فَٱنقَلَبُوا۟ بِنِعْمَةٍ مِّنَ ٱللَّهِ وَفَضْلٍ لَّمْ يَمْسَسْهُمْ سُوٓءٌ وَٱتَّبَعُوا۟ رِضْوَٰنَ ٱللَّهِ ۗ وَٱللَّهُ ذُو فَضْلٍ عَظِيمٍ ﴾

174. So they returned with Grace and Bounty from Allâh. No harm touched them; and they followed the good Pleasure of Allâh. And Allâh is the Owner of Great Bounty.

﴿ إِنَّمَا ذَلِكُمُ ٱلشَّيْطَانُ يُخَوِّفُ أَوْلِيَآءَهُ فَلَا تَخَافُوهُمْ وَخَافُونِ إِن كُنتُم مُّؤْمِنِينَ ﴾

175. It is only Shaitân (Satan) that suggests to you the fear of his Auliyâ' (supporters and friends (polytheists, disbelievers in the Oneness of Allâh and in His Messenger, Muhammad (peace be upon him))) so fear them not, but fear Me, if you are (true) believers.

Transliteration

169. Wala tahsabanna allatheena qutiloo fee sabeeli Allahi amwatan bal ahyaon AAinda rabbihim yurzaqoona 170. Fariheena bima atahumu Allahu min fadlihi wayastabshiroona biallatheena lam yalhaqoo bihim min khalfihim alla khawfun AAalayhim wala hum yahzanoona 171. Yastabshiroona biniAAmatin mina Allahi wafadlin waanna Allaha la yudeeAAu ajra almu/mineena 172. Allatheena istajaboo lillahi waalrrasooli min baAAdi ma asabahumu alqarhu lillatheena ahsanoo minhum waittaqaw ajrun AAatheemun 173. Allatheena qala lahumu alnnasu inna alnnasa qad jamaAAoo lakum faikhshawhum fazadahum eemanan waqaloo hasbuna Allahu waniAAma alwakeelu 174. Fainqalaboo biniAAmatin mina Allahi wafadlin lam yamsashum soo-on waittabaAAoo ridwana Allahi waAllahu thoo fadlin AAatheemin 175. Innama thalikumu alshshaytanu yukhawwifu awliyaahu fala takhafoohum wakhafooni in kuntum mu/mineena

Tafsir Ibn Kathir

Virtues of the Martyrs

Allah states that even though the martyrs were killed in this life, their souls are alive and receiving provisions in the Dwelling of Everlasting Life. In his Sahih, Muslim recorded that Masruq said, "We asked `Abdullah about this Ayah,

(Think not of those as dead who are killed in the way of Allah. Nay, they are alive, with their Lord, and they have provision.)

He said, `We asked the Messenger of Allah the same question and he said,

«أَرْوَاحُهُمْ فِي جَوْفِ طَيْرٍ خُضْرٍ، لَهَا قَنَادِيلُ مُعَلَّقَةٌ بِالْعَرْشِ، تَسْرَحُ مِنَ الْجَنَّةِ حَيْثُ شَاءَتْ، ثُمَّ تَأْوِي إِلَى تِلْكَ الْقَنَادِيلِ، فَاطَّلَعَ إِلَيْهِمْ رَبُّهُمُ اطِّلَاعَةً فَقَالَ: هَلْ تَشْتَهُونَ شَيْئًا؟ فَقَالُوا: أَيَّ شَيْءٍ نَشْتَهِي وَنَحْنُ نَسْرَحُ مِنَ الْجَنَّةِ حَيْثُ شِئْنَا؟ فَفَعَلَ ذَلِكَ بِهِمْ ثَلَاثَ مَرَّاتٍ، فَلَمَّا رَأَوْا أَنَّهُمْ لَنْ يُتْرَكُوا مِنْ أَنْ يُسْأَلُوا،

قَالُوا: يَا رَبِّ نُرِيدُ أَنْ تَرُدَّ أَرْوَاحَنَا فِي أَجْسَادِنَا حَتَّى نُقْتَلَ فِي سَبِيلِكَ مَرَّةً أُخْرَى، فَلَمَّا رَأَى أَنْ لَيْسَ لَهُمْ حَاجَةٌ، تُرِكُوا»

(Their souls are inside green birds that have lamps, which are hanging below the Throne (of Allah), and they wander about in Paradise wherever they wish. Then they return to those lamps. Allah looks at them and says, `Do you wish for anything' They say, `What more could we wish for, while we go wherever we wish in Paradise' Allah asked them this question thrice, and when they realize that He will keep asking them until they give an answer, they say, `O Lord! We wish that our souls be returned to our bodies so that we are killed in Your cause again.' Allah knew that they did not have any other wish, so they were left.)''' There are several other similar narrations from Anas and Abu Sa`id.

Imam Ahmad recorded that Anas said that the Messenger of Allah said,

«مَا مِنْ نَفْسٍ تَمُوتُ، لَهَا عِنْدَ اللهِ خَيْرٌ، يَسُرُّهَا أَنْ تَرْجِعَ إِلَى الدُّنْيَا، إِلَّا الشَّهِيدُ، فَإِنَّهُ يَسُرُّهُ أَنْ يَرْجِعَ إِلَى الدُّنْيَا فَيُقْتَلَ مَرَّةً أُخْرَى، لِمَا يَرَى مِنْ فَضْلِ الشَّهَادَة»

(No soul that has a good standing with Allah and dies would wish to go back to the life of this world, except for the martyr. He would like to be returned to this life so that he could be martyred again, for he tastes the honor achieved from martyrdom.) Muslim collected this Hadith

In addition, Imam Ahmad recorded that, Ibn `Abbas said that the Messenger of Allah said,

«لَمَّا أُصِيبَ إِخْوَانُكُمْ بِأُحُدٍ، جَعَلَ اللهُ أَرْوَاحَهُمْ فِي أَجْوَافِ طَيْرٍ خُضْرٍ، تَرِدُ أَنْهَارَ الْجَنَّةِ، وَتَأْكُلُ مِنْ ثِمَارِهَا، وَتَأْوِي إِلَى قَنَادِيلَ مِنْ ذَهَبٍ فِي ظِلِّ الْعَرْشِ، فَلَمَّا وَجَدُوا طِيبَ مَشْرَبِهِمْ وَمَأْكَلِهِمْ، وَحُسْنَ مُتَقَلَّبِهِمْ قَالُوا: يَا لَيْتَ إِخْوَانَنَا يَعْلَمُونَ مَا صَنَعَ اللهُ لَنَا، لِئَلَّا يَزْهَدُوا فِي الْجِهَادِ، وَلَا يَنْكُلُوا عَنِ الْحَرْبِ، فَقَالَ اللهُ عَزَّ وَجَلَّ: أَنَا أُبَلِّغُهُمْ عَنْكُم»

(When your brothers were killed in Uhud, Allah placed their souls inside green birds that tend to the rivers of Paradise and eat from its fruits. They then return to golden lamps hanging in the shade of the Throne. When they tasted the delight of their food, drink and dwelling, they said, `We wish that our brothers knew what Allah gave us so that they will not abandon Jihad or warfare.' Allah said, `I will convey the news for you.') Allah revealed these and the following Ayat,

(Think not of those as dead who are killed in the way of Allah. Nay, they are alive, with their Lord, and they have provision.)

Qatadah, Ar-Rabi` and Ad-Dahhak said that these Ayat were revealed about the martyrs of Uhud.

Abu Bakr Ibn Marduwyah recorded that Jabir bin `Abdullah said, "The Messenger of Allah looked at me one day and said, `O Jabir! Why do I see you sad' I said, `O Messenger of Allah! My father was martyred and left behind debts and children.' He said,

«أَلَا أُخْبِرُكَ؟ مَا كَلَّمَ اللهُ أَحَدًا قَطُّ إِلَّا مِنْ وَرَاءِ حِجَابٍ، وَإِنَّهُ كَلَّمَ أَبَاكَ كِفَاحًا»

(Should I tell you that Allah never spoke to anyone except from behind a veil However, He spoke to your father directly. He said,

«قَالَ: سَلْنِي أُعْطِكَ. قَالَ: أَسْأَلُكَ أَنْ أُرَدَّ إِلَى الدُّنْيَا فَأُقْتَلَ فِيكَ ثَانِيَةً، فَقَالَ الرَّبُّ عَزَّ وَجَلَّ: إِنَّهُ قَدْ سَبَقَ مِنِّي الْقَوْلُ: إِنَّهُمْ إِلَيْهَا لَا يَرْجِعُونَ. قَالَ: أَيْ رَبِّ فَأَبْلِغْ مَنْ وَرَائِي»

`Ask Me and I will give you.' He said, `I ask that I am returned to life so that I am killed in Your cause again.' The Lord, Exalted He be, said, `I have spoken the word that they shall not be returned back to it (this life).' He said, `O Lord! Then convey the news to those I left behind.') Allah revealed,

(Think not of those as dead who are killed in the way of Allah...)"

Imam Ahmad recorded that Ibn `Abbas said that the Messenger of Allah said,

«الشُّهَدَاءُ عَلَى بَارِقِ نَهْرٍ بِبَابِ الْجَنَّةِ، فِي قُبَّةٍ خَضْرَاءَ، يَخْرُجُ عَلَيْهِمْ رِزْقُهُمْ مِنَ الْجَنَّةِ بُكْرَةً وَعَشِيًّا»

(The martyrs convene at the shore of a river close to the door of Paradise, in a green tent, where their provisions are brought to them from Paradise day and night.)

Ahmad and Ibn Jarir collected this Hadith, which has a good chain of narration. It appears that the martyrs are of different types, some of them wander in Paradise, and some remain close to this river by the door of Paradise. It is also possible that the river is where all the souls of the martyrs convene and where they are provided with their provision day and night, and Allah knows best. Imam Ahmad narrated a Hadith that contains good news for every believer that his soul will be wandering in Paradise, as well, eating from its fruits, enjoying its delights and happiness and tasting the honor that Allah has prepared in it for him. This Hadith has a unique, authentic chain of narration that includes three of the Four Imams. Imam Ahmad narrated this Hadith from Muhammad bin Idris Ash-Shafi`i who narrated it from Malik bin Anas Al-Asbuhi, from Az-Zuhri, from `Abdur-Rahman bin Ka`b bin Malik that his father said that the Messenger of Allah said,

«نَسَمَةُ الْمُؤْمِنِ طَائِرٌ يَعْلُقُ فِي شَجَرِ الْجَنَّةِ حَتَّى يَرْجِعَهُ اللهُ إِلَى جَسَدِهِ يَوْمَ يَبْعَثُهُ»

(The soul of the believer becomes a bird that feeds on the trees of Paradise, until Allah sends him back to his body when He resurrects him.)

This Hadith states that the souls of the believers are in the shape of a bird in Paradise. As for the souls of martyrs, they are inside green birds, like the stars to the rest of the believing souls. We ask Allah the Most Generous that He makes us firm on the faith.

Allah's statement,

(They rejoice in what Allah has bestowed upon them) indicates that the martyrs who were killed in Allah's cause are alive with Allah, delighted because of the bounty and happiness they are enjoying. They are also awaiting their brethren, who will die in Allah's cause after them, for they will be meeting them soon. These martyrs do not have fear about the future or sorrow for what they left behind. We ask Allah to grant us Paradise. The Two Sahihs record from Anas, the story of the seventy Ansar Companions who were murdered at Bir Ma`unah in one night. In this Hadith, Anas reported that the Prophet used to supplicate to Allah in Qunut in prayer against those who killed them. Anas said, "A part of the Qur'an was revealed about them, but was later abrogated, `Convey to our people that we met Allah and He was pleased with us and made us pleased.'"

Allah said next,

(They rejoice in a grace and a bounty from Allah, and that Allah will not waste the reward of the believers) (3:171).

Muhammad bin Ishaq commented, "They were delighted and pleased because of Allah's promise that was fulfilled for them, and for the tremendous rewards they earned." `Abdur-Rahman bin Zayd bin Aslam said, "This Ayah encompasses all the believers, martyrs and otherwise. Rarely does Allah mention a bounty and a reward that He granted to the Prophets, without following that with what He has granted the believers after them."

The Battle of Hamra' Al-Asad

Allah said,

(Those who answered (the Call of) Allah and the Messenger after being wounded) (3:172).

This occurred on the day of Hamra' Al-Asad. After the idolators defeated the Muslims (at Uhud), they started on their way back home, but soon they were concerned because they did not finish off the Muslims in Al-Madinah, so they set out to make that battle the final one. When the Messenger of Allah got news of this, he commanded the Muslims to march to meet the disbelievers, to bring fear to their hearts and to demonstrate that the Muslims still had strength to fight. The Prophet only allowed those who were present during Uhud to accompany him, except for Jabir bin `Abdullah Al-Ansari, as we will mention. The Muslims mobilized, even though they were still suffering from their injuries, in obedience to Allah and His Messenger.

Ibn Abi Hatim recorded that `Ikrimah said, "When the idolators returned (towards Makkah) after Uhud, they said, `You neither killed Muhammad nor collected female captives. Woe to you for what you did. Let us go back.' When the Messenger of Allah heard this news, he mobilized the Muslim forces, and they marched until they reached Hamra Al-Asad. The idolators said, `Rather, we will meet next year', and the Messenger of Allah went back (to Al-Madinah), and this was considered a Ghazwah (battle). Allah sent down,

(Those who answered (the Call of) Allah and the Messenger after being wounded; for those of them who did good deeds and feared Allah, there is a great reward.)

Al-Bukhari recorded that `A'ishah said to `Urwah about the Ayah;

(Those who answered (the Call of) Allah and the Messenger)

"My nephew! Your fathers Az-Zubayr and Abu Bakr were among them. After the Prophet suffered the calamity at Uhud and the idolators went back, he feared that the idolators might try to come back and he said, `Who would follow them' Seventy men, including Az-Zubayr and Abu Bakr, volunteered." This was recorded by Al-Bukhari alone.

As for Allah's statement,

(Those unto whom the people said, "Verily, the people have gathered against you, therefore, fear them." But it (only) increased them in faith) (3:173), it means, those who threatened the people, saying that the disbelievers have amassed against them, in order to instill fear in them, but this did not worry them, rather, they trusted in Allah and sought His help,

(and they said: "Allah is Sufficient for us, and He is the Best Disposer of affairs.")

Al-Bukhari recorded that Ibn `Abbas said,

("Allah Alone is Sufficient for us and He is the Best Disposer of affairs for us.")

"Ibrahim said it when he was thrown in fire. Muhammad said it when the people said, `Verily, the people have gathered against you, therefore, fear them.' But it only increased them in faith, and they said, `Allah is Sufficient for us and He is the Best Disposer of affairs for us.'" Abu Bakr Ibn Marduwyah recorded that Anas bin Malik said that the Prophet was told on the day of Uhud, "Verily, the people have gathered against you, therefore, fear them." Thereafter, Allah sent down this Ayah (3:173).

This is why Allah said,

(So they returned with grace and bounty from Allah. No harm touched them;) for when they relied on Allah, Allah took care of their worries, He confounded the plots of their enemies, and the Muslims returned to their land,

(with grace and bounty from Allah. No harm touched them;) safe from the wicked plots of their enemies,

(and they followed the pleasure of Allah. And Allah is the Owner of great bounty.)

Al-Bayhaqi recorded that Ibn `Abbas said about Allah's statement,

(So they returned with grace and bounty from Allah,) "The `Grace' was that they were saved. The `Bounty' was that a caravan passed by, and those days were (Hajj) season days. Thus the Messenger of Allah bought and sold and made a profit, which he divided between his Companions."

Allah then said,

(It is only Shaytan that suggests to you the fear of his friends,) (3:175) meaning, Shaytan threatens you with his friends and tries to pretend they are powerful and fearsome. Allah said next,

(so fear them not, but fear Me, if you are indeed believers.) meaning, "If Shaytan brings these thoughts to you, then depend on Me and seek refuge with Me. Indeed, I shall suffice you and make you prevail over them." Similarly, Allah said,

(Is not Allah Sufficient for His servant Yet they try to frighten you with those besides Him!) (39: 36), until,

(Say: "Sufficient for me is Allah; in Him those who trust must put their trust.") (39:38). Allah said,

(So fight you against the friends of Shaytan; ever feeble indeed is the plot of Shaytan.) (4:76) and

(They are the party of Shaytan. Verily, it is the party of Shaytan that will be the losers!) (58:19),

(Allah has decreed: "Verily, it is I and My Messengers who shall be the victorious." Verily, Allah is All-Powerful, All-Mighty.) (58:21) and

(Verily, Allah will help those who help His (cause).) (22:40) and

(O you who believe! If you help (in the cause of) Allah, He will help you) (47:7), and,

(Verily, We will indeed make victorious Our Messengers and those who believe, in this world's life and on the Day when the witnesses will stand forth. The Day when their excuses will be of no profit to wrongdoers. Theirs will be the curse, and theirs will be the evil abode.) (40:51,52)

Surah: 3 Ayah: 176, Ayah: 177, Ayah: 178, Ayah: 179 & Ayah: 180

﴿ وَلاَ يَحْزُنكَ ٱلَّذِينَ يُسَٰرِعُونَ فِى ٱلْكُفْرِ إِنَّهُمْ لَن يَضُرُّواْ ٱللَّهَ شَيْـًٔا يُرِيدُ ٱللَّهُ أَلَّا يَجْعَلَ لَهُمْ حَظًّا فِى ٱلْءَاخِرَةِ وَلَهُمْ عَذَابٌ عَظِيمٌ ۝ ﴾

176. And let not those grieve you (O Muhammad (peace be upon him)) who rush with haste to disbelieve; verily, not the least harm will they do to Allâh. It is Allâh's Will to give them no portion in the Hereafter. For them there is a great torment.

﴿ إِنَّ ٱلَّذِينَ ٱشْتَرَوُاْ ٱلْكُفْرَ بِٱلْإِيمَٰنِ لَن يَضُرُّواْ ٱللَّهَ شَيْـًٔا وَلَهُمْ عَذَابٌ أَلِيمٌ ۝ ﴾

177. Verily, those who purchase disbelief at the price of Faith, not the least harm will they do to Allâh. For them, there is a painful torment.

﴿ وَلَا يَحْسَبَنَّ ٱلَّذِينَ كَفَرُوٓاْ أَنَّمَا نُمْلِى لَهُمْ خَيْرٌ لِّأَنفُسِهِمْ إِنَّمَا نُمْلِى لَهُمْ لِيَزْدَادُوٓاْ إِثْمًا وَلَهُمْ عَذَابٌ مُّهِينٌ ۝ ﴾

178. And let not the disbelievers think that Our postponing of their punishment is good for them. We postpone the punishment only so that they may increase in sinfulness. And for them is a disgracing torment.

﴿ مَّا كَانَ ٱللَّهُ لِيَذَرَ ٱلْمُؤْمِنِينَ عَلَىٰ مَآ أَنتُمْ عَلَيْهِ حَتَّىٰ يَمِيزَ ٱلْخَبِيثَ مِنَ ٱلطَّيِّبِ وَمَا كَانَ ٱللَّهُ لِيُطْلِعَكُمْ عَلَى ٱلْغَيْبِ وَلَٰكِنَّ ٱللَّهَ يَجْتَبِى مِن رُّسُلِهِ مَن يَشَآءُ فَـَٔامِنُواْ بِٱللَّهِ وَرُسُلِهِ ۚ وَإِن تُؤْمِنُواْ وَتَتَّقُواْ فَلَكُمْ أَجْرٌ عَظِيمٌ ۝ ﴾

179. Allâh will not leave the believers in the state in which you are now, until He distinguishes the wicked from the good. Nor will Allâh disclose to you the secrets of the Ghaib (unseen), but Allâh chooses of His Messengers whom He wills. So believe in Allâh and His Messengers. And if you believe and fear Allâh, then for you there is a great reward.

﴿ وَلَا يَحْسَبَنَّ ٱلَّذِينَ يَبْخَلُونَ بِمَآ ءَاتَىٰهُمُ ٱللَّهُ مِن فَضْلِهِۦ هُوَ خَيْرًا لَّهُم ۖ بَلْ هُوَ شَرٌّ لَّهُمْ ۖ سَيُطَوَّقُونَ مَا بَخِلُواْ بِهِۦ يَوْمَ ٱلْقِيَٰمَةِ ۗ وَلِلَّهِ مِيرَٰثُ ٱلسَّمَٰوَٰتِ وَٱلْأَرْضِ ۗ وَٱللَّهُ بِمَا تَعْمَلُونَ خَبِيرٌ ﴾

180. And let not those who covetously withhold of that which Allâh has bestowed on them of His Bounty (Wealth) think that it is good for them (and so they do not pay the obligatory Zakât). Nay, it will be worse for them; the things which they covetously withheld shall be tied to their necks like a collar on the Day of Resurrection. And to Allâh belongs the heritage of the heavens and the earth; and Allâh is Well-Acquainted with all that you do.

Transliteration

176. Wala yahzunka allatheena yusariAAoona fee alkufri innahum lan yadurroo Allaha shay-an yureedu Allahu alla yajAAala lahum haththan fee al-akhirati walahum AAathabun AAatheemun   177. Inna allatheena ishtarawoo alkufra bial-eemani lan yadurroo Allaha shay-an walahum AAathabun aleemun   178. Wala yahsabanna allatheena kafaroo annama numlee lahum khayrun li-anfusihim innama numlee lahum liyazdadoo ithman walahum AAathabun muheenun   179. Ma kana Allahu liyathara almu/mineena AAala ma antum AAalayhi hatta yameeza alkhabeetha mina alttayyibi wama kana Allahu liyutliAAakum AAala alghaybi walakinna Allaha yajtabee min rusulihi man yashao faaminoo biAllahi warusulihi wa-in tu/minoo watattaqoo falakum ajrun AAatheemun   180. Wala yahsabanna allatheena yabkhaloona bima atahummu Allahu min fadlihi huwa khayran lahum bal huwa sharrun lahum sayutawwaqoona ma bakhiloo bihi yawma alqiyamati walillahi meerathu alssamawati waal-ardi waAllahu bima taAAmaloona khabeerun

Tafsir Ibn Kathir

Comforting the Messenger of Allah

Allah said to His Prophet,

(And let not those grieve you who rush with haste to disbelieve) (3:176).

Because the Prophet was eager for people's benefit, he would become sad when the disbelievers would resort to defiance, rebellion and stubbornness. Allah said, `Do not be saddened by this behavior,' (verily, not the least harm will they do to Allah. It is Allah's will to give them no portion in the Hereafter.) for He decided with His power and wisdom that they shall not acquire any share in the Hereafter,

(For them there is a great torment.)

Allah said about the disbelievers,

(Verily, those who purchase disbelief at the price of faith,) by exchanging disbelief for faith,

(not the least harm will they do to Allah.) Rather, they will only harm themselves,

(For them, there is a painful torment.)

Allah said next,

(And let not the disbelievers think that Our postponing their punishment is good for them. We postpone the punishment only so that they may increase in sinfulness. And for them is a disgraceful torment) (3:178).

This statement is similar to Allah's other statements,

(Do they think that because We have given them abundant wealth and children, (that) We hasten unto them with good things. Nay, but they perceive not.) (23:55,56) and

(Then leave Me Alone with such as belie this Qur'an. We shall punish them gradually from directions they perceive not.) (68:44), and,

(And let not their wealth or their children amaze you. Allah's plan is to punish them with these things in this world, and that their souls shall depart (die) while they are disbelievers) (9:85).

Allah then said,

(Allah will not leave the believers in the state in which you are now, until He distinguishes the wicked from the good.) (3:179), meaning, He allows a calamity to happen, and during this calamity His friend becomes known and His enemy exposed, the patient believer recognized and the sinful hypocrite revealed. This Ayah refers to Uhud, since Allah tested the believers in that battle, thus making known the faith, endurance, patience, firmness and obedience to Allah and His Messenger that the believers had. Allah exposed the hypocrites in their defiance, reverting from Jihad, and the treachery they committed against Allah and His Messenger. This is why Allah said,

(Allah will not leave the believers in the state in which you are now, until He distinguishes the wicked from the good.)

Mujahid commented, "He distinguished between them during the day of Uhud." Qatadah said, "He distinguished between them in Jihad and Hijrah." Allah said next,

(Nor will Allah disclose to you the secrets of the Unseen.) meaning, you do not have access to Allah's knowledge of His creation so that you can distinguish between the believer and the hypocrite, except by the signs of each type that Allah uncovers. Allah's statement,

(but Allah chooses of His Messengers whom He wills.) is similar to another Ayah,

((He Alone is) the All-Knower of the Unseen, and He reveals to none His Unseen. Except to a Messenger (from mankind) whom He has chosen, and then He makes a band of watching guards (angels) to march before him and behind him.) (72:26,27). Allah then said,

(So believe in Allah and His Messengers.) Obey Allah and His Messenger and adhere to the law that he legislated for you,

(and if you believe and fear Allah, then for you there is a great reward.)

The Censure of Selfishness, and Warning Against it

Allah said,

(And let not those who are stingy with that which Allah has bestowed on them of His bounty (wealth) think that it is good for them. Nay, it will be worse for them.) (3:180)

Therefore, the Ayah says that the miser should not think that collecting money will benefit him. Rather, it will harm him in his religion and worldly affairs. Allah mentions the money that the miser collected on the Day of Resurrection,

(the things that they stingy with shall be tied to their necks like a collar on the Day of Resurrection.)

Al-Bukhari recorded that Abu Hurayrah said that the Messenger of Allah said,

«مَنْ آتَاهُ اللهُ مَالًا فَلَمْ يُؤَدِّ زَكَاتَهُ، مُثِّلَ لَهُ شُجَاعًا أَقْرَعَ، لَهُ زَبِيبَتَانِ، يُطَوَّقُهُ يَوْمَ الْقِيَامَةِ، يَأْخُذُ بِلِهْزِمَتَيْهِ يَعْنِي بِشِدْقَيْهِ يَقُولُ: أَنَا مَالُكَ، أَنَا كَنْزُكَ»

(Whoever Allah makes wealthy and he does not pay the Zakah due on his wealth, then (on the Day of Resurrection) his wealth will be made in the likeness of a bald-headed poisonous male snake with two black spots over the eyes. The snake will encircle his neck and bite his cheeks and proclaim, `I am your wealth, I am your treasure.')

The Prophet then recited the Ayah,

[وَلاَ يَحْسَبَنَّ الَّذِينَ يَبْخَلُونَ بِمَآ ءَاتَـٰهُمُ اللَّهُ مِن فَضْلِهِ هُوَ خَيْراً لَّهُم بَلْ هُوَ شَرٌّ لَّهُمْ]

(And let not those who are stingy with that which Allah has bestowed on them of His bounty think that it is good for them. Nay, it will be worse for them), until the end. Al-Bukhari, but not Muslim, collected this Hadith using this chain of narration, Ibn Hibban also collected it in his Sahih.

Imam Ahmad recorded that `Abdullah said that the Prophet said,

«مَا مِنْ عَبْدٍ لَا يُؤَدِّي زَكَاةَ مَالِهِ إِلَّا جُعِلَ لَهُ شُجَاعٌ أَقْرَعُ يَتْبَعُهُ، يَفِرُّ مِنْهُ وَهُوَ يَتْبَعُهُ، فَيَقُولُ: أَنَا كَنْزُك»

(Every person who does not pay the Zakah due on his wealth, will have his money made into the shape of a bald-headed, poisonous male snake who will follow him. The person will run away from the snake, who will follow him and proclaim, `I am your treasure.')

`Abdullah then recited the Ayah in Allah's Book that testifies to this fact,

[سَيُطَوَّقُونَ مَا بَخِلُواْ بِهِ يَوْمَ الْقِيَـٰمَةِ]

(the things that they were stingy with shall be tied to their necks like a collar on the Day of Resurrection.)

This was recorded by At-Tirmidhi, An-Nasa'i, and Ibn Majah, and At-Tirmidhi said, "Hasan Sahih."

Allah's statement,

(And to Allah belongs the inheritance of the heavens and the Earth), means,

(and spend of that whereof He has made you trustees) (57: 7). Therefore, since all affairs are under Allah's control, then spend from your money so it will benefit you on the Day of Return,

(and Allah is Well-Acquainted with all that you do.) with your intentions and what your hearts conceal.

Surah: 3 Ayah: 181, Ayah: 182, Ayah: 183 & Ayah: 184

﴿ لَّقَدْ سَمِعَ ٱللَّهُ قَوْلَ ٱلَّذِينَ قَالُوٓاْ إِنَّ ٱللَّهَ فَقِيرٌ وَنَحْنُ أَغْنِيَآءُ ۘ سَنَكْتُبُ مَا قَالُواْ وَقَتْلَهُمُ ٱلْأَنۢبِيَآءَ بِغَيْرِ حَقٍّ وَنَقُولُ ذُوقُواْ عَذَابَ ٱلْحَرِيقِ ﴿١٨١﴾

181. Indeed, Allâh has heard the statement of those (Jews) who say: "Truly, Allâh is poor and we are rich!" We shall record what they have said and their killing of the Prophets unjustly, and We shall say: "Taste you the torment of the burning (Fire)."

﴿ ذَٰلِكَ بِمَا قَدَّمَتْ أَيْدِيكُمْ وَأَنَّ ٱللَّهَ لَيْسَ بِظَلَّامٍ لِّلْعَبِيدِ ﴿١٨٢﴾

182. This is because of that (evil) which your hands have sent before you. And certainly, Allâh is never unjust to (His) slaves.

﴿ ٱلَّذِينَ قَالُوٓاْ إِنَّ ٱللَّهَ عَهِدَ إِلَيْنَآ أَلَّا نُؤْمِنَ لِرَسُولٍ حَتَّىٰ يَأْتِيَنَا بِقُرْبَانٍ تَأْكُلُهُ ٱلنَّارُ ۗ قُلْ قَدْ جَآءَكُمْ رُسُلٌ مِّن قَبْلِى بِٱلْبَيِّنَٰتِ وَبِٱلَّذِى قُلْتُمْ فَلِمَ قَتَلْتُمُوهُمْ إِن كُنتُمْ صَٰدِقِينَ ﴿١٨٣﴾

183. Those (Jews) who said: "Verily, Allâh has taken our promise not to believe in any Messenger unless he brings to us an offering which the fire (from heaven) shall devour." Say: "Verily, there came to you Messengers before me, with clear signs and even with what you speak of; why then did you kill them, if you are truthful?"

﴿ فَإِن كَذَّبُوكَ فَقَدْ كُذِّبَ رُسُلٌ مِّن قَبْلِكَ جَآءُو بِٱلْبَيِّنَٰتِ وَٱلزُّبُرِ وَٱلْكِتَٰبِ ٱلْمُنِيرِ ﴿١٨٤﴾

184. Then if they reject you (O Muhammad (peace be upon him)) so were Messengers rejected before you, who came with Al-Baiyinât (clear signs, proofs, evidences) and the Scripture and the Book of Enlightenment.

Transliteration

181. Laqad samiAAa Allahu qawla allatheena qaloo inna Allaha faqeerun wanahnu aghniyaon sanaktubu ma qaloo waqatlahumu al-anbiyaa bighayri haqqin wanaqoolu thooqoo AAathaba alhareeqi   182. Thalika bima qaddamat aydeekum waanna Allaha laysa bithallamin lilAAabeedin   183. Allatheena qaloo inna Allaha AAahida ilayna alla nu/mina lirasoolin hatta ya/tiyana biqurbanin ta/kuluhu alnnaru qul qad jaakum rusulun min qablee bialbayyinati wabiallathee qultum falima qataltumoohum in kutum sadiqeena   184. Fa-in kaththabooka faqad kuththiba rusulun min qablika jaoo bialbayyinati waalzzuburi waalkitabi almuneeri

Tafsir Ibn Kathir

Allah Warns the Idolators

Sa`id bin Jubayr said that Ibn `Abbas said, "When Allah's statement,

(Who is he that will lend to Allah a goodly loan so that He may multiply it to him many times) (2:245) was revealed, the Jews said, `O Muhammad! Has your Lord become poor so that He asks His servants to give Him a loan' Allah sent down,

(Indeed, Allah has heard the statement of those (Jews) who say: "Truly, Allah is poor and we are rich!") (3:181)."

This Hadith was collected by Ibn Marduwyah and Ibn Abi Hatim.

Allah's statement,

(We shall record what they have said) contains a threat and a warning that Allah followed with His statement,

(and their killing of the Prophets unjustly,)

This is what they say about Allah and this is how they treat His Messengers. Allah will punish them for these deeds in the worst manner,

(and We shall say: "Taste you the torment of the burning (Fire)." This is because of that which your hands have sent before you. And certainly, Allah is never unjust to (His) servants.)

They will be addressed like this as a way of chastising, criticism, disgrace and humiliation.

Allah said,

(Those (Jews) who said: "Verily, Allah has taken our promise not to believe in any Messenger unless he brings to us an offering which the fire (from heaven) shall devour.")

Allah refuted their claim that in their Books, Allah took a covenant from them to only believe in the Messenger whose miracles include fire coming down from the sky that consumes the charity offered by a member of the Messenger's nation, as Ibn `Abbas and Al-Hasan stated. Allah replied,

(Say: "Verily, there came to you Messengers before me, with Al-Bayinat...") with proofs and evidence,

(and even with what you speak of) a fire that consumes the accepted charity, as you asked,

(why then did you kill them) Why did you meet these Prophets with denial, defiance, stubbornness and even murder, (if you are truthful), if you follow the truth and obey the Messengers.

Allah then comforts His Prophet Muhammad ,

(Then if they reject you, so were Messengers rejected before you, who came with Al-Baiyyinat and the Scripture, and the Book of Enlightenment.) meaning, do not be sad because they deny you, for you have an example in the Messengers who came before you. These Messengers were rejected although they brought clear proofs, plain evidence and unequivocal signs,

(and the Zubur), the divinely revealed Books that were sent down to the Messengers,

(and the Book of Enlightenment) meaning the clarification and best explanation.

Surah: 3 Ayah: 185 & Ayah: 186

﴿ كُلُّ نَفْسٍ ذَآئِقَةُ ٱلْمَوْتِ ۗ وَإِنَّمَا تُوَفَّوْنَ أُجُورَكُمْ يَوْمَ ٱلْقِيَٰمَةِ ۖ فَمَن زُحْزِحَ عَنِ ٱلنَّارِ وَأُدْخِلَ ٱلْجَنَّةَ فَقَدْ فَازَ ۗ وَمَا ٱلْحَيَوٰةُ ٱلدُّنْيَآ إِلَّا مَتَٰعُ ٱلْغُرُورِ ﴾

185. Everyone shall taste death. And only on the Day of Resurrection shall you be paid your wages in full. And whoever is removed away from the Fire and admitted to Paradise, he indeed is successful. The life of this world is only the enjoyment of deception (a deceiving thing).

﴿ ۞ لَتُبْلَوُنَّ فِىٓ أَمْوَٰلِكُمْ وَأَنفُسِكُمْ وَلَتَسْمَعُنَّ مِنَ ٱلَّذِينَ أُوتُوا۟ ٱلْكِتَٰبَ مِن قَبْلِكُمْ وَمِنَ ٱلَّذِينَ أَشْرَكُوٓا۟ أَذًى كَثِيرًا ۚ وَإِن تَصْبِرُوا۟ وَتَتَّقُوا۟ فَإِنَّ ذَٰلِكَ مِنْ عَزْمِ ٱلْأُمُورِ ﴾

186. You shall certainly be tried and tested in your wealth and properties and in your personal selves, and you shall certainly hear much that will grieve you from those who received the Scripture before you (Jews and Christians) and from those who ascribe partners to Allâh; but if you persevere patiently, and become Al-Muttaqûn (the pious - see V.2:2) then verily, that will be a determining factor in all affairs (and that is from the great matters which you must hold on with all your efforts).

Transliteration

185. Kullu nafsin tha-iqatu almawti wa-innama tuwaffawna ojoorakum yawma alqiyamati faman zuhziha AAani alnnari waodkhila aljannata faqad faza wama alhayatu alddunya illa mataAAu alghuroori 186. Latublawunna fee amwalikum waanfusikum walatasmaAAunna mina allatheena ootoo alkitaba min qablikum wamina allatheena ashrakoo athan katheeran wa-in tasbiroo watattaqoo fa-inna Thalika min AAazmi al-omoori

Tafsir Ibn Kathir

Every Soul Shall Taste Death

Allah issues a general and encompassing statement that every living soul shall taste death. In another statement, Allah said,

(Whatsoever is on it (the earth) will perish. And the Face of your Lord full of majesty and honor will remain forever) (55:26,27).

Therefore, Allah Alone is the Ever-Living Who never dies, while the Jinn, mankind and angels, including those who carry Allah's Throne, shall die. The Irresistible One and Only, will alone remain for ever and ever, remaining Last, as He was the First. This Ayah comforts all creation, since every soul that exists on the earth shall die. When the term of this life comes to an end and the sons of Adam no longer have any new generations, and thus this world ends, Allah will command that the Day of Resurrection commence. Allah will then recompense the creation for their deeds, whether minor or major, many or few, big or small. Surely, Allah will not deal unjustly with anyone, even the weight of an atom, and this is why He said,

(And only on the Day of Resurrection shall you be paid your wages in full) (3:185).

Who Shall Gain Ultimate Victory

Allah said,

(And whoever is moved away from the Fire and admitted to Paradise, he indeed is successful.) meaning, whoever is kept away from the Fire, saved from it and entered into Paradise, will have achieved the ultimate success.

Ibn Abi Hatim recorded that Abu Hurayrah said that the Messenger of Allah said,

«مَوْضِعُ سَوْطٍ فِي الْجَنَّةِ خَيْرٌ مِنَ الدُّنْيَا وَمَا فِيهَا، اقْرَأُوا إِنْ شِئْتُمْ»

(A place in Paradise as small as that which is occupied by a whip is better than the world and whatever is on its surface. Read if you will),

[فَمَن زُحْزِحَ عَنِ النَّارِ وَأُدْخِلَ الْجَنَّةَ فَقَدْ فَازَ]

(And whoever is removed away from the Fire and admitted to Paradise, he indeed is successful). This was collected in the Two Sahihs, but using another chain of narration and without the addition (the Ayah.) Abu Hatim Ibn Hibban recorded it in his Sahih without the addition as did Al-Hakim in his Mustadrak.

Allah said,

(The life of this world is only the enjoyment of deception.) belittling the value of this life and degrading its importance. This life is short, little and finite, just as Allah said,

(Nay, you prefer the life of this world. Although the Hereafter is better and more lasting.) (87:16,17), and,

(And whatever you have been given is an enjoyment of the life of (this) world and its adornment, and that (Hereafter) which is with Allah is better and will remain forever) (28:60). A Hadith states,

«وَاللهِ مَا الدُّنْيَا فِي الْآخِرَةِ إِلَّا كَمَا يَغْمِسُ أَحَدُكُمْ أُصْبُعَهُ فِي الْيَمِّ، فَلْيَنْظُرْ بِمَ تَرْجِعُ إِلَيْهِ»

(By Allah! This life, compared to the Hereafter, is just as insignificant as when one of you dips his finger in the sea; let him contemplate what his finger will come back with.)

Qatadah commented on Allah's statement,

(The life of this world is only the enjoyment of deception.) "Life is a delight. By Allah, other than Whom there is no deity, it will soon fade away from its people. Therefore, take obedience to Allah from this delight, if you can. Verily, there is no power except from Allah."

The Believer is Tested and Hears Grieving Statements from the Enemy

Allah said,

(You shall certainly be tried and tested in your wealth and properties and in yourselves), just as He said in another Ayah,

(And certainly, We shall test you with something of fear, hunger, loss of wealth, lives and fruits) (2:155).

Therefore, the believer shall be tested, in his wealth, himself, his offspring and family. The believer shall be tested according to the degree of his faith, and when his faith is stronger, the test is larger.

(and you shall certainly hear much that will grieve you from those who received the Scripture before you (Jews and Christians) and from those who ascribe partners to Allah) (3:186).

Allah said to the believers upon their arrival at Al-Madinah, before Badr, while comforting them against the harm they suffered from the People of the Scriptures and the polytheists;

(but if you persevere patiently, and have Taqwa, then verily, that will be a determining factor in all affairs.)

Therefore, Allah commanded the believers to be forgiving, patient and forbearing until He brought His awaited aid.

Al-Bukhari recorded that Usamah bin Zayd said that Allah's Messenger rode a donkey with a saddle covered by a velvet sheet and let Usamah ride behind him (on the donkey). The Prophet wanted to visit Sa`d bin `Ubadah in Bani Al-Harith bin Al-Khazraj, and this occurred before the battle of Badr. The Prophet passed by a gathering in which `Abdullah bin Ubayy bin Salul was sitting, before `Abdullah bin Ubayy became Muslim. That gathering was made up of various Muslims as well as Mushriks, who worshipped the idols, and some Jews. `Abdullah bin Rawahah was sitting in that gathering. When the Prophet reached `Abdullah bin Ubayy, the donkey caused some sand to fall on the group. Then, `Abdullah bin Ubayy covered his nose with his robe and said, `Do not fill us with sand.' The Messenger of Allah greeted the gathering with Salam, called them to Allah and recited some of the Qur'an to them. `Abdullah bin Ubayy said, `O fellow! No other speech is better than what you said, if it was true! However, do not bother us in our gatherings. Go back to your place and whoever came to you, narrate your stories to him.' `Abdullah bin Rawahah said, `Rather, O Messenger of Allah! Attend our gatherings for we like that.' The Muslims, Mushriks and Jews then cursed each other, and they almost fought with each other. The Prophet tried to calm them down, until they finally settled. The Prophet rode his donkey and went to Sa`d bin `Ubadah, saying, `O Sa`d! Have you heard what Abu Hubbab said (meaning `Abdullah bin Ubayy) He said such and such things. ' Sa`d said, `O Messenger of Allah! Forgive and pardon him. By Allah, Who sent down the Book to you, Allah brought us the truth that you came with at a time when the people of this city almost appointed him king. When Allah changed all that with the truth that He gave you, he choked on it, and this is the reason behind the behavior you saw from him.' The Messenger of Allah forgave him. Indeed, the Messenger of Allah and his Companions used to forgive the Mushriks and the People of the Scriptures, just as Allah commanded them, and they used to tolerate the harm that they suffered. Allah said,

(and you shall certainly hear much that will grieve you from those who received the Scripture before you (Jews and Christians) and from those who ascribe partners to Allah;) (3:186), and,

(Many of the People of the Scripture (Jews and Christians) wish that they could turn you away as disbelievers after you have believed, out of envy from their own selves, even after the truth has become manifest unto them. But forgive and overlook, till Allah brings His command) (2:109).

The Prophet used to implement the pardon that Allah commanded him until He gave His command (to fight the disbelievers). When the Messenger fought at Badr, and Allah killed, by his hand, the leaders of the disbelievers from Quraysh, `Abdullah bin Ubayy bin Salul and the Mushriks and idol worshippers who were with him said, `This matter has prevailed,' and they gave their pledge to the Prophet and became Muslims."

Therefore, every person who stands for truth, enjoins righteousness and forbids evil, will be harmed in some manner. In such cases, there is no cure better than being patient in Allah's cause, trusting in Him and returning to Him.

Surah: 3 Ayah: 187, Ayah: 188 & Ayah: 189

﴿ وَإِذْ أَخَذَ ٱللَّهُ مِيثَٰقَ ٱلَّذِينَ أُوتُوا۟ ٱلْكِتَٰبَ لَتُبَيِّنُنَّهُۥ لِلنَّاسِ وَلَا تَكْتُمُونَهُۥ فَنَبَذُوهُ وَرَآءَ ظُهُورِهِمْ وَٱشْتَرَوْا۟ بِهِۦ ثَمَنًا قَلِيلًا ۖ فَبِئْسَ مَا يَشْتَرُونَ ۞ ﴾

187. (And remember) when Allâh took a covenant from those who were given the Scripture (Jews and Christians) to make it (the news of the coming of Prophet Muhammad (peace be upon him) and the religious knowledge) known and clear to mankind, and not to hide it, but they threw it away behind their backs, and purchased with it some miserable gain! And indeed worst is that which they bought.

﴿ لَا تَحْسَبَنَّ ٱلَّذِينَ يَفْرَحُونَ بِمَآ أَتَوا۟ وَّيُحِبُّونَ أَن يُحْمَدُوا۟ بِمَا لَمْ يَفْعَلُوا۟ فَلَا تَحْسَبَنَّهُم بِمَفَازَةٍ مِّنَ ٱلْعَذَابِ ۖ وَلَهُمْ عَذَابٌ أَلِيمٌ ۞ ﴾

188. Think not that those who rejoice in what they have done (or brought about), and love to be praised for what they have not done,- think not you that they are rescued from the torment, and for them is a painful torment.

﴿ وَلِلَّهِ مُلْكُ ٱلسَّمَٰوَٰتِ وَٱلْأَرْضِ ۗ وَٱللَّهُ عَلَىٰ كُلِّ شَىْءٍ قَدِيرٌ ۞ ﴾

189. And to Allâh belongs the dominion of the heavens and the earth, and Allâh has power over all things.

Transliteration

187. Wa-ith akhatha Allahu meethaqa allatheena ootoo alkitaba latubayyinunnahu lilnnasi wala taktumoonahu fanabathoohu waraa thuhoorihim waishtaraw bihi thamanan qaleelan fabi/sa ma yashtaroona 188. La tahsabanna allatheena yafrahoona bima ataw wayuhibboona an yuhmadoo bima lam yafAAaloo fala tahsabannahum bimafazatin mina alAAathabi walahum AAathabun aleemun 189. Walillahi mulku alssamawati waal-ardi waAllahu AAala kulli shay-in qadeerun

Tafsir Ibn Kathir

Chastising the People of the Scriptures for Breaking the Covenant and Hiding the Truth

In this Ayah, Allah chastises the People of the Scriptures, from whom Allah took the covenant by the words of their Prophets, that they would believe in Muhammad and describe him to the people, so that they would recognize and follow him when Allah sent him. However, they hid this truth and preferred the the small amounts and the material gains instead of the rewards of this life and the Hereafter that they were promised. This is a losing deal and a failing trade, indeed.

These Ayat also contain a warning for the scholars not to imitate their behavior, so that they do not suffer the same fate and become like them. Therefore, the scholars are required to spread the beneficial knowledge that they have, encouraging the various righteous good deeds. They are also warned against hiding any part of their knowledge. A Hadith states that the Prophet said,

«مَنْ سُئِلَ عَنْ عِلْمٍ فَكَتَمَهُ، أُلْجِمَ يَوْمَ الْقِيَامَةِ بِلِجَامٍ مِنْ نَارٍ»

(Whoever was asked about knowledge that he knew but did not disclose it, will be tied with a bridle made of fire on the Day of Resurrection.)

Chastising Those Who Love to be Praised for What They Have not Done

Allah's statement,

(Think not that those who rejoice in what they have done, and love to be praised for what they have not done), refers to those who show off, rejoice in what they do and claim to do what they have not done. The Two Sahihs recorded that the Prophet said,

«مَنِ ادَّعَى دَعْوَةً كَاذِبَةً لِيَتَكَثَّرَ بِهَا، لَمْ يَزِدْهُ اللهُ إِلَّا قِلَّةً»

(Whoever issues a false claim to acquire some type of gain, then Allah will only grant him decrease.)

The Sahih also recorded;

«الْمُتَشَبِّعُ بِمَا لَمْ يُعْطَ، كَلَابِسِ ثَوْبَيْ زُورٍ»

(He who claims to do what he has not done, is just like a person who wears two robes made of falsehood.)

Imam Ahmad recorded that Marwan told his guard Rafi` to go to Ibn `Abbas and proclaim to him, "If every person among us who rejoices with what he has done and loves to be praised for what he has not done will be tormented, we all will be tormented." Ibn `Abbas said, "This Ayah was revealed about the People of the Scriptures." He then recited the Ayah,

((And remember) when Allah took a covenant from those who were given the Scripture (Jews and Christians) to make it (the truth) known and clear to mankind, and not to hide it, but they threw it away behind their backs, and purchased with it some miserable gain! And indeed worst is that which they bought.) then the Ayah,

(Think not that those who rejoice in what they have done, and love to be praised for what they have not done)

Ibn `Abbas said, "The Prophet asked them about something, and they hid its knowledge, giving him an incorrect answer. They parted after showing off and rejoicing in front of him because they answered him, so they pretended, and they were delighted that they hid the correct news about what he had asked them." This was recorded by Al-Bukhari, Muslim, At-Tirmidhi and An-Nasa'i.

Al-Bukhari recorded that Abu Sa`id Al-Khudri said, "During the time of the Messenger of Allah , when the Messenger would go to battle, some hypocrite men would remain behind and rejoice because they did not accompany the Prophet in battle. When the Messenger would come back, they would ask him to excuse them swearing to having some excuse, and wanting to be praised for that which they did not do. So Allah revealed,

(Think not that those who rejoice in what they have done, and love to be praised for what they have not done),"

to the end of the Ayah." And Muslim recorded similarly.

Allah said;

(think not that they are rescued from the torment,) Do not think that they will be saved from punishment, rather it will certainly strike them. So Allah said;

(and for them is a painful torment.) Allah then said,

(And to Allah belongs the dominion of the heavens and the earth, and Allah has power over all things.) He is the Owner of everything, able to do all things and nothing escapes His might. Therefore, fear Him, never defy Him and beware of His anger and revenge. He is the Most Great, none is greater than Him, and the Most Able, none is more able than He is.

Surah: 3 Ayah: 190, Ayah: 191, Ayah: 192, Ayah: 193 & Ayah: 194

﴿ إِنَّ فِى خَلْقِ ٱلسَّمَٰوَٰتِ وَٱلْأَرْضِ وَٱخْتِلَٰفِ ٱلَّيْلِ وَٱلنَّهَارِ لَءَايَٰتٍ لِّأُو۟لِى ٱلْأَلْبَٰبِ ۝ ﴾

190. Verily! In the creation of the heavens and the earth, and in the alternation of night and day, there are indeed signs for men of understanding.

﴿ ٱلَّذِينَ يَذْكُرُونَ ٱللَّهَ قِيَٰمًا وَقُعُودًا وَعَلَىٰ جُنُوبِهِمْ وَيَتَفَكَّرُونَ فِى خَلْقِ ٱلسَّمَٰوَٰتِ وَٱلْأَرْضِ رَبَّنَا مَا خَلَقْتَ هَٰذَا بَٰطِلًا سُبْحَٰنَكَ فَقِنَا عَذَابَ ٱلنَّارِ ۝ ﴾

191. Those who remember Allâh (always, and in prayers) standing, sitting, and lying down on their sides, and think deeply about the creation of the heavens and the earth, (saying): "Our Lord! You have not created (all) this without purpose, glory to You! (Exalted are You above all that they associate with You as partners). Give us salvation from the torment of the Fire.

﴿ رَبَّنَآ إِنَّكَ مَن تُدْخِلِ ٱلنَّارَ فَقَدْ أَخْزَيْتَهُۥ ۖ وَمَا لِلظَّـٰلِمِينَ مِنْ أَنصَارٍ ۝ ﴾

192. "Our Lord! Verily, whom You admit to the Fire, indeed, You have disgraced him; and never will the Zâlimûn (polytheists and wrong-doers) find any helpers.

﴿ رَّبَّنَآ إِنَّنَا سَمِعْنَا مُنَادِيًا يُنَادِى لِلْإِيمَـٰنِ أَنْ ءَامِنُوا۟ بِرَبِّكُمْ فَـَٔامَنَّا ۚ رَبَّنَا فَٱغْفِرْ لَنَا ذُنُوبَنَا وَكَفِّرْ عَنَّا سَيِّـَٔاتِنَا وَتَوَفَّنَا مَعَ ٱلْأَبْرَارِ ۝ ﴾

193. "Our Lord! Verily, we have heard the call of one (Muhammad (peace be upon him)) calling to Faith: 'Believe in your Lord,' and we have believed. Our Lord! Forgive us our sins and expiate from us our evil deeds, and make us die (in the state of righteousness) along with Al-Abrâr (the believers of Islâmic Monotheism, the pious and righteous).

﴿ رَبَّنَا وَءَاتِنَا مَا وَعَدتَّنَا عَلَىٰ رُسُلِكَ وَلَا تُخْزِنَا يَوْمَ ٱلْقِيَـٰمَةِ ۗ إِنَّكَ لَا تُخْلِفُ ٱلْمِيعَادَ ۝ ﴾

194. "Our Lord! Grant us what You promised unto us through Your Messengers and disgrace us not on the Day of Resurrection, for You never break (Your) Promise."

Transliteration

190. Inna fee khalqi alssamawati waal-ardi waikhtilafi allayli waalnnahari laayatin li-olee al-albabi 191. Allatheena yathkuroona Allaha qiyaman waquAAoodan waAAala junoobihim wayatafakkaroona fee khalqi alssamawati waal-ardi rabbana ma khalaqta hatha batilan subhanaka faqina AAathaba alnnari 192. Rabbana innaka man tudkhili alnnara faqad akhzaytahu wama lilththalimeena min ansarin 193. Rabbana innana samiAAna munadiyan yunadee lil-eemani an aminoo birabbikum faamanna rabbana faighfir lana thunoobana wakaffir AAanna sayyi-atina watawaffana maAAa al-abrari 194. Rabbana waatina ma waAAadtana AAala rusulika wala tukhzina yawma alqiyamati innaka la tukhlifu almeeAAada

Tafsir Ibn Kathir

The Proofs of Tawhid for People of Understanding, their Characteristics, Speech, and Supplications

Allah said,

(Verily, in the creation of the heavens and the Earth,) (3:190), referring to the sky in its height and spaciousness, the earth in its expanse and density, the tremendous features they have of rotating planets, seas, mountains, deserts, trees, plants, fruits, animals, metals and various beneficial colors, scents, tastes and elements.

(And in the alternation of night and day), as one follows and takes from the length of the other. For instance, at times one of them becomes longer than the other, shorter than the other at times and equal to the other at other times, and the same is repeated again and again, and all this occurs by the decision of the Almighty, Most Wise. This is why Allah said,

(there are indeed signs for men of understanding), referring to the intelligent and sound minds that contemplate about the true reality of things, unlike the deaf and mute who do not have sound comprehension. Allah said about the latter type,

(And how many a sign in the heavens and the earth they pass by, while they are averse therefrom. And most of them believe not in Allah except that they attribute partners unto Him) (12:105,106).

Allah then describes those who have good minds,

(Those who remember Allah standing, sitting, and lying down on their sides) (3:191).

Al-Bukhari recorded that `Imran bin Husayn said that, the Messenger of Allah said,

«صَلِّ قَائِمًا، فَإِنْ لَمْ تَسْتَطِعْ فَقَاعِدًا، فَإِنْ لَمْ تَسْتَطِعْ فَعَلَى جَنْبٍ»

(Pray while standing, and if you can't, pray while sitting, and if you cannot do even that, then pray lying on your side.) These people remember Allah in all situations, in their heart and speech,

(and think deeply about the creation of the heavens and the Earth), contemplating about signs in the sky and earth that testify to the might, ability, knowledge, wisdom, will and mercy of the Creator. Allah criticizes those who do not contemplate about His creation, which testifies to His existence, Attributes, Shari`ah, His decree and Ayat. Allah said,

(And how many a sign in the heavens and the Earth they pass by, while they are averse therefrom. And most of them believe not in Allah except that they attribute partners unto Him) (12:105,106).

Allah also praises His believing servants,

(Those who remember Allah standing, sitting, and lying down on their sides, and think deeply about the creation of the heavens and the earth), supplicating;

("Our Lord! You have not created this without purpose,")

You did not create all this in jest and play. Rather, You created it in truth, so that You recompense those who do evil in kind, and reward those who do righteous deeds with what is better.

The faithful believers praise Allah and deny that He does anything in jest and without purpose, saying,

("glory to You,"), for You would never create anything without purpose,

("Give us salvation from the torment of the Fire."), meaning, "O You Who created the creation in truth and justice, Who is far from any shortcomings, or doing things without purpose or with jest, save us from the torment of the Fire with Your power and strength. Direct us to perform the deeds that make You pleased with us. Guide us to righteous work from which You admit us into the delightful Paradise, and save us from Your painful torment."

They next supplicate,

("Our Lord! Verily, whom You admit to the Fire, indeed, You have disgraced him;), by humiliating and disgracing him before all people on the Day of Gathering,

("and never will the wrongdoers find any helpers."), on the Day of Judgment, who would save them from You. Therefore, there is no escaping whatever fate You decided for them.

("Our Lord! Verily, we have heard the call of one calling to faith,"), a caller who calls to faith, referring to the Messenger of Allah ,

(`Believe in your Lord,' and we have believed), accepted his call and followed him.

("Our Lord! Forgive us our sins"), on account of our faith and obeying Your Prophet

("Forgive us our sins"), and cover them,

("and expiate from us our evil deeds"), between us and You, in private,

("and make us die along with Al-Abrar."), join us with the righteous people.

("Our Lord! Grant us what You promised unto us through Your Messengers") for our faith in Your Messengers, or, and this explanation is better; grant us what You promised us by the words of Your Messengers,

("and disgrace us not on the Day of Resurrection,"), before all creation,

("for You never break (Your) Promise."), for surely, the promise that You conveyed to Your Messengers, which includes us being resurrected before You, shall certainly come to pass.

It was the Prophet's tradition to recite the ten Ayat at the end of (Surah) Al `Imran when he woke up at night for (voluntary) prayer. Al-Bukhari recorded that Ibn `Abbas said, "I slept one night at the house of my aunt, Maymunah. The Messenger of Allah spoke with his wife for a while and then went to sleep. When it was the third part of the night, he stood up, looked at the sky and recited,

(Verily, in the creation of the heavens and the earth, and in the alternation of night and day, there are indeed signs for men of understanding) (3:190).

The Prophet then stood up, performed ablution, used Siwak (to clean his teeth) and prayed eleven units of prayer. When Bilal said the Adhan, the Prophet prayed two units of prayer, went out (to the Masjid) and led the people in the Dawn prayer." This was also collected by Muslim.

Ibn Marduwyah recorded that `Ata' said, "I, Ibn `Umar and `Ubayd bin `Umayr went to `A'ishah and entered her room, and there was a screen between us and her. She said, `O `Ubayd! What prevents you from visiting us' He said, `What the poet said, `Visit every once in a while, and you will be loved more.' Ibn `Umar said, `Tell us about the most unusual thing you witnessed from the Messenger of Allah .' She cried and said, `All his matters were amazing. On night, he came close to me until his skin touched my skin and said, `Let me worship my Lord.' I said, `By Allah I love your being close to me. I also love that you worship your Lord.' He used the water-skin and performed ablution, but did not use too much water. He then stood up in prayer and cried until his beard became wet. He prostrated and cried until he made the ground wet. He then laid down on his side and cried. When Bilal came to alert the Prophet for the Dawn prayer, he said, `O Messenger of Allah! What makes you cry, while Allah has forgiven you your previous and latter sins' He said,

»وَيْحَكَ يَا بِلَالُ، وَمَا يَمْنَعُنِي أَنْ أَبْكِيَ، وَقَدْ أُنْزِلَ عَلَيَّ فِي هذِهِ اللَّيْلَةِ«

(O Bilal! What prevents me from crying, when this night, this Ayah was revealed to me,)

(Verily, in the creation of the heavens and the earth, and in the alternation of night and day, there are indeed signs for men of understanding.)

(Woe to he who recites it but does not contemplate it.).''

Surah: 3 Ayah: 195

﴿فَاسْتَجَابَ لَهُمْ رَبُّهُمْ أَنِّي لَا أُضِيعُ عَمَلَ عَامِلٍ مِّنكُم مِّن ذَكَرٍ أَوْ أُنثَىٰ بَعْضُكُم مِّنْ بَعْضٍ فَالَّذِينَ هَاجَرُوا وَأُخْرِجُوا مِن دِيَارِهِمْ وَأُوذُوا فِي سَبِيلِي وَقَاتَلُوا وَقُتِلُوا لَأُكَفِّرَنَّ عَنْهُمْ سَيِّئَاتِهِمْ وَلَأُدْخِلَنَّهُمْ جَنَّاتٍ تَجْرِي مِن تَحْتِهَا الْأَنْهَارُ ثَوَابًا مِّنْ عِندِ اللَّهِ وَاللَّهُ عِندَهُ حُسْنُ الثَّوَابِ ۱۹۵﴾

195. So their Lord accepted of them (their supplication and answered them), "Never will I allow to be lost the work of any of you, be he male or female. You are (members) one of another, so those who emigrated and were driven out from their homes, and suffered harm in My Cause, and who fought, and were killed (in My Cause), verily, I will exoiate from them their evil deeds and admit them into Gardens under which rivers flow (in Paradise); a reward from Allâh, and with Allâh is the best of rewards."

Transliteration

195. Faistajaba lahum rabbuhum annee la odeeAAu AAamala AAamilin minkum min thakarin aw ontha baAAdukum min baAAdin faallatheena hajaroo waokhrijoo min diyarihim waoothoo fee sabeelee waqataloo waqutiloo laokaffiranna AAanhum sayyi-atihim walaodkhilannahum jannatin tajree min tahtiha al-anharu thawaban min AAindi Allahi waAllahu AAindahu husnu alththawabi

Tafsir Ibn Kathir

Allah Accepts the Supplication of Men of Understanding

Allah said,

(So their Lord accepted of them), answered their invocation. Sa`id bin Mansur recorded that Salamah, a man from the family of Umm Salamah said, "Umm Salamah said, `O Messenger of Allah! Allah does not mention women in connection with Hijrah (Migration).' Allah sent down the Ayah,

(So their Lord accepted of them (their supplication and answered them), "Never will I allow to be lost the work of any of you, be he male or female.)

The Ansar say that Umm Salamah was the first woman to migrate to them." Al-Hakim collected this Hadith in his Mustadrak, and said, "It is Sahih according to the criteria of Al-Bukhari but they (Al-Bukhari and Muslim) did not collect it".

Allah's statement,

("Never will I allow to be lost the work of any of you, be he male or female,) explains the type of answer Allah gave them, stating that no deed of any person is ever lost with Him. Rather, He will completely reward each person for his or her good deeds. Allah's statement,

(You are (members) one of another) means, you are all equal in relation to gaining My reward. Therefore,

(those who emigrated), by leaving the land of Shirk and migrating to the land of faith, leaving behind their loved ones, brethren, friends and neighbors,

(and were driven out from their homes), when the Mushriks tormented them and forced them to migrate,

(and suffered harm in My cause), for their only wrong, to the people, was that they believed in Allah Alone. In similar Ayat, Allah said,

(and have driven out the Messenger and yourselves because you believe in Allah your Lord!) (60:1), and,

(And they had no fault except that they believed in Allah, the Almighty, Worthy of all praise!) (85:8) . Allah's statement, (and who fought and were killed (in My cause),) (3:195) refers to the highest rank there is, that one fights in the cause of Allah and dies in the process, with his face covered in dust and blood. It is recorded in the Sahih that a man said,

('O Messenger of Allah! If I was killed in Allah's cause, observing patience, awaiting Allah's reward, attacking, not retreating, would Allah forgive my sins' The Prophet said,

«نَعَم»

`Yes.' The Prophet then asked the man,

«كَيْفَ قُلْتَ؟»

`What did you ask' When the man repeated the question, the Prophet said,

«نَعَمْ، إِلَّا الدَّيْنَ، قَالَهُ لِي جِبْرِيلُ آنِفًا»

`Yes, except for the debt, for Jibril conveyed this to me right now'.)

This is why Allah said here,

(verily, I will expiate from them their evil deeds and admit them into Gardens under which rivers flow), within Paradise, where there are rivers of various drinks: milk, honey, wine and fresh water. There is what no eye has ever seen, no ear has ever heard and no heart has ever imagined (of delights in Paradise). Allah's statement,

(a reward from Allah) testifies to His might, for the Mighty and Most Great only gives tremendous rewards. Allah's statement,

(and with Allah is the best of rewards.") for those who perform good deeds.

Surah: 3 Ayah: 196, Ayah: 197 & Ayah: 198

﴿ لَا يَغُرَّنَّكَ تَقَلُّبُ ٱلَّذِينَ كَفَرُواْ فِي ٱلْبِلَٰدِ ۝ ﴾

196. Let not the free disposal (and affluence) of the disbelievers throughout the land deceive you.

﴿ مَتَٰعٌ قَلِيلٌ ثُمَّ مَأْوَىٰهُمْ جَهَنَّمُ وَبِئْسَ ٱلْمِهَادُ ۝ ﴾

197. A brief enjoyment; then, their ultimate abode is Hell; and worst indeed is that place for rest.

$$\text{﴿ لَٰكِنِ ٱلَّذِينَ ٱتَّقَوْا۟ رَبَّهُمْ لَهُمْ جَنَّٰتٌ تَجْرِى مِن تَحْتِهَا ٱلْأَنْهَٰرُ خَٰلِدِينَ فِيهَا نُزُلًا مِّنْ عِندِ ٱللَّهِ ۗ وَمَا عِندَ ٱللَّهِ خَيْرٌ لِّلْأَبْرَارِ ﴾}$$

198. But, for those who fear their Lord, are Gardens under which rivers flow (in Paradise); therein are they to dwell (for ever), an entertainment from Allâh; and that which is with Allâh is the Best for Al-Abrâr (the believers of Islâmic Monotheism, the pious and righteous).

Transliteration

196. La yaghurrannaka taqallubu allatheena kafaroo fee albiladi 197. MataAAun qaleelun thumma ma/wahum jahannamu wabi/sa almihadu 198. Lakini allatheena ittaqaw rabbahum lahum jannatun tajree min tahtiha al-anharu khalideena feeha nuzulan min AAindi Allahi wama AAinda Allahi khayrun lil-abrari

Tafsir Ibn Kathir

Warning Against Being Deceived by This Life; the Rewards of the Righteous Believers

Allah said, do not look at the disbelievers, who are enjoying various delights and joys. Soon, they will loose all this and be tied to their evil works, for verily, we are only giving them time, which deceives them, when all they have is,

(A brief enjoyment; then their ultimate abode is Hell; and worst indeed is that place for rest.)

This Ayah is similar to several other Ayat, such as,

(None disputes in the Ayat of Allah but those who disbelieve. So, let not their ability of going about here and there through the land deceive you!) (40:4),

(Verily, those who invent a lie against Allah, will never be successful. (A brief) enjoyment in this world! and then unto Us will be their return, then We shall make them taste the severest torment because they used to disbelieve.) (10:69,70),

(We let them enjoy for a little while, then in the end We shall oblige them to (enter) a great torment.) (31:24),

(So, give a respite to the disbelievers; deal gently with them for a while.) (86:17), and,

(Is he whom We have promised an excellent promise (Paradise) which he will find true -- like him whom We have made to enjoy the luxuries of the life of (this) world, then on the Day of Resurrection, he will be among those brought up (to be punished in the Hell-fire)) (28:61).

After Allah mentioned the condition of the disbelievers in this life and their destination to the Fire, He said,

(But, for those who have Taqwa of their Lord, are Gardens under which rivers flow (in Paradise); therein are they to dwell, an entertainment from Allah,) (3:198), for certainly,

(and that which is with Allah is the best for Al-Abrar.)

Ibn Jarir recorded that Abu Ad-Darda' used to say, "Death is better for every believer. Death is better for every disbeliever, and those who do not believe me should read Allah's statements,

(and that which is with Allah is the best for Al-Abrar), and,

(And let not the disbelievers think that Our postponing of their punishment is good for them. We postpone the punishment only so that they may increase in sinfulness. And for them is a disgraceful torment.) (3:178)."

Surah: 3 Ayah: 199 & Ayah: 200

﴿ وَإِنَّ مِنْ أَهْلِ ٱلْكِتَٰبِ لَمَن يُؤْمِنُ بِٱللَّهِ وَمَآ أُنزِلَ إِلَيْكُمْ وَمَآ أُنزِلَ إِلَيْهِمْ خَٰشِعِينَ لِلَّهِ لَا يَشْتَرُونَ بِـَٔايَٰتِ ٱللَّهِ ثَمَنًا قَلِيلًا أُو۟لَٰٓئِكَ لَهُمْ أَجْرُهُمْ عِندَ رَبِّهِمْ إِنَّ ٱللَّهَ سَرِيعُ ٱلْحِسَابِ ﴾ ۱۹۹

199. And there are, certainly, among the people of the Scripture (Jews and Christians), those who believe in Allâh and in that which has been revealed to you, and in that which has been revealed to them, humbling themselves before Allâh. They do not sell the Verses of Allâh for a little price, for them is a reward with their Lord. Surely, Allâh is Swift in account.

﴿ يَٰٓأَيُّهَا ٱلَّذِينَ ءَامَنُوا۟ ٱصْبِرُوا۟ وَصَابِرُوا۟ وَرَابِطُوا۟ وَٱتَّقُوا۟ ٱللَّهَ لَعَلَّكُمْ تُفْلِحُونَ ﴾ ۲۰۰

200. O you who believe! Endure and be more patient (than your enemy), and guard your territory by stationing army units permanently at the places from where the enemy can attack you, and fear Allâh, so that you may be successful.

Transliteration

199. Wa-inna min ahli alkitabi laman yu/minu biAllahi wama onzila ilaykum wama onzila ilayhim khashiAAeena lillahi la yashtaroona bi-ayati Allahi thamanan qaleelan ola-ika lahum ajruhum AAinda rabbihim inna Allaha sareeAAu alhisabi 200. Ya ayyuha allatheena amanoo isbiroo wasabiroo warabitoo waittaqoo Allaha laAAallakum tuflihoona

Tafsir Ibn Kathir

The Condition of Some of the People of the Scriptures and their Rewards

Allah states that some of the People of the Book truly believe in Him and in what was sent down to Muhammad , along with believing in the previously revealed Books, and they are obedient to Him and humble themselves before Allah.

(They do not sell the verses of Allah for a small price) (3:199), for they do not hide what they know of the glad tidings about the description of Muhammad , his Prophethood, and the description of his Ummah. Indeed, these are the best people among the People of the Book, whether they were Jews or Christians. Allah said in Surat Al-Qasas,

(Those to whom We gave the Scripture before it, they believe in it (the Qur'an). And when it is recited to them, they say: "We believe in it. Verily, it is the truth from our Lord. Indeed even before it we were Muslims. These will be given their reward twice over, because they are patient,) (28:52-54). Allah said,

(Those to whom We gave the Book, recite it (follow it) as it should be recited (i.e. followed), they are the ones who believe therein.) (2:121),

(And of the people of Musa there is a community who lead with truth and establish justice therewith.) (7:159),

(Not all of them are alike; a party of the people of the Scripture stand for the right, they recite the verses of Allah during the hours of the night, prostrating themselves in prayer.) (3:113), and,

(Say: "Believe in it (the Qur'an) or do not believe (in it). Verily, those who were given knowledge before it, when it is recited to them, fall down on their faces in humble prostration." And they say: "Glory be to our Lord! Truly, the promise of our Lord must be fulfillled." And they fall down on their faces weeping and it increases their humility.) (17:107-109).

These qualities exist in some of the Jews, but only a few of them. For instance, less than ten Jewish rabbis embraced the Islamic faith, such as `Abdullah bin Salam. Many among the Christians, on the other hand, embraced the Islamic faith. Allah said,

(Verily, you will find the strongest among men in enmity to the believers the Jews and those who commit Shirk, and you will find the nearest in love to the believers those who say: "We are Christians.") (5:82), until,

(So because of what they said, Allah rewarded them Gardens under which rivers flow (in Paradise), they will abide therein forever) (5:85). In this Ayah,

Allah said,

(for them is a reward with their Lord) (3:199).

When Ja`far bin Abi Talib recited Surah Maryam (chapter 19) to An-Najashi, King of Ethiopia, in the presence of Christian priests and patriarchs, he and they cried until their beards became wet from crying. The Two Sahihs record that when An-Najashi died, the Prophet conveyed the news to his Companions and said,

«إِنَّ أَخًا لَكُمْ بِالْحَبَشَةِ قَدْ مَاتَ، فَصَلُّوا عَلَيْهِ»

(A brother of yours from Ethiopia has passed, come to offer the funeral prayer.) He went out with the Companions to the Musalla lined them up in rows, and after that led the prayer.

Ibn Abi Najih narrated that Mujahid said that,

(And there are, certainly, among the People of the Scripture), refers to those among them who embraced Islam. `Abbad bin Mansur said that he asked Al-Hasan Al-Basri about Allah's statement,

(And there are, certainly, among the People of the Scripture, those who believe in Allah).

Al-Hasan said, "They are the People of the Book, before Muhammad was sent, who believed in Muhammad and recognized Islam. Allah gave them a double reward, for the faith that they had before Muhammad , and for believing in Muhammad (after he was sent as Prophet)." Ibn Abi Hatim recorded both of these statements. The Two Sahihs record that Abu Musa said that the Messenger of Allah said,

«ثَلَاثَةٌ يُؤْتَوْنَ أَجْرَهُمْ مَرَّتَيْنِ»

(Three persons will acquire a double reward.)

He mentioned among them,

«وَرَجُلٌ مِنْ أَهْلِ الْكِتَابِ آمَنَ بِنَبِيِّهِ وَآمَنَ بِي»

(A person from among the People of the Book who believed in his Prophet and in me.)

Allah's statement,

(They do not sell the verses of Allah for a small price), means, they do not hide the knowledge that they have, as the cursed ones among them have done. Rather, they share the knowledge without a price, and this is why Allah said,

(for them is a reward with their Lord. surely, Allah is Swift in account.)

Mujahid commented on the verse,

((Surely, Allah is) swift in account), "He is swift in reckoning," as Ibn Abi Hatim and others have recorded from him.

The Command for Patience and Ribat

Allah said,

(O you who believe! Endure and be more patient, and Rabitu) (3:200).

Al-Hasan Al-Basri said, "The believers are commanded to be patient in the religion that Allah chose for them, Islam. They are not allowed to abandon it in times of comfort or hardship, ease or calamity, until they die as Muslims. They are also commanded to endure against their enemies, those who hid the truth about their religion." Similar explanation given by several other scholars among the Salaf.

As for Murabatah, it is to endure in acts of worship and perseverance. It also means to await prayer after prayer, as Ibn `Abbas, Sahl bin Hanif and Muhammad bin Ka`b Al-Qurazi stated. Ibn Abi Hatim collected a Hadith that was also collected by Muslim and An-Nasa'i from Abu Hurayrah that the Prophet said,

«أَلَا أُخْبِرُكُمْ بِمَا يَمْحُو اللَّهُ بِهِ الْخَطَايَا، وَيَرْفَعُ بِهِ الدَّرَجَاتِ؟ إِسْبَاغُ الْوُضُوءِ عَلَى الْمَكَارِهِ، وَكَثْرَةُ الْخُطَا إِلَى الْمَسَاجِدِ، وَانْتِظَارُ الصَّلَاةِ بَعْدَ الصَّلَاةِ، فَذلِكُمُ الرِّبَاطُ، فَذلِكُمُ الرِّبَاطُ، فَذلِكُمُ الرِّبَاطُ»

(Should I tell you about actions with which Allah forgives sins and raises the grade Performing perfect ablution in unfavorable conditions, the many steps one takes to the Masajid, and awaiting prayer after the prayer, for this is the Ribat, this is the Ribat, this is the Ribat.)

They also say that the Murabatah in the above Ayah refers to battles against the enemy, and manning Muslim outposts to protect them from enemy incursions inside Muslim territory. There are several Hadiths that encourage Murabatah and mention its rewards. Al-Bukhari recorded that Sahl bin Sa`d As-Sa`idi said that the Messenger of Allah said,

«رِبَاطُ يَوْمٍ فِي سَبِيلِ اللهِ خَيْرٌ مِنَ الدُّنْيَا وَمَا عَلَيْهَا»

(A Day of Ribat in the cause of Allah is better than this life and all that is in it.)

Muslim recorded that Salman Al-Farisi said that the Messenger of Allah said,

Chapter 3: Al-i-'Imran (The Family of Imran), Verses 093-200

«رِبَاطُ يَوْمٍ وَلَيْلَةٍ خَيْرٌ مِنْ صِيَامِ شَهْرٍ وَقِيَامِهِ، وَإِنْ مَاتَ جَرَى عَلَيْهِ عَمَلُهُ الَّذِي كَانَ يَعْمَلُهُ، وَأُجْرِيَ عَلَيْهِ رِزْقُهُ، وَأَمِنَ الْفَتَّانَ»

(Ribat for a day and a night is better than fasting the days of a month and its Qiyam (voluntary prayer at night). If one dies in Ribat, his regular righteous deeds that he used to perform will keep being added to his account, and he will receive his provision, and will be saved from the trials of the grave.)

Imam Ahmad recorded that Fadalah bin `Ubayd said that he heard the Messenger of Allah saying,

«كُلُّ مَيِّتٍ يُخْتَمُ عَلَى عَمَلِهِ إِلَّا الَّذِي مَاتَ مُرَابِطًا فِي سَبِيلِ اللهِ، فَإِنَّهُ يَنْمِي لَهُ عَمَلُهُ إِلَى يَوْمِ الْقِيَامَةِ، وَيَأْمَنُ فِتْنَةَ الْقَبْرِ»

(Every dead person will have his record of deeds sealed, except for whoever dies while in Ribat in the cause of Allah, for his work will keep increasing until the Day of Resurrection, and he will be safe from the trial of the grave.)

This is the same narration collected by Abu Dawud and At-Tirmidhi, who said, "Hasan Sahih". Ibn Hibban also collected this Hadith in his Sahih. fAt-Tirmidhi recorded that Ibn `Abbas said that he heard the Messenger of Allah saying,

«عَيْنَانِ لَا تَمَسُّهُمَا النَّارُ: عَيْنٌ بَكَتْ مِنْ خَشْيَةِ اللهِ، وَعَيْنٌ بَاتَتْ تَحْرُسُ فِي سَبِيلِ اللهِ»

(Two eyes shall not be touched by the Fire: an eye that cried for fear from Allah and an eye that spent the night guarding in Allah's cause.)

Al-Bukhari recorded in his Sahih that Abu Hurayrah said that the Messenger of Allah said,

«تَعِسَ عَبْدُ الدِّينَارِ وَعَبْدُ الدِّرْهَمِ وَعَبْدُ الْخَمِيصَةِ، إِنْ أُعْطِيَ رَضِيَ، وَإِنْ لَمْ يُعْطَ سَخِطَ، تَعِسَ وَانْتَكَسَ، وَإِذَا شِيكَ فَلَا انْتَقَشَ، طُوبَى لِعَبْدٍ آخِذٍ بِعِنَانِ فَرَسِهِ فِي سَبِيلِ اللهِ، أَشْعَثَ رَأْسُهُ، مُغْبَرَّةٍ قَدَمَاهُ، إِنْ كَانَ فِي الْحِرَاسَةِ كَانَ فِي

الْحِرَاسَةِ، وَإِنْ كَانَ فِي السَّاقَةِ كَانَ فِي السَّاقَةِ، إِنِ اسْتَأْذَنَ لَمْ يُؤْذَنْ لَهُ، وَإِنْ شَفَعَ لَمْ يُشَفَّعْ»

(Let the servant of the Dinar, the servant of the Dirham and the servant of the Khamisah (of clothes) perish, as he is pleased if these things are given to him, and if not, he is displeased. Let such a person perish and be humiliated, and if he is pierced with a thorn, let him not find anyone to take it out for him. Paradise is for him who holds the reins of his horse, striving in Allah's cause, with his hair unkempt and feet covered with dust: if he is appointed to the vanguard, he is perfectly satisfied with his post of guarding, and if he is appointed in the rearguard, he accepts his post with satisfaction; if he asks for permission he is not permitted, and if he intercedes, his intercession is not accepted.)

Ibn Jarir recorded that Zayd bin Aslam said, "Abu `Ubaydah wrote to `Umar bin Al-Khattab and mentioned to him that the Romans were mobilizing their forces. `Umar wrote back, `Allah will soon turn whatever hardship a believing servant suffers, to ease, and no hardship shall ever overcome two types of ease. Allah says in His Book,

(O you who believe! Endure and be more patient, and Rabitu, and have Taqwa of Allah, so that you may be successful)' (3:200)."

Al-Hafiz Ibn `Asakir mentioned in the biography of `Abdullah bin Al-Mubarak, that Muhammad bin Ibrahim bin Abi Sakinah said, "While in the area of Tarsus, `Abdullah bin Al-Mubarak dictated this poem to me when I was greeting him goodbye. He sent the poem with me to Al-Fudayl bin `Iyad in the year one hundred and seventy, `O he who worships in the vicinity of the Two Holy Masjids! If you but see us, you will realize that you are only jesting in worship. He who brings wetness to his cheek with his tears, should know that our necks are being wet by our blood. He who tires his horses without purpose, know that our horses are getting tired in battle. Scent of perfume is yours, while our scent is the glimmer of spears and the stench of dust (in battle). We were narrated about in the speech of our Prophet, an authentic statement that never lies. That the dust that erupts by Allah's horses and which fills the nostrils of a man shall never be combined with the smoke of a raging Fire. This, the Book of Allah speaks among us that the martyr is not dead, and the truth in Allah's Book cannot be denied.' I met Al-Fudayl Ibn `Iyad in the Sacred Masjid and gave him the letter. When he read it, his eyes became tearful and he said, `Abu `Abdur-Rahman (`Abdullah bin Al-Mubarak) has said the truth and offered sincere advice to me.' He then asked me, `Do you write the Hadith' I said, `Yes.' He said, `Write this Hadith as reward for delivering the letter of Abu `Abdur-Rahman to me. He then dictated, `Mansur bin Al-Mu`tamir narrated to us that Abu Salih narrated from Abu Hurayrah that a man asked, `O Messenger of Allah! Teach me a good deed that will earn me the reward of the Mujahidin in Allah's cause.' The Prophet said,

«هَلْ تَسْتَطِيعُ أَنْ تُصَلِّيَ فَلَا تَفْتُرَ، وَتَصُومَ فَلَا تُفْطِرَ؟»

(Are you able to pray continuously and fast without breaking the fast) The man said, `O Messenger of Allah! I cannot bear it.' The Prophet said,

«فَوَالَّذِي نَفْسِي بِيَدِهِ لَوْ طُوِّقْتَ ذَلِكَ مَا بَلَغْتَ الْمُجَاهِدِينَ فِي سَبِيلِ اللهِ، أَوَ مَا عَلِمْتَ أَنَّ فَرَسَ الْمُجَاهِدِ لَيَسْتَنُّ فِي طِوَلِهِ، فَيُكْتَبُ لَهُ بِذَلِكَ الْحَسَنَاتُ»

(By He in Whose Hand is my soul! Even if you were able to do it, you will not achieve the grade of the Mujahidin in Allah's cause. Did you not know that the horse of the Mujahid earns rewards for him as long as it lives.)

Allah said next,

(and have Taqwa of Allah), concerning all your affairs and situations. For instance, the Prophet said to Mu`adh when he sent him to Yemen,

«اتَّقِ اللهَ حَيْثُمَا كُنْتَ، وَأَتْبِعِ السَّيِّئَةَ الْحَسَنَةَ تَمْحُهَا، وَخَالِقِ النَّاسَ بِخُلُقٍ حَسَنٍ»

(Have Taqwa of Allah wherever you may be, follow the evil deed with a good deed and it will erase it, and deal with people in a good manner.)

Allah said next,

(so that you may be successful.), in this life and the Hereafter. Ibn Jarir recorded that Muhammad bin Ka`b Al-Qurazi said that, Allah's statement,

(and have Taqwa of Allah, so that you may be successful.) means, "Fear Me concerning what is between you and Me, so that you may acquire success when you meet Me tomorrow."

The Tafsir of Surah Al `Imran ends here, all praise is due to Allah, and we ask Him that we die while on the path of the Qur'an and Sunnah, Amin.

INTRODUCTION TO CHAPTER (SURAH) 4: AN-NISAA (THE WOMEN)

Ibn Kathir's Introduction

Virtues of Surat An-Nisa, A Madinan Surah

Al-`Awfi reported that Ibn `Abbas said that Surat An-Nisa' was revealed in Al-Madinah. Ibn Marduwyah recorded similar statements from `Abdullah bin Az-Zubayr and Zayd bin Thabit. In his Mustadrak, Al-Hakim recorded that `Abdullah bin Mas`ud said, "There are five Ayat in Surat An-Nisa' that I would prefer to the life of this world and all that is in it,

(Surely, Allah wrongs not even the weight of an atom,) (4:40),

(If you avoid the great sins which you are forbidden to do) (4:31),

(Verily, Allah forgives not that partners should be set up with Him (in worship), but He forgives except that (anything else) to whom He wills) (4:48),

(If they (hypocrites), when they had been unjust to themselves, had come to you) (4:64), and,

(And whoever does evil or wrongs himself, but afterwards seeks Allah's forgiveness, he will find Allah Oft-Forgiving, Most Merciful) (4:110)." Al-Hakim recorded that Ibn `Abbas said, "Ask me about Surat An-Nisa', for I learned the Qur'an when I was still young." Al-Hakim said, "This Hadith is Sahih according to the criteria of the Two Sahihs, and they did not collect it."

CHAPTER (SURAH) 4: AN-NISAA (THE WOMEN), VERSES 001-023

﴿ بِسْمِ ٱللَّهِ ٱلرَّحْمَٰنِ ٱلرَّحِيمِ ﴾

In the Name of Allâh, the Most Gracious, the Most Merciful.

Surah: 4 Ayah: 1

﴿ يَٰٓأَيُّهَا ٱلنَّاسُ ٱتَّقُواْ رَبَّكُمُ ٱلَّذِى خَلَقَكُم مِّن نَّفْسٍ وَٰحِدَةٍ وَخَلَقَ مِنْهَا زَوْجَهَا وَبَثَّ مِنْهُمَا رِجَالاً كَثِيرًا وَنِسَآءً وَٱتَّقُواْ ٱللَّهَ ٱلَّذِى تَسَآءَلُونَ بِهِۦ وَٱلْأَرْحَامَ إِنَّ ٱللَّهَ كَانَ عَلَيْكُمْ رَقِيبًا ﴾

1. O mankind! Be dutiful to your Lord, Who created you from a single person (Adam), and from him (Adam) He created his wife (Hawwâ (Eve)) and from them both He created many men and women; and fear Allâh through Whom you demand (your mutual rights), and (do not cut the relations of) the wombs (kinship). Surely, Allâh is Ever an All-Watcher over you.

Transliteration

1. Ya ayyuha alnnasu ittaqoo rabbakumu allathee khalaqakum min nafsin wahidatin wakhalaqa minha zawjaha wabaththa minhuma rijalan katheeran wanisaan waittaqoo Allaha allathee tasaaloona bihi waal-arhama inna Allaha kana AAalaykum raqeeban

Tafsir Ibn Kathir

The Command to have Taqwa, a Reminder about Creation, and Being Kind to Relatives

Allah commands His creatures to have Taqwa of Him by worshipping Him Alone without partners. He also reminds to them of His ability, in that He created them all from a single person, Adam, peace be unto him.

(And from him He created his wife) Hawwa' (Eve), who was created from Adam's left rib, from his back while he was sleeping. When Adam woke up and saw Hawwa', he liked her and had affection for her, and she felt the same toward him. An authentic Hadith states,

«إِنَّ الْمَرْأَةَ خُلِقَتْ مِنْ ضِلَعٍ، وَإِنَّ أَعْوَجَ شَيْءٍ فِي الضِّلَعِ أَعْلَاهُ، فَإِنْ ذَهَبْتَ تُقِيمُهُ كَسَرْتَهُ، وَإِنِ اسْتَمْتَعْتَ بِهَا اسْتَمْتَعْتَ بِهَا وَفِيهَا عِوَجٌ»

(Woman was created from a rib. Verily, the most curved portion of the rib is its upper part, so, if you should try to straighten it, you will break it, but if you leave it as it is, it will remain crooked.) Allah's statement,

(And from them both He created many men and women;) means, Allah created from Adam and Hawwa' many men and women and distributed them throughout the world in various shapes, characteristics, colors and languages. In the end, their gathering and return will be to Allah. Allah then said,

(And have Taqwa of Allah through Whom you demand your mutual (rights) and revere the wombs), protect yourself from Allah by your acts of obedience to Him. Allah's statement,

(through Whom you demand your mutual (rights)), is in reference to when some people say, "I ask you by Allah, and then by the relation of the Rahim (the womb, i.e. my relationship to you)", according to Ibrahim, Mujahid and Al-Hasan. Ad-Dahhak said; "Fear Allah Whom you invoke when you conduct transactions and contracts." "And revere the womb by not cutting the relations of the womb, but keep and honor them, as Ibn `Abbas, `Ikrimah, Mujahid, Al-Hasan, Ad-Dahhak, Ar-Rabi`, and others have stated. Allah's statement,

(Surely, Allah is always watching over you.) means, He watches all your deeds and sees your every circumstance. In another Ayah, Allah said;

(And Allah is Witness over all things.) (58:6). An authentic Hadith states,

«اعْبُدِ اللهَ كَأَنَّكَ تَرَاهُ، فَإِنْ لَمْ تَكُنْ تَرَاهُ، فَإِنَّهُ يَرَاكَ»

(Worship Allah as if you see Him, for even though you cannot see Him, He sees you.) This part of the Ayah encourages having a sense of certainty that Allah is always watching, in a complete and perfect manner. Allah mentioned that He has created mankind from a single father and a single mother, so that they feel compassion for each other and are kind to the weaker among them. In his Sahih, Muslim recorded that Jarir bin `Abdullah Al-Bajali said that a delegation from Mudar came to the Messenger of Allah , and he saw their state, wearing striped woolen clothes due to poverty. After the Zuhr prayer, the Messenger of Allah stood up and gave a speech in which he recited,

(O mankind! Have Taqwa of your Lord, Who created you from a single person,) until the end of the Ayah. He also recited,

(O you who believe! Have Taqwa of Allah. And let every person look to what he has sent forth for the tomorrow) (59:18). He also encouraged them to give charity, saying,

«تَصَدَّقَ رَجُلٌ مِنْ دِينَارِهِ، مِنْ دِرْهَمِهِ، مِنْ صَاعِ بُرِّهِ، مِنْ صَاعِ تَمْرِهِ»

(A man gave Sadaqah from his Dinar, from his Dirham, from his Sa` of wheat, from his Sa` of dates) until the end of the Hadith. This narration was also collected by Ahmad and the Sunan compilers from Ibn Mas`ud.

Surah: 4 Ayah: 2, Ayah: 3 & Ayah: 4

﴿ وَءَاتُواْ ٱلْيَتَـٰمَىٰٓ أَمْوَٰلَهُمْ ۖ وَلَا تَتَبَدَّلُواْ ٱلْخَبِيثَ بِٱلطَّيِّبِ ۖ وَلَا تَأْكُلُوٓاْ أَمْوَٰلَهُمْ إِلَىٰٓ أَمْوَٰلِكُمْ ۚ إِنَّهُۥ كَانَ حُوبًا كَبِيرًا ﴿٢﴾ ﴾

2. And give unto orphans their property and do not exchange (your) bad things for (their) good ones; and devour not their substance (by adding it) to your substance. Surely, this is a great sin.

﴿ وَإِنْ خِفْتُمْ أَلَّا تُقْسِطُواْ فِى ٱلْيَتَـٰمَىٰ فَٱنكِحُواْ مَا طَابَ لَكُم مِّنَ ٱلنِّسَآءِ مَثْنَىٰ وَثُلَـٰثَ وَرُبَـٰعَ ۖ فَإِنْ خِفْتُمْ أَلَّا تَعْدِلُواْ فَوَٰحِدَةً أَوْ مَا مَلَكَتْ أَيْمَـٰنُكُمْ ۚ ذَٰلِكَ أَدْنَىٰٓ أَلَّا تَعُولُواْ ﴿٣﴾ ﴾

3. And if you fear that you shall not be able to deal justly with the orphan-girls then marry (other) women of your choice, two or three, or four; but if you fear that you shall not be able to deal justly (with them), then only one or (the slaves) that your right hands possess. That is nearer to prevent you from doing injustice.

Chapter 4: An-Nisaa (The Women), Verses 001-023

﴿ وَءَاتُواْ ٱلنِّسَآءَ صَدُقَـٰتِهِنَّ نِحْلَةً ۚ فَإِن طِبْنَ لَكُمْ عَن شَىْءٍ مِّنْهُ نَفْسًا فَكُلُوهُ هَنِيٓـًٔا مَّرِيٓـًٔا ۝ ﴾

4. And give to the women (whom you marry) their Mahr (obligatory bridal money given by the husband to his wife at the time of marriage) with a good heart; but if they, of their own good pleasure, remit any part of it to you, take it, and enjoy it without fear of any harm (as Allâh has made it lawful).

Transliteration

2. Waatoo alyatama amwalahum wala tatabaddaloo alkhabeetha bialttayyibi wala ta/kuloo amwalahum ila amwalikum innahu kana hooban kabeeran 3. Wa-in khiftum alla tuqsitoo fee alyatama fainkihoo ma taba lakum mina alnnisa-i mathna wathulatha warubaAAa fa-in khiftum alla taAAdiloo fawahidatan aw ma malakat aymanukum Thalika adna alla taAAooloo 4. Waatoo alnnisaa saduqatihinna nihlatan fa-in tibna lakum AAan shay-in minhu nafsan fakuloohu hanee-an maree-an

Tafsir Ibn Kathir

Protecting the Property of the Orphans

Allah commands that the property of the orphans be surrendered to them in full when they reach the age of adolescence, and He forbids using or confiscating any part of it. So He said;

(and do not exchange (your) bad things for (their) good ones;) Sa`id bin Al-Musayyib and Az-Zuhri commented, "Do not substitute a weak animal of yours for a fat animal (of the orphans)." Ibrahim An-Nakha`i and Ad-Dahhak commented, "Do not give something of bad quality for something of good quality." As-Suddi said, "One of them (caretakers of orphans) would take a fat sheep from the orphan's property and put in its place, a weak sheep of his, saying, `A sheep for a sheep.' He would also take a good Dirham and exchange it for a fake Dirham, saying, `A Dirham for a Dirham.'" Allah's statement,

(and devour not their substance to your substance.) means, do not mix them together so that you eat up both, as Mujahid, Sa`id bin Jubayr, Muqatil bin Hayyan, As-Suddi and Sufyan bin Hassin stated. Allah said,

(Surely, this is a great sin.), a major and substantial sin, according to Ibn `Abbas. This was also reported from Mujahid, `Ikrimah, Sa`id bin Jubayr, Al-Hasan, Ibn Sirin, Qatadah, Muqatil bin Hayyan, Ad-Dahhak, Abu Malik, Zayd bin Aslam and Abu Sinan. The meaning above is: adding their property to your property is a grave sin and a major mistake, so avoid it.

The Prohibition of Marrying Female Orphans Without Giving a Dowry

Allah said,

(And if you fear that you shall not be able to deal justly with the orphan girls, then marry (other) women of your choice, two) Allah commands, when one of you is the caretaker of a female orphan and he fears that he might not give her a dowry that is suitable for women of her status, he should marry other women, who are plenty as Allah has not restricted him. Al-Bukhari recorded that `A'ishah said, "A man was taking care of a female orphan and he married her, although he did not desire to marry her. That girl's money was mixed with his, and he was keeping her portion from her. Afterwards, this Ayah was revealed about his case;

(If you fear that you shall not be able to deal justly)" Al-Bukhari recorded that `Urwah bin Az-Zubayr said that he asked `A'ishah about the meaning of the statement of Allah,

(If you fear that you shall not be able to deal justly with the orphan girls.) She said, "O my nephew! This is about the orphan girl who lives with her guardian and shares his property. Her wealth and beauty may tempt him to marry her without giving her an adequate dowry which might have been given by another suitor. So, such guardians were forbidden to marry such orphan girls unless they treated them justly and gave them the most suitable dowry; otherwise they were ordered to marry woman besides them." `A'ishah further said, "After that verse, the people again asked the Messenger of Allah (about marriage with orphan girls), so Allah revealed the Ayah,

(They ask your instruction concerning the women..) (4:127)." She said, "Allah's statement in this Ayah,

(yet whom you desire to marry) (4:127) refers to the guardian who does not desire to marry an orphan girl under his supervision because she is neither wealthy nor beautiful. The guardians were forbidden to marry their orphan girls possessing property and beauty without being just to them, as they generally refrain from marrying them (when they are neither beautiful nor wealthy)."

The Permission to Marry Four Women

Allah's statement,

(two or three, or four), means, marry as many women as you like, other than the orphan girls, two, three or four. We should mention that Allah's statement in another Ayah,

(Who made the angels messengers with wings, - two or three or four) (35:1), does not mean that other angels do not have more than four wings, as there are proofs that some angels do have more wings. Yet, men are prohibited from marrying more than four wives, as the Ayah decrees, since the Ayah specifies what men are allowed of wives, as Ibn `Abbas and the majority of scholars stated. If it were allowed for them to have more than four wives, the Ayah would have mentioned it. Imam Ahmad recorded that Salim said that his father said that Ghilan bin Salamah Ath-Thaqafi had ten wives when he became Muslim, and the Prophet said to him, "Choose any four of them (and divorce the rest)." During the reign of `Umar, Ghilan divorced his remaining wives and divided his money between his children. When `Umar heard news of this, he said to Ghilan, "I think that the devil has conveyed to your heart the news of your imminent death, from what the devil hears during his eavesdropping. It may as well be that you will not remain alive but for a little longer. By Allah! You will take back your wives and your money, or I will take possession of this all and will order that your grave be stoned as is the case with the grave of Abu Righal (from Thamud, who was saved from their fate because he was in the Sacred Area. But, when he left it, he was tormented like they were)." Ash-Shafi`i, At-Tirmidhi, Ibn Majah, Ad-Daraqutni and Al-Bayhaqi collected this Hadith up to the Prophet's statement, "Choose any four of them." Only Ahmad collected the full version of this Hadith. Therefore, had it been allowed for men to marry more than four women at the same time, the Prophet would have allowed Ghilan to keep more than four of his wives since they all embraced Islam with him. When the Prophet commanded him to keep just four of them and divorce the rest, this indicated that men are not allowed to keep more than four wives at a time under any circumstances. If this is the case concerning those who already had more than four wives upon embracing Islam, then this ruling applies even more so to marrying more than four.

Marrying Only One Wife When One Fears He Might not Do Justice to His Wives

Allah's statement,

(But if you fear that you will not be able to deal justly (with them), then only one or what your right hands possess.) The Ayah commands, if you fear that you will not be able to do justice between your wives by marrying more than one, then marry only one wife, or satisfy yourself with only female captives, for it is not obligatory to treat them equally, rather it is recommended. So if one does so, that is good, and if not, there is no harm on him. In another Ayah, Allah said,

(You will never be able to do perfect justice between wives even if it is your ardent desire) (4:129). Allah said,

(That is nearer to prevent you from Ta`ulu), meaning, from doing injustice. Ibn Abi Hatim, Ibn Marduwyah and Abu Hatim Ibn Hibban, in his Sahih, recorded that `A'ishah said that, the Prophet said that the Ayah,

(That is nearer to prevent you from Ta`ulu), means, from doing injustice. However, Ibn Abi Hatim said that his father said that this Hadith to the Prophet is a mistake, for it should be attributed to `A'ishah not the Prophet . Ibn Abi Hatim reported from Ibn `Abbas, `A'ishah, Mujahid, `Ikrimah, Al-Hasan, Abu Malik, Abu Razin, An-Nakha`i, Ash-Sha`bi, Ad-Dahhak, `Ata' Al-Khurasani, Qatadah, As-Suddi and Muqatil bin Hayyan that Ta`ulu means to deviate (from justice).

Giving the Dowry is Obligatory

`Ali bin Abi Talhah reported Ibn `Abbas saying, Nihlah, in Allah's statement,

(And give to the women (whom you marry) their Saduqat Nihlah) refers to the dowry. Muhammad bin Ishaq narrated from Az-Zuhri that `Urwah said that `A'ishah said that `Nihlah' means `obligatory'. Muqatil, Qatadah and Ibn Jurayj said, `Nihlah' means `obligatory' Ibn Jurayj added: `specified.' Ibn Zayd said, "In Arabic, Nihlah, refers to what is necessary. So Allah is commanding: Do not marry unless you give your wife something that is her right. No person after the Prophet is allowed to marry a woman except with the required dowry, nor by giving false promises about the dowry (intended)." Therefore, the man is required to pay a dowry to his wife with a good heart, just as he gives a gift with a good heart. If the wife gives him part or all of that dowry with a good heart, her husband is allowed to take it, as it is lawful for him in this case. This is why Allah said afterwards,

(But if they, of their own pleasure, remit any part of it to you, take it, and enjoy it without fear of any harm.)

Surah: 4 Ayah: 5 & Ayah: 6

﴿ وَلَا تُؤْتُوا ٱلسُّفَهَآءَ أَمْوَٰلَكُمُ ٱلَّتِى جَعَلَ ٱللَّهُ لَكُمْ قِيَٰمًا وَٱرْزُقُوهُمْ فِيهَا وَٱكْسُوهُمْ وَقُولُوا۟ لَهُمْ قَوْلًا مَّعْرُوفًا ۝ ﴾

5. And give not unto the foolish your property which Allâh has made a means of support for you, but feed and clothe them therewith, and speak to them words of kindness and justice.

﴿ وَٱبْتَلُوا۟ ٱلْيَتَٰمَىٰ حَتَّىٰٓ إِذَا بَلَغُوا۟ ٱلنِّكَاحَ فَإِنْ ءَانَسْتُم مِّنْهُمْ رُشْدًا فَٱدْفَعُوٓا۟ إِلَيْهِمْ أَمْوَٰلَهُمْ وَلَا تَأْكُلُوهَآ إِسْرَافًا وَبِدَارًا أَن يَكْبَرُوا۟ وَمَن كَانَ غَنِيًّا فَلْيَسْتَعْفِفْ وَمَن كَانَ فَقِيرًا فَلْيَأْكُلْ بِٱلْمَعْرُوفِ فَإِذَا دَفَعْتُمْ إِلَيْهِمْ أَمْوَٰلَهُمْ فَأَشْهِدُوا۟ عَلَيْهِمْ وَكَفَىٰ بِٱللَّهِ حَسِيبًا ۝ ﴾

6. And try orphans (as regards their intelligence) until they reach the age of marriage; if then you find sound judgement in them, release their property to them, but consume it not wastefully, and hastily fearing that they should grow up, and whoever (amongst guardians) is rich, he should take no wages, but if he is poor, let him have for himself what is just and reasonable (according to his labor). And when you release their property to them, take witness in their presence; and Allâh is All-Sufficient in taking account.

Transliteration

5. Wala tu/too alssufahaa amwalakumu allatee jaAAala Allahu lakum qiyaman waorzuqoohum feeha waoksoohum waqooloo lahum qawlan maAAroofan   6. Waibtaloo alyatama hatta itha balaghoo alnnikaha fa-in anastum minhum rushdan faidfaAAoo ilayhim amwalahum wala ta/kulooha israfan wabidaran an yakbaroo waman kana ghaniyyan falyastaAAfif waman kana faqeeran falya/kul bialmaAAroofi fa-itha dafaAAtum ilayhim amwalahum faashhidoo AAalayhim wakafa biAllahi haseeban

Tafsir Ibn Kathir

Holding the Property of the Unwise in Escrow

Allah prohibited giving the unwise the freedom to do as they wish with wealth, which Allah has made as a means of support for people. This ruling sometimes applies because of being young, as young people are incapable of making wise decisions. It also applies in cases of insanity, erratic behavior and having a weak intellect or religious practice. It applies in cases of bankruptcy, when the debtors ask that the property of a bankrupt person is put in escrow, when his debts cannot be paid off with his money. Ad-Dahhak reported that Ibn `Abbas said that Allah's statement,

(And give not unto the unwise your property) refers to children and women. Similar was also said by Ibn Mas`ud, Al-Hakam bin `Uyaynah, Al-Hasan and Ad-Dahhak: "Women and boys." Sa`id bin Jubayr said that `the unwise' refers to the orphans. Mujahid, `Ikrimah and Qatadah said; "They are women."

Spending on the Unwise with Fairness

Allah said,

(but feed and clothe them therewith, and speak to them words of kindness and justice.) `Ali bin Abi Talhah said that Ibn `Abbas commented, "Do not give your wealth, what Allah has made you responsible for and made a means of sustenance to you, to your wife or children. Rather, hold on to your money, take care of it, and be the one who spends on them for clothes, food and provision." Mujahid said that the Ayah,

(and speak to them words of kindness and justice.) refers to kindness and keeping good relations. This honorable Ayah commands kind treatment, in deed, with family and those under one's care. One should spend on them for clothes and provisions, and be good to them, such as saying good words to them.

Giving Back the Property of the Orphans When They Reach Adulthood

Allah said,

(And test orphans) meaning, test their intelligence, as Ibn `Abbas, Mujahid, Al-Hasan, As-Suddi and Muqatil bin Hayyan stated.

(until they reach the age of marriage), the age of puberty, according to Mujahid. The age of puberty according to the majority of scholars comes when the child has a wet dream. In his Sunan, Abu Dawud recorded that `Ali said, "I memorized these words from the Messenger of Allah ,

«لَا يُتْمَ بَعْدَ احْتِلَامٍ، وَلَا صُمَاتَ يَوْمٍ إِلَى اللَّيْلِ»

(There is no orphan after the age of puberty nor vowing to be silent throughout the day to the night.) In another Hadith, `A'ishah and other Companions said that the Prophet said,

«رُفِعَ الْقَلَمُ عَنْ ثَلَاثَةٍ، عَنِ الصَّبِيِّ حَتَّى يَحْتَلِمَ، وَعَنِ النَّائِمِ حَتَّى يَسْتَيْقِظَ، وَعَنِ الْمَجْنُونِ حَتَّى يُفِيقَ»

(The pen does not record the deeds of three persons: the child until the age of puberty, the sleeping person until waking up, and the senile until sane.) Or, the age of fifteen is considered the age of adolescence. In the Two Sahihs, it is recorded that Ibn `Umar said, "I was presented in front of the Prophet on the eve of the battle of Uhud, while I was fourteen years of age, and he did not allow me to take part in that battle. But I was presented in front of him on the eve of the battle of Al-Khandaq (The Trench) when I was fifteen years old, and he allowed me (to join that battle)." `Umar bin `Abdul-`Aziz commented when this Hadith reached him, "This is the difference between a child and an adult." There is a difference of opinion over whether pubic hair is considered a sign of adulthood, and the correct opinion is that it is. The Sunnah supports this view, according to a Hadith collected by Imam Ahmad from `Atiyah Al-Qurazi who said, We were presented to the Prophet on the day of Qurizah, whoever had pubic hair was killed, whoever did not was left free to go, I was one of those who did not, so I was left free." The Four Sunan compilers also recorded similar to it. At-Tirmidhi said, "Hasan Sahih." Allah's statement,

(if then you find sound judgment in them, release their property to them,) Sa`id bin Jubayr said that this portion of the Ayah means, when you find them to be good in the religion and wise with their money. Similar was reported from Ibn `Abbas, Al-Hasan Al-Basri and others among the Imams. The scholars of Fiqh stated that when the child becomes good in the religion and wise concerning with money, then the money that his caretaker was keeping for him should be surrendered to him.

Poor Caretakers are Allowed to Wisely Spend from the Money of the Orphan Under Their Care, to Compensate for Their Work

Allah said,

(But consume it not wastefully and hastily, fearing that they should grow up.) Allah commands that the money of the orphan should not be spent unnecessarily,

(Wastefully and hastily) for fear they might grow up. Allah also commands,

(And whoever among guardians is rich, he should take no wages,) Hence, the guardian who is rich and does not need the orphan's money, should not take any of it as wages.

(but if he is poor, let him have for himself what is just and reasonable.) Ibn Abi Hatim recorded that `A'ishah said, "This Ayah,

(And whoever among guardians is rich, he should take no wages, but if he is poor, let him have for himself what is just and reasonable.) was revealed about the guardian of the orphan and pertains to whatever work he does for the orphan's estate. " Al-Bukhari also collected this Hadith. Imam Ahmad recorded that `Amr bin Shu`ayb said that his father said that his father told him that a man asked the Messenger of Allah , "I do not have money, but I have an orphan under my care." The Messenger said,

«كُلْ مِنْ مَالِ يَتِيمِكَ غَيْرَ مُسْرِفٍ وَلَا مُبَذِّرٍ وَلَا مُتَأَثِّلٍ مَالًا، وَمِنْ غَيْرِ أَنْ تَقِيَ مَالَكَ أَوْ قَالَ تَفْدِيَ مَالَكَ بِمَالِهِ»

(Eat from your orphan's wealth without extravagance or wastefulness, or mixing it, and without saving your money by spending his.)" Allah said,

(And when you release their property to them.) after they become adults, and you see that they are wise, then,

(take a witness in their presence;) Allah commands the guardians of orphans to surrender the property of the orphans who become consenting adults, in the presence of witnesses, so that none of them denies the fact that he received his money. Allah said next,

(and Allah is All-Sufficient in taking account.) meaning, Allah is sufficient as Witness, Reckoner and Watcher over their work for orphans, and when they surrender their money to them, whether their property was complete and whole, or deficient and less. Indeed, Allah knows all of that. In his Sahih, Muslim recorded that the Messenger of Allah said,

«يَا أَبَا ذَرَ إِنِّي أَرَاكَ ضَعِيفًا، وَإِنِّي أُحِبُّ لَكَ مَا أُحِبُّ لِنَفْسِي، لَا تَأَمَّرَنَّ عَلَى اثْنَيْنِ، وَلَا تَلِيَنَّ مَالَ يَتِيمٍ»

(O Abu Dharr! Verily, you are weak, and I love for you what I love for myself. Do not become a leader of two nor assume guardianship of an orphan's property.)

Surah: 4 Ayah: 7, Ayah: 8, Ayah: 9 & Ayah: 10

﴿ لِلرِّجَالِ نَصِيبٌ مِّمَّا تَرَكَ ٱلْوَالِدَانِ وَٱلْأَقْرَبُونَ وَلِلنِّسَآءِ نَصِيبٌ مِّمَّا تَرَكَ ٱلْوَالِدَانِ وَٱلْأَقْرَبُونَ مِمَّا قَلَّ مِنْهُ أَوْ كَثُرَ نَصِيبًا مَّفْرُوضًا ۝ ﴾

7. There is a share for men and a share for women from what is left by parents and those nearest related, whether the property be small or large - a legal share.

﴿ وَإِذَا حَضَرَ ٱلْقِسْمَةَ أُوْلُواْ ٱلْقُرْبَىٰ وَٱلْيَتَـٰمَىٰ وَٱلْمَسَـٰكِينُ فَٱرْزُقُوهُم مِّنْهُ وَقُولُواْ لَهُمْ قَوْلاً مَّعْرُوفًا ۝ ﴾

8. And when the relatives and the orphans and Al-Masâkin (the poor) are present at the time of division, give them out of the property, and speak to them words of kindness and justice.

﴿ وَلْيَخْشَ ٱلَّذِينَ لَوْ تَرَكُوا۟ مِنْ خَلْفِهِمْ ذُرِّيَّةً ضِعَـٰفًا خَافُوا۟ عَلَيْهِمْ فَلْيَتَّقُوا۟ ٱللَّهَ وَلْيَقُولُوا۟ قَوْلًا سَدِيدًا ۝ ﴾

9. And let those (executors and guardians) have the same fear in their minds as they would have for their own, if they had left weak offspring behind. So let them fear Allâh and speak right words.

﴿ إِنَّ ٱلَّذِينَ يَأْكُلُونَ أَمْوَٰلَ ٱلْيَتَـٰمَىٰ ظُلْمًا إِنَّمَا يَأْكُلُونَ فِى بُطُونِهِمْ نَارًا وَسَيَصْلَوْنَ سَعِيرًا ۝ ﴾

10. Verily, those who unjustly eat up the property of orphans, they eat up only fire into their bellies, and they will be burnt in the blazing Fire!

Transliteration

7. Lilrrijali naseebun mimma taraka alwalidani waal-aqraboona walilnnisa-i naseebun mimma taraka alwalidani waal-aqraboona mimma qalla minhu aw kathura naseeban mafroodan 8. Wa-itha hadara alqismata oloo alqurba waalyatama waalmasakeenu faorzuqoohum minhu waqooloo lahum qawlan maAAroofan 9. Walyakhsha allatheena law tarakoo min khalfihim thurriyyatan diAAafan khafoo AAalayhim falyattaqoo Allaha walyaqooloo qawlan sadeedan 10. Inna allatheena ya/kuloona amwala alyatama thulman innama ya/kuloona fee butoonihim naran wasayaslawna saAAeeran

Tafsir Ibn Kathir

The Necessity of Surrendering the Inheritance According to the Portions that Allah Ordained

Sa`id bin Jubayr and Qatadah said, "The idolators used to give adult men a share of inheritance and deprive women and children of it. Allah revealed;

(There is a share for men from what is left by parents and those nearest in relation)." Therefore, everyone is equal in Allah's decision to inherit, even though their shares vary according to the degree of their relationship to the deceased, whether being a relative, spouse, etc. Ibn Marduwyah reported that Jabir said, "Umm Kujjah came to the Messenger of Allah and said to him, `O Messenger of Allah! I have two daughters whose father died, and they do not own anything.' So Allah revealed;

(There is a share for men from what is left by parents and those nearest in relation.)" We will mention this Hadith when explaining the two Ayat about inheritance. Allah knows best. Allah said,

Chapter 4: An-Nisaa (The Women), Verses 001-023

(are present at the time of division,) those who do not have a share in the inheritance,

(and the orphans and the poor), are also present upon dividing the inheritance, give them a share of the inheritance. Al-Bukhari recorded that Ibn `Abbas said that the Ayah,

(And when the relatives and the orphans and the poor are present at the time of division), was not abrogated. Ibn Jarir recorded that Ibn `Abbas said that this Ayah still applies and should be implemented. Ath-Thawri said that Ibn Abi Najih narrated from Mujahid that implementing this Ayah, "Is required from those who have anything to inherit, paid from whatever portions their hearts are satisfied with giving away." Similar explanation was reported from Ibn Mas`ud, Abu Musa, `Abdur-Rahman bin Abi Bakr, Abu Al-`Aliyah, Ash-Sha`bi and Al-Hasan. Ibn Sirin, Sa`id bin Jubayr, Makhul, Ibrahim An-Nakha`i, `Ata' bin Abi Rabah, Az-Zuhri and Yahya bin Ya`mar said this payment is obligatory. Others say that this refers to the bequeathal at the time of death. And others say that it was abrogated. Al-`Awfi reported that Ibn `Abbas said that this Ayah,

(And when are present at the time of division), refers to divisions of inheritance. So, when poor relatives, who are ineligible for inheritance, orphans, and the poor attend the division of the inheritance, which is sometimes substantial, their hearts will feel eager to have a share, seeing each eligible person assuming his share; while they are desperate, yet are not given anything. Allah the Most Kind, Most Compassionate, commands that they should have a share in the inheritance as an act of kindness, charity, compassion and mercy for them.

Observing Fairness in the Will

Allah said, (And let those have the same fear in their minds as they would have for their own, if they had left behind...) `Ali bin Abi Talhah reported that Ibn `Abbas said that this part of the Ayah, "Refers to a man who is near death and he dictates a will and testament that harms some of the rightful inheritors. Allah commands whoever hears such will to fear Allah, and direct the dying man to do what is right and to be fair, being as eager to protect the inheritors of the dying man as he would be with his own." Similar was reported from Mujahid and several others. The Two Sahihs record that when the Messenger of Allah visited Sa`d bin Abi Waqqas during an illness he suffered from, Sa`d said to the Messenger, "O Messenger of Allah! I am wealthy and have no inheritors except a daughter. Should I give two-thirds of my property in charity" He said, "No." Sa`d asked, "Half" He said, "No." Sa`d said, "One-third" The Prophet said;

»الثُّلُثُ، وَالثُّلُثُ كَثِيرٌ«

(One-third, and even one-third is too much.) The Messenger of Allah then said,

»إِنَّكَ أَنْ تَذَرَ وَرَثَتَكَ أَغْنِيَاءَ خَيْرٌ مِنْ أَنْ تَذَرَهُمْ عَالَةً يَتَكَفَّفُونَ النَّاسَ«

(You'd better leave your inheritors wealthy rather than leaving them poor, begging from others.)

A Stern Warning Against Those Who Use Up the Orphan's Wealth

It was also said that the Ayah

(consume it not wastefully and hastily, fearing that they should grow up,) means, let them have Taqwa of Allah when taking care of the orphan's wealth, as Ibn Jarir recorded from Al-`Awfi who reported this explanation from Ibn `Abbas. This is a sound opinion that is supported by the warning that follows against consuming the orphan's wealth unjustly. In this case, the meaning becomes: Just as you would want your offspring to be treated fairly after you, then treat other people's offspring fairly when you are given the responsibility of caring for them. Allah proclaims that those who unjustly consume the wealth of orphans, will be eating fire into their stomach, this is why Allah said,

(Verily, those who unjustly eat up the property of orphans, they eat up only a fire into their bellies, and they will be burnt in the blazing Fire!) meaning, when you consume the orphan's wealth without a right, then you are only consuming fire, which will kindle in your stomach on the Day of Resurrection. It is recorded in the Two Sahihs that Abu Hurayrah said that the Messenger of Allah said,

«اجْتَنِبُوا السَّبْعَ الْمُوبِقَاتِ»

(Avoid the seven great destructive sins.) The people asked, "O Allah's Messenger! What are they" He said,

«الشِّرْكُ بِاللهِ، وَالسِّحْرُ، وَقَتْلُ النَّفْسِ الَّتِي حَرَّمَ اللهُ إِلَّا بِالْحَقِّ، وَأَكْلُ الرِّبَا، وَأَكْلُ مَالِ الْيَتِيمِ، وَالتَّوَلِّي يَوْمَ الزَّحْفِ، وَقَذْفُ الْمُحْصَنَاتِ الْمُؤْمِنَاتِ الْغَافِلَاتِ»

(To join others in worship along with Allah, magic, to kill the life which Allah has forbidden except for a just cause, to consume interest, to consume an orphan's property, to turn your back to the enemy and flee from the battlefield at the time of fighting, and to accuse chaste women who never even think of anything harmful to their chastity being good believers.)

Surah: 4 Ayah: 11

﴿ يُوصِيكُمُ ٱللَّهُ فِىٓ أَوْلَٰدِكُمْ ۖ لِلذَّكَرِ مِثْلُ حَظِّ ٱلْأُنثَيَيْنِ ۚ فَإِن كُنَّ نِسَآءً فَوْقَ ٱثْنَتَيْنِ فَلَهُنَّ ثُلُثَا مَا تَرَكَ ۖ وَإِن كَانَتْ وَٰحِدَةً فَلَهَا ٱلنِّصْفُ ۚ وَلِأَبَوَيْهِ لِكُلِّ وَٰحِدٍ

مِّنْهُمَا ٱلسُّدُسُ مِمَّا تَرَكَ إِن كَانَ لَهُۥ وَلَدٌ ۚ فَإِن لَّمْ يَكُن لَّهُۥ وَلَدٌ وَوَرِثَهُۥٓ أَبَوَاهُ فَلِأُمِّهِ ٱلثُّلُثُ ۚ فَإِن كَانَ لَهُۥٓ إِخْوَةٌ فَلِأُمِّهِ ٱلسُّدُسُ ۚ مِنۢ بَعْدِ وَصِيَّةٍ يُوصِى بِهَآ أَوْ دَيْنٍ ۗ ءَابَآؤُكُمْ وَأَبْنَآؤُكُمْ لَا تَدْرُونَ أَيُّهُمْ أَقْرَبُ لَكُمْ نَفْعًا ۚ فَرِيضَةً مِّنَ ٱللَّهِ ۗ إِنَّ ٱللَّهَ كَانَ عَلِيمًا حَكِيمًا ۝

11. Allâh commands you as regards your children's (inheritance): to the male, a portion equal to that of two females; if (there are) only daughters, two or more, their share is two-thirds of the inheritance; if only one, her share is half. For parents, a sixth share of inheritance to each if the deceased left children; if no children, and the parents are the (only) heirs, the mother has a third; if the deceased left brothers or (sisters), the mother has a sixth. (The distribution in all cases is) after the payment of legacies he may have bequeathed or debts. You know not which of them, whether your parents or your children, are nearest to you in benefit; (these fixed shares) are ordained by Allâh. And Allâh is Ever All-Knower, All-Wise.

Transliteration

11. Yooseekumu Allahu fee awladikum liththakari mithlu haththi alonthayayni fa-in kunna nisaan fawqa ithnatayni falahunna thulutha ma taraka wa-in kanat wahidatan falaha alnnisfu wali-abawayhi likulli wahidin minhuma alssudusu mimma taraka in kana lahu waladun fa-in lam yakun lahu waladun wawarithahu abawahu fali-ommihi alththuluthu fa-in kana lahu ikhwatun fali-ommihi alssudusu min baAAdi wasiyyatin yoosee biha aw daynin abaokum waabnaokum la tadroona ayyuhum aqrabu lakum nafAAan fareedatan mina Allahi inna Allaha kana AAaleeman hakeeman

Tafsir Ibn Kathir

Learning the Various Shares of the Inheritance is Encouraged

This, the following, and the last honorable Ayah in this Surah contain the knowledge of Al-Fara'id, inheritance. The knowledge of Al-Fara'id is derived from these three Ayat and from the Hadiths on this subject which explain them. Learning this knowledge is encouraged, especially the specific things mentioned in the Ayat. Ibn `Uyaynah said; "Knowledge of Al-Fara'id was called half of knowledge, because it effects all people."

The Reason Behind Revealing Ayah 4:11

Explaining this Ayah, Al-Bukhari recorded that Jabir bin `Abdullah said, "Allah's Messenger came visiting me on foot with Abu Bakr at Banu Salamah's (dwellings), and the Prophet found me unconscious. He asked for some water, performed ablution with it, then poured it on me, and I regained consciousness. I said, `What do you command me to do with my money, O Allah's Messenger' this Ayah was later revealed,

(Allah commands you for your children's (inheritance); to the male, a portion equal to that of two females)." This is how it was recorded by Muslim and An-Nasa'i. The remainder of the Six compilers also collected this Hadith. Another Hadith from Jabir concerning the reason behind revealing Ayah 4:11 Ahmad recorded from Jabir that he said, "The wife of Sa`d bin Ar-Rabi` came to Allah's Messenger and said to him, `O Allah's Messenger! These are the two daughters of Sa`d bin Ar-Rabi`, who was killed as a martyr at Uhud. Their uncle took their money and did not leave anything for them. They will not be married unless they have money.' The Messenger said, `Allah will decide on this matter.' The Ayah about the inheritance was later revealed and the Messenger of Allah sent word to their uncle commanding him,

«أَعْطِ ابْنَتَيْ سَعْدٍ الثُّلُثَيْنِ، وَأُمَّهُمَا الثُّمُنَ، وَمَا بَقِيَ فَهُوَ لَكَ»

(Give two-thirds (of Sa`d's money) to Sa`d's two daughters and one eighth for their mother, and whatever is left is yours.)" Abu Dawud, At-Tirmidhi, and Ibn Majah collected this Hadith. It is apparent, however, that the first Hadith from Jabir was about the case of the last Ayah in the Surah (4:176, rather than 4:11), for at the time this incident occurred, Jabir had sisters and did not have daughters, parents or offspring to inherit from him. Yet, we mentioned the Hadith here just as Al-Bukhari did.

Males Get Two Times the Share of Females for Inheritance

Allah said,

(Allah commands you for your children's (inheritance): to the male, a portion equal to that of two females;) Allah commands: observe justice with your children. The people of Jahiliyyah used to give the males, but not the females, a share in the inheritance. Therefore, Allah commands that both males and females take a share in the inheritance, although the portion of the males is twice as much as that of the females. There is a distinction because men need money to spend on their dependants, commercial transactions, work and fulfilling their obligations. Consequently, men get twice the portion of the inheritance that females get. Allah's statement,

(Allah commands you for your children's (inheritance): to the male, a portion equal to that of two females;) testifies to the fact that Allah is more merciful with children than their own parents are with them, since He commands the parents to be just and fair with their own children. An authentic Hadith stated that a captured woman was looking for her child and when she found him, she held him, gave him her breast and nursed him. The Messenger of Allah said to his Companions,

«أَتَرَوْنَ هَذِهِ طَارِحَةً وَلَدَهَا فِي النَّارِ وَهِيَ تَقْدِرُ عَلَى ذَلِكَ»

؟ (Do you think that this woman would willingly throw her child in the fire) They said, "No, O Messenger of Allah." He said,

Chapter 4: An-Nisaa (The Women), Verses 001-023

«فَوَاللَّهِ للَّهُ أَرْحَمُ بِعِبَادِهِ مِنْ هذِهِ بِوَلَدِهَا»

(By Allah! Allah is more merciful with His servants than this woman is with her own child.) Al-Bukhari recorded that Ibn `Abbas said, "The custom (in old days) was that the property of the deceased would be inherited by his offspring; as for the parents (of the deceased), they would inherit by the will of the deceased. Then Allah cancelled whatever He willed from that custom and ordained that the male get twice the amount inherited by the female, and for each parent a sixth (of the whole legacy), for the wife an eighth or a fourth, and for the husband a half or a fourth."

The Share of the Females When They Are the Only Eligible Heirs

Allah said,

(if only daughters, two or more, their share is two-thirds of the inheritance;) We should mention here that some people said the Ayah only means two daughters, and that `more' is redundant, which is not true. Nothing in the Qur'an is useless or redundant. Had the Ayah been talking about only two women, it would have said, "The share of both of them is two-thirds." As for the daughters, two or more, the ruling that they get two-thirds was derived from this Ayah, stating that the two sisters get two-thirds. We also mentioned the Hadith in which the Prophet commanded that two-thirds be the share of the two daughters of Sa`d bin Ar-Rabi`. So this is proven in the Book and the Sunnah.

(if only one, her share is half.) If there are two daughters, then there are texts to prove they share a half. Therefore, two-thirds is the share of the two daughters or sisters, and Allah knows best.

Share of the Parents in the Inheritance

Allah said,

(For parents, a sixth share of inheritance to each) There are several forms of the share that the parents get in the inheritance. 1. If the deceased left behind children, the parents get a sixth each. When the deceased had only one daughter, she gets half of the inheritance and the parents each one sixth, and another sixth is given to the father. 2. When the parents are the only inheritors, the mother gets one-third while the father gets the remaining two-thirds. In this case, the father's share will be twice the mother's share. If the deceased had a surviving spouse, the spouse gets half, in the case of a husband, or a fourth in the case of a surviving wife. In both cases, the mother of the deceased gets one-third of the remaining inheritance. This is because the remaining portion of the inheritance is treated just as the entire legacy in regard to the parents' share. Allah has given the mother one-half of what the father gets. Therefore, the mother gets a third of the remaining inheritance while the father gets two-thirds. 3. If the deceased left behind surviving brothers and sisters, whether half brothers, half sisters or from the same father and mother, their presence does not cause reduction in the father's share. Yet, their presence reduces the share of the mother to one-sixth instead of one-third, and the father gets the rest, when there are no other heirs. Ibn Abi Hatim recorded that Qatadah commented on the Ayah,

(If the deceased left brothers or (sisters), the mother has a sixth.) "Their presence will reduce the share of the mother, but they will not inherit. If there is only one surviving brother, the mother's share will remain one-third, but her share will be reduced if there is more than one surviving brother. The people of knowledge attribute this reduction in the mother's share from one-third (to one-sixth) to the fact that the father is the one who helps the brothers (and sisters) of the deceased get married, spending from his own money for this purpose. The mother does not spend from her money for this purpose." This is a sound opinion.

First the Debts are Paid Off, then the Will, then the Fixed Inheritance

Allah said,

((The distribution in all cases is) after the payment of legacies he may have bequeathed or debts.) The scholars of the Salaf and the Khalaf agree that paying debts comes before fulfilling the will, and this is apparent to those who read the Ayah carefully. Allah said next,

(You know not which of them, whether your parents or your children, are nearest to you in benefit.) This Ayah means: We have appointed a share to the parents and children, contrary to the practice of Jahiliyyah and the early Islamic era, when the inheritance would go to the children, and parents get a share only if they were named in the will, as Ibn `Abbas stated. Allah abrogated this practice and appointed a fixed share for the children and for the parents. One may derive benefit in this life or for the Hereafter from his parents, the likes of which he could not get from his children. The opposite of this could also be true. Allah said,

(You know not which of them, whether your parents or your children, are nearest to you in benefit,): since benefit could come from one or the other of these relatives, We appointed a fixed share of inheritance for each. Allah knows best. Allah said,

(ordained by Allah), meaning: These appointed shares of inheritance that We mentioned and which give some inheritors a bigger share than others, is a commandment from Allah that He has decided and ordained,

(And Allah is Ever All-Knower, All-Wise.), Who places everything in its rightful place and gives each his rightful share.

Surah: 4 Ayah: 12

﴿ ۞ وَلَكُمْ نِصْفُ مَا تَرَكَ أَزْوَاجُكُمْ إِن لَّمْ يَكُن لَّهُنَّ وَلَدٌ فَإِن كَانَ لَهُنَّ وَلَدٌ فَلَكُمُ الرُّبُعُ مِمَّا تَرَكْنَ مِنْ بَعْدِ وَصِيَّةٍ يُوصِينَ بِهَا أَوْ دَيْنٍ وَلَهُنَّ الرُّبُعُ مِمَّا تَرَكْتُمْ إِن لَّمْ يَكُن لَّكُمْ وَلَدٌ فَإِن كَانَ لَكُمْ وَلَدٌ فَلَهُنَّ

ٱلثُّمُنُ مِمَّا تَرَكْتُمْ مِّنۢ بَعْدِ وَصِيَّةٍ تُوصُونَ بِهَآ أَوْ دَيْنٍ ۗ وَإِن كَانَ رَجُلٌ يُورَثُ كَلَـٰلَةً أَوِ ٱمْرَأَةٌ وَلَهُۥٓ أَخٌ أَوْ أُخْتٌ فَلِكُلِّ وَٰحِدٍ مِّنْهُمَا ٱلسُّدُسُ ۚ فَإِن كَانُوٓا۟ أَكْثَرَ مِن ذَٰلِكَ فَهُمْ شُرَكَآءُ فِى ٱلثُّلُثِ ۚ مِنۢ بَعْدِ وَصِيَّةٍ يُوصَىٰ بِهَآ أَوْ دَيْنٍ غَيْرَ مُضَآرٍّ ۚ وَصِيَّةً مِّنَ ٱللَّهِ ۗ وَٱللَّهُ عَلِيمٌ حَلِيمٌ ﴿١٢﴾

12. In that which your wives leave, your share is a half if they have no child; but if they leave a child, you get a fourth of that which they leave after payment of legacies that they may have bequeathed or debts. In that which you leave, their (your wives) share is a fourth if you leave no child; but if you leave a child, they get an eighth of that which you leave after payment of legacies that you may have bequeathed or debts. If the man or woman whose inheritance is in question has left neither ascendants nor descendants, but has left a brother or a sister, each one of the two gets a sixth; but if more than two, they share in a third, after payment of legacies he (or she) may have bequeathed or debts, so that no loss is caused (to anyone). This is a Commandment from Allâh; and Allâh is Ever All-Knowing, Most-Forbearing.

Transliteration

12. Walakum nisfu ma taraka azwajukum in lam yakun lahunna waladun fa-in kana lahunna waladun falakumu alrrubuAAu mimma tarakna min baAAdi wasiyyatin yooseena biha aw daynin walahunna alrrubuAAu mimma taraktum in lam yakun lakum waladun fa-in kana lakum waladun falahunna alththumunu mimma taraktum min baAAdi wasiyyatin toosoona biha aw daynin wa-in kana rajulun yoorathu kalalatan awi imraatun walahu akhun aw okhtun falikulli wahidin minhuma alssudusu fa-in kanoo akthara min thalika fahum shurakao fee alththuluthi min baAAdi wasiyyatin yoosa biha aw daynin ghayra mudarrin wasiyyatan mina Allahi waAllahu AAaleemun haleemun

Tafsir Ibn Kathir

Share of the Spouses in the Inheritance

Allah says to the husband, you get half of what your wife leaves behind if she dies and did not have a child. If she had a child, you get one-fourth of what she leaves behind, after payment of legacies that she may have bequeathed, or her debts. We mentioned before that payment of debts comes before fulfilling the will, and then comes the will, then the inheritance, and there is a consensus on this matter among the scholars. And the rule applies to the grandchildren as well as the children, even if they are great-grandchildren (or even further in generation) Allah then said,

(In that which you leave, their (your wives) share is a fourth) and if there is more than one wife, they all share in the fourth, or one-eighth that the wife gets. Earlier, we explained Allah's statement,

(After payment of legacies)

The Meaning of Kalalah

Allah said,

(If the man or woman whose inheritance is in question was left in Kalalah.) Kalalah is a derivative of Iklil; the crown that surrounds the head. The meaning of Kalalah in this Ayah is that the person's heirs come from other than the first degree of relative. Ash-Sha`bi reported that when Abu Bakr As-Siddiq was asked about the meaning of Kalalah, he said, "I will say my own opinion about it, and if it is correct, then this correctness is from Allah. However, if my opinion is wrong, it will be my error and because of the evil efforts of Shaytan, and Allah and His Messenger have nothing to do with it. Kalalah refers to the man who has neither descendants nor ascendants." When `Umar became the Khalifah, he said, "I hesitate to contradict an opinion of Abu Bakr." This was recorded by Ibn Jarir and others. In his Tafsir, Ibn Abi Hatim recorded that Ibn `Abbas said, "I was among the last persons to see `Umar bin Al-Khattab, and he said to me, `What you said was the correct opinion.' I asked, `What did I say' He said, `That Kalalah refers to the person who has no child or parents.'" This is also the opinion of `Ali bin Abi Talib, Ibn Mas`ud, Ibn `Abbas, Zayd bin Thabit, Ash-Sha`bi, An-Nakha`i, Al-Hasan Al-Basri, Qatadah, Jabir bin Zayd and Al-Hakam . This is also the view of the people of Al-Madinah, Kufah, Basrah, the Seven Fuqaha', the Four Imams and the majority of scholars of the past and present, causing some scholars to declare that there is a consensus on this opinion.

The Ruling Concerning Children of the Mother From Other Than the Deceased's Father

Allah said,

(But has left a brother or a sister), meaning, from his mother's side, as some of the Salaf stated, including Sa`d bin Abi Waqqas. Qatadah reported that this is the view of Abu Bakr As-Siddiq.

(Each one of the two gets a sixth; but if more than two, they share in a third.) There is a difference between the half brothers from the mother's side and the rest of the heirs. First, they get a share in the inheritance on account of their mother. Second, the males and females among them get the same share. Third, they only have a share in the inheritance when the deceased's estate is inherited in Kalalah, for they do not have a share if the deceased has a surviving father, grandfather, child or grandchild. Fourth, they do not have more than a third, no matter how numerous they were. aAllah's statement,

(After payment of legacies he (or she) may have bequeathed or debts, so that no loss is caused (to anyone).) means, let the will and testament be fair and free of any type of harm, without depriving some rightful heirs from all, or part of their share, or adding to the fixed portion that Allah or dained for some heirs. Indeed, whoever does this, will have disputed with Allah concerning His decision and division. An authentic Hadith states,

Chapter 4: An-Nisaa (The Women), Verses 001-023

»إِنَّ اللَّهَ قَدْ أَعْطَى كُلَّ ذِي حَقٍّ حَقَّهُ فَلَا وَصِيَّةَ لِوَارِثٍ«

(Allah has given each his fixed due right. Therefore, there is no will for a rightful inheritor.)

Surah: 4 Ayah: 13 & Ayah: 14

﴿تِلْكَ حُدُودُ ٱللَّهِ ۚ وَمَن يُطِعِ ٱللَّهَ وَرَسُولَهُ يُدْخِلْهُ جَنَّـٰتٍ تَجْرِى مِن تَحْتِهَا ٱلْأَنْهَـٰرُ خَـٰلِدِينَ فِيهَا ۚ وَذَٰلِكَ ٱلْفَوْزُ ٱلْعَظِيمُ ﴿١٣﴾﴾

13. These are the limits (set by) Allâh (or ordainments as regards laws of inheritance), and whosoever obeys Allâh and His Messenger (Muhammad (peace be upon him)) will be admitted to Gardens under which rivers flow (in Paradise), to abide therein, and that will be the great success.

﴿وَمَن يَعْصِ ٱللَّهَ وَرَسُولَهُ وَيَتَعَدَّ حُدُودَهُ يُدْخِلْهُ نَارًا خَـٰلِدًا فِيهَا وَلَهُ عَذَابٌ مُّهِينٌ ﴿١٤﴾﴾

14. And whosoever disobeys Allâh and His Messenger (Muhammad (peace be upon him)) and transgresses His limits, He will cast him into the Fire, to abide therein; and he shall have a disgraceful torment.

Transliteration

13. Tilka hudoodu Allahi waman yutiAAi Allaha warasoolahu yudkhilhu jannatin tajree min tahtiha alanharu khalideena feeha wathalika alfawzu alAAatheemu 14. Waman yaAAsi Allaha warasoolahu wayataAAadda hudoodahu yudkhilhu naran khalidan feeha walahu AAathabun muheenun

Tafsir Ibn Kathir

Warning Against Transgressing the Limits for Inheritance

Meaning, the Fara'id are Allah's set limits. This includes what Allah has aloted for the heirs, according to the degree of relation they have to the deceased, and their degree of dependency on him. Therefore, do not transgress or violate them. So Allah said;

(And whosoever obeys Allah and His Messenger,) regarding the inheritance, and does not add or decrease any of these fixed shares by use of tricks and plots. Rather, he gives each his appointed share as Allah commanded, ordained and decided,

(Will be admitted to Gardens under which rivers flow (in Paradise), to abide therein, and is the great success. And whosoever disobeys Allah and His Messenger, and transgresses His (set) limits, He will cast him into the Fire, to abide therein; and he shall have a disgraceful torment.) This is because he changed what Allah has ordained and disputed with His judgment. Indeed, this is the behavior of those who do not agree with what Allah has decided and divided, and this is why Allah punishes them with humiliation in the eternal, painful torment. Imam Ahmad recorded that Abu Hurayrah said that, the Messenger of Allah said,

«إِنَّ الرَّجُلَ لَيَعْمَلُ بِعَمَلِ أَهْلِ الْخَيْرِ سَبْعِينَ سَنَةً، فَإِذَا أَوْصَى حَافَ فِي وَصِيَّتِهِ، فَيُخْتَمُ لَهُ بِشَرِّ عَمَلِهِ، فَيَدْخُلُ النَّارَ، وَإِنَّ الرَّجُلَ لَيَعْمَلُ بِعَمَلِ أَهْلِ الشَّرِّ سَبْعِينَ سَنَةً، فَيَعْدِلُ فِي وَصِيَّتِهِ فَيُخْتَمُ لَهُ بِخَيْرِ عَمَلِهِ فَيَدْخُلُ الْجَنَّةَ»

(A man might perform the actions of righteous people for seventy years, but when it is time to compile his will, he commits injustice. So his final work will be his worst, and he thus enters the Fire. A man might perform the deeds of evil people for seventy years, yet he is fair in his will. So his final work will be his best, and he thus enters Paradise.) Abu Hurayrah said, "Read, if you will,

(These are the limits (set by) Allah) until,

(a disgraceful torment.)." In the chapter on injustice in the will, Abu Dawud recorded in his Sunan that Abu Hurayrah said that the Messenger of Allah said,

«إِنَّ الرَّجُلَ لَيَعْمَلُ أَوِ الْمَرْأَةَ بِطَاعَةِ اللهِ سِتِّينَ سَنَةً، ثُمَّ يَحْضُرُهُمَا الْمَوْتُ، فَيُضَارَّانِ فِي الْوَصِيَّةِ، فَتَجِبُ لَهُمَا النَّارُ»

(A man or a woman might perform actions in obedience to Allah for sixty years. Yet, when they are near death, they leave an unfair will and thus acquire the Fire.) Abu Hurayrah then recited the Ayah,

(After payment of legacies he (or she) may have bequeathed or debts, so that no loss is caused), until,

(and that is the great success.) This was also recorded by At-Tirmidhi and Ibn Majah, and At-Tirmidhi said, "Hasan Gharib".

Surah: 4 Ayah: 15 & Ayah: 16

﴿وَاللَّاتِي يَأْتِينَ الْفَاحِشَةَ مِن نِّسَآئِكُمْ فَاسْتَشْهِدُواْ عَلَيْهِنَّ أَرْبَعَةً مِّنكُمْ فَإِن شَهِدُواْ فَأَمْسِكُوهُنَّ فِي الْبُيُوتِ حَتَّىٰ يَتَوَفَّاهُنَّ الْمَوْتُ أَوْ يَجْعَلَ اللَّهُ لَهُنَّ سَبِيلاً﴾

15. And those of your women who commit illegal sexual intercourse, take the evidence of four witnesses from amongst you against them; and if they testify,

confine them (i.e. women) to houses until death comes to them or Allâh ordains for them some (other) way.

﴿ وَٱلَّذَانِ يَأْتِيَٰنِهَا مِنكُمْ فَـَٔاذُوهُمَاۖ فَإِن تَابَا وَأَصْلَحَا فَأَعْرِضُوا۟ عَنْهُمَآۗ إِنَّ ٱللَّهَ كَانَ تَوَّابًۭا رَّحِيمًۭا ۝ ﴾

16. And the two persons (man and woman) among you who commit illegal sexual intercourse, hurt them both. And if they repent (promise Allâh that they will never repeat, i.e. commit illegal sexual intercourse and other similar sins) and do righteous good deeds, leave them alone. Surely, Allâh is Ever All-Forgiving (the One Who accepts repentance), (and He is) Most Merciful.

Transliteration

15. Waallatee ya/teena alfahishata min nisa-ikum faistashhidoo AAalayhinna arbaAAatan minkum fain shahidoo faamsikoohunna fee albuyooti hatta yatawaffahunna almawtu aw yajAAala Allahu lahunna sabeelan 16. Waallathani ya/tiyaniha minkum faathoohuma fa-in taba waaslaha faaAAridoo AAanhuma inna Allaha kana tawwaban raheeman

Tafsir Ibn Kathir

The Adulteress is Confined in her House; A Command Later Abrogated

At the begining of Islam, the ruling was that if a woman commits adultery as stipulated by sufficient proof, she was confined to her home, without leave, until she died. Allah said,

(And those of your women who commit illegal sexual intercourse, take the evidence of four witnesses from among you against them; and if they testify, confine them (i.e. women) to houses until death comes to them or Allah ordains for them some (other) way.) `Some other way' mentioned here is the abrogation of this ruling that came later. Ibn `Abbas said, "The early ruling was confinement, until Allah sent down Surat An-Nur (chapter 24) which abrogated that ruling with the ruling of flogging (for fornication) or stoning to death (for adultery).'' Similar was reported from `Ikrimah, Sa`id bin Jubayr, Al-Hasan, `Ata' Al-Khurasani, Abu Salih, Qatadah, Zayd bin Aslam and Ad-Dahhak, and this is a matter that is agreed upon. Imam Ahmad recorded that `Ubadah bin As-Samit said, "When the revelation descended upon the Messenger of Allah , it would affect him and his face would show signs of strain. One day, Allah sent down a revelation to him, and when the Messenger was relieved of its strain, he said,

«خُذُوا عَنِّي، قَدْ جَعَلَ اللهُ لَهُنَّ سَبِيلًا، الثَّيِّبُ بِالثَّيِّبِ، وَالْبِكْرُ بِالْبِكْرِ، الثَّيِّبُ جَلْدُ مِائَةٍ، وَرَجْمٌ بِالْحِجَارَةِ، وَالْبِكْرُ جَلْدُ مِائَةٍ ثُمَّ نَفْيُ سَنَة»

(Take from me: Allah has made some other way for them. The married with the married, the unmarried with the unmarried. The married gets a hundred lashes and stoning to death, while the unmarried gets a hundred lashes then banishment for a year.)" Muslim and the collectors of the Sunan recorded that `Ubadah bin As-Samit said that the Prophet said,

«خُذُوا عَنِّي خُذُوا عَنِّي، قَدْ جَعَلَ اللهُ لَهُنَّ سَبِيلًا، الْبِكْرُ بِالْبِكْرِ جَلْدُ مِائَةٍ وَتَغْرِيبُ عَامٍ، وَالثَّيِّبُ بِالثَّيِّبِ جَلْدُ مِائَةٍ وَالرَّجْمُ»

(Take from me, take from me. Allah has made some other way for them: the (unmarried) gets a hundred lashes and banishment for one year, while the (married) gets a hundred lashes and stoning to death.) At-Tirmidhi said, "Hasan Sahih". Allah said,

(And the two persons among you who commit illegal sexual intercourse, punish them both.) Ibn `Abbas and Sa`id bin Jubayr said that this punishment includes cursing, shaming them and beating them with sandals. This was the ruling until Allah abrogated it with flogging or stoning, as we stated. Mujahid said, "It was revealed about the case of two men who do it." As if he was referring to the actions of the people of Lut, and Allah knows best. The collectors of Sunan recorded that Ibn `Abbas said that the Messenger of Allah said,

«مَنْ رَأَيْتُمُوهُ يَعْمَلُ عَمَلَ قَوْمِ لُوطٍ، فَاقْتُلُوا الْفَاعِلَ وَالْمَفْعُولَ بِهِ»

(Whoever you catch committing the act of the people of Lut (homosexuality), then kill both parties to the act.) Allah said,

(And if they repent and do righteous good deeds), by refraining from that evil act, and thereafter their actions become righteous,

(leave them alone), do not verbally abuse them after that, since he who truly repents is just like he who has no sin,

(Surely, Allah is Ever the One Who accepts repentance, Most Merciful.) The following is recorded in the Two Sahihs:

«إِذَا زَنَتْ أَمَةُ أَحَدِكُمْ، فَلْيَجْلِدْهَا الْحَدَّ، وَلَا يُثَرِّبْ عَلَيْهَا»

(When the slave-girl of one of you commits illegal sexual intercouse, let him flog her and not chastise her afterwards.) because the lashes she receives erase the sin that she has committed.

Surah: 4 Ayah: 17 & Ayah: 18

﴿ إِنَّمَا ٱلتَّوْبَةُ عَلَى ٱللَّهِ لِلَّذِينَ يَعْمَلُونَ ٱلسُّوٓءَ بِجَهَٰلَةٍ ثُمَّ يَتُوبُونَ مِن قَرِيبٍ فَأُو۟لَٰٓئِكَ يَتُوبُ ٱللَّهُ عَلَيْهِمْ ۗ وَكَانَ ٱللَّهُ عَلِيمًا حَكِيمًا ﴾

17. Allâh accepts only the repentance of those who do evil in ignorance and foolishness and repent soon afterwards; it is they whom Allâh will forgive and Allâh is Ever All-Knower, All-Wise.

﴿ وَلَيْسَتِ ٱلتَّوْبَةُ لِلَّذِينَ يَعْمَلُونَ ٱلسَّيِّئَاتِ حَتَّىٰٓ إِذَا حَضَرَ أَحَدَهُمُ ٱلْمَوْتُ قَالَ إِنِّى تُبْتُ ٱلْـَٰٔنَ وَلَا ٱلَّذِينَ يَمُوتُونَ وَهُمْ كُفَّارٌ ۚ أُو۟لَٰٓئِكَ أَعْتَدْنَا لَهُمْ عَذَابًا أَلِيمًا ﴾

18. And of no effect is the repentance of those who continue to do evil deeds until death faces one of them and he says: "Now I repent;" nor of those who die while they are disbelievers. For them We have prepared a painful torment.

Transliteration

17. Innama alttawbatu AAala Allahi lillatheena yaAAmaloona alssoo-a bijahalatin thumma yatooboona min qareebin faola-ika yatoobu Allahu AAalayhim wakana Allahu AAaleeman hakeeman 18. Walaysati alttawbatu lillatheena yaAAmaloona alssayyi-ati hatta itha hadara ahadahumu almawtu qala innee tubtu al-ana wala allatheena yamootoona wahum kuffarun ola-ika aAAtadna lahum AAathaban aleeman

Tafsir Ibn Kathir

Repentance is Accepted Until one Faces death

Allah states that He accepts repentance of the servant who commits an error in ignorance and then repents, even just before he sees the angel who captures the soul, before his soul reaches his throat. Mujahid and others said, "Every person who disobeys Allah by mistake, or intentionally is ignorant, until he refrains from the sin." Qatadah said that Abu Al-`Aliyah narrated that the Companions of the Messenger of Allah used to say, "Every sin that the servant commits, he commits out of ignorance." `Abdur-Razzaq narrated that, Ma`mar said that Qatadah said that, the Companions of the Messenger of Allah agreed that every sin that is committed by intention or otherwise, is committed in ignorance." Ibn Jurayj said, "Abdullah bin Kathir narrated to me that Mujahid said, `Every person who disobeys Allah (even willfully), is ignorant while committing the act of disobedience.'" Ibn Jurayj said, "`Ata' bin Abi Rabah told me something similar." Abu Salih said that Ibn `Abbas commented, "It is because of one's ignorance that he commits the error." `Ali bin Abi Talhah reported that Ibn `Abbas said about the Ayah, (and repent soon (afterwards)), "Until just before he (or she) looks at the angel of death." Ad-Dahhak said, "Every thing before death is `soon (afterwards).'" Al-Hasan Al-Basri said about the Ayah,

(and repent soon afterwards), "Just before his last breath leaves his throat." `Ikrimah said, "All of this life is `soon (afterwards).'" Imam Ahmad recorded that Ibn `Umar said that the Messenger said,

《إِنَّ اللهَ يَقْبَلُ تَوْبَةَ الْعَبْدِ مَا لَمْ يُغَرْغِرْ》

(Allah accepts the repentance of the servant as long as the soul does not reach the throat.) This Hadith was also collected by At-Tirmidhi and Ibn Majah, and At-Tirmidhi said, "Hasan Gharib". By mistake, Ibn Majah mentioned that this Hadith was narrated through `Abdullah bin `Amr. However, what is correct is that `Abdullah bin `Umar bin Al-Khattab was the narrator. Allah said,

(It is they to whom Allah will forgive and Allah is Ever All-Knower, All-Wise.) Surely, when hope in continued living diminishes, the angel of death comes forth and the soul reaches the throat, approaches the chest and arrives at the state where it is being gradually pulled out, then there is no accepted repentance, nor a way out of that certain end. Hence Allah's statements,

(And of no effect is the repentance of those who continue to do evil deeds until death faces one of them and he says: "Now I repent,") and,

(So when they saw Our punishment, they said: "We believe in Allah Alone...") (40:84) Allah decided that repentance shall not be accepted from the people of the earth when the sun rises from the west, as Allah said,

(The day that some of the signs of your Lord do come, no good will it do to a person to believe then, if he believed not before, nor earned good through his faith.) (6:158). Allah said,

(nor of those who die while they are disbelievers.) Consequently, when the disbeliever dies while still a disbeliever and polytheist, his sorrow and repentance shall not avail him. If he were to ransom himself, even with the earth's fill of gold, it will not be accepted from him. Ibn `Abbas, Abu Al-`Aliyah and Ar-Rabi` bin Anas said that the Ayah:

(nor of those who die while they are disbelievers), was revealed about the people of Shirk. Imam Ahmad recorded that Usamah bin Salman said that Abu Dharr said that the Messenger of Allah said,

《إِنَّ اللهَ يَقْبَلُ تَوْبَةَ عَبْدِهِ أَوْ يَغْفِرُ لِعَبْدِهِ مَا لَمْ يَقَعِ الْحِجَابُ》

(Allah accepts the repentance of His servant, or forgives His servant, as long as the veil does not drop.) They asked, "And what does the drop of the veil mean " He said,

«أَنْ تَخْرُجَ النَّفْسُ وَهِيَ مُشْرِكَةٌ»

(When the soul is removed while one is a polythiest.) Allah then said,

(For them We have prepared a painful torment), torment that is severe, eternal and enormous.

Surah: 4 Ayah: 19, Ayah: 20, Ayah: 21 & Ayah: 22

﴿ يَٰٓأَيُّهَا ٱلَّذِينَ ءَامَنُواْ لَا يَحِلُّ لَكُمْ أَن تَرِثُواْ ٱلنِّسَآءَ كَرْهًا ۖ وَلَا تَعْضُلُوهُنَّ لِتَذْهَبُواْ بِبَعْضِ مَآ ءَاتَيْتُمُوهُنَّ إِلَّآ أَن يَأْتِينَ بِفَٰحِشَةٍ مُّبَيِّنَةٍ ۚ وَعَاشِرُوهُنَّ بِٱلْمَعْرُوفِ ۚ فَإِن كَرِهْتُمُوهُنَّ فَعَسَىٰٓ أَن تَكْرَهُواْ شَيْـًٔا وَيَجْعَلَ ٱللَّهُ فِيهِ خَيْرًا كَثِيرًا ﴾

19. O you who believe! You are forbidden to inherit women against their will; and you should not treat them with harshness, that you may take away part of the Mahr you have given them, unless they commit open illegal sexual intercourse; And live with them honorably. If you dislike them, it may be that you dislike a thing and Allâh brings through it a great deal of good.

﴿ وَإِنْ أَرَدتُّمُ ٱسْتِبْدَالَ زَوْجٍ مَّكَانَ زَوْجٍ وَءَاتَيْتُمْ إِحْدَىٰهُنَّ قِنطَارًا فَلَا تَأْخُذُواْ مِنْهُ شَيْـًٔا ۚ أَتَأْخُذُونَهُۥ بُهْتَٰنًا وَإِثْمًا مُّبِينًا ﴾

20. But if you intend to replace a wife by another and you have given one of them a Qintar (of gold i.e. a great amount) as Mahr, take not the least bit of it back; would you take it wrongfully without a right and (with) a manifest sin?

﴿ وَكَيْفَ تَأْخُذُونَهُۥ وَقَدْ أَفْضَىٰ بَعْضُكُمْ إِلَىٰ بَعْضٍ وَأَخَذْنَ مِنكُم مِّيثَٰقًا غَلِيظًا ﴾

21. And how could you take it (back) while you have gone in unto each other, and they have taken from you a firm and strong covenant?

﴿ وَلَا تَنكِحُواْ مَا نَكَحَ ءَابَآؤُكُم مِّنَ ٱلنِّسَآءِ إِلَّا مَا قَدْ سَلَفَ ۚ إِنَّهُۥ كَانَ فَٰحِشَةً وَمَقْتًا وَسَآءَ سَبِيلًا ﴾

22. And marry not women whom your fathers married, except what has already passed; indeed it was shameful and most hateful, and an evil way.

Transliteration

19. Ya ayyuha allatheena amanoo la yahillu lakum an tarithoo alnnisaa karhan wala taAAduloohunna litathhaboo bibaAAdi ma ataytumoohunna illa an ya/teena bifahishatin mubayyinatin waAAashiroohunna bialmaAAroofi fa-in karihtumoohunna faAAasa an takrahoo shay-an wayajAAala Allahu feehi khayran katheeran 20. Wa-in aradtumu istibdala zawjin makana zawjin waataytum ihdahunna qintaran fala ta/khuthoo minhu shay-an ata/khuthoonahu buhtanan wa-ithman mubeenan 21. Wakayfa ta/khuthoonahu waqad afda baAAdukum ila baAAdin waakhathna minkum meethaqan ghaleethan 22. Wala tankihoo ma nakaha abaokum mina alnnisa-i illa ma qad salafa innahu kana fahishatan wamaqtan wasaa sabeelan

Tafsir Ibn Kathir

Meaning of `Inheriting Women Against Their Will

Al-Bukhari recorded that Ibn `Abbas said about the Ayah,

(O you who believe! You are not permitted to inherit women against their will,) "Before, the practice was that when a man dies, his male relatives used to have the right to do whatever they wanted with his wife. If one of them wants, he would marry her, give her in marriage, or prevent her from marriage, for they had more right to her than her own family. Thereafter, this Ayah was revealed about this practice,

(O you who believe! You are not permitted to inherit women against their will)."

Women Should not Be Treated with Harshness

Allah said,

(nor to prevent them from marriage, in order to take part of what you have given them,) Allah commands: Do not treat the woman harshly so that she gives back all or part of the dowry that she was given, or forfeits one of her rights by means of coercion and oppression. Allah's statement,

(unless they commit open Fahishah.) Ibn Mas`ud, Ibn `Abbas, Sa`id bin Al-Musayyib, Ash-Sha`bi, Al-Hasan Al-Basri, Muhammad bin Sirin, Sa`id bin Jubayr, Mujahid, `Ikrimah, `Ata' Al-Khurasani, Ad-Dahhak, Abu Qilabah, Abu Salih, As-Suddi, Zayd bin Aslam and Sa`id bin Abi Hilal said that this refers to illicit sex. Meaning that if the wife commits adultery, you are allowed to take back the dowry you gave her. You are also allowed to annoy her, until she gives back the dowry in return for a Khula`." In Surat Al-Baqarah, Allah said,

(And it is not lawful for you (men) to take back (from your wives) any of what you have given them, except when both parties fear that they would be unable to keep the limits ordained by Allah) (2:229). Ibn `Abbas, `Ikrimah and Ad-Dahhak said that Fahishah refers to disobedience and defiance. Ibn Jarir chose the view that it is general, encompasses all these meanings, adultery, disobedience, defiance, rudeness, and so forth. Meaning that he is allowed to annoy his wife when she does any of these acts until she forfeits all or part of her rights and he then separates from her, and this (view) is good, and Allah knows best.

Live With Women Honorably

Allah said,

(And live with them honorably), by saying kind words to them, treating them kindly and making your appearance appealing for them, as much as you can, just as you like the same from them. Allah said in another Ayah,

(And they have rights similar over them to what is reasonable) (2:228). The Messenger of Allah said,

«خَيْرُكُمْ خَيْرُكُمْ لِأَهْلِهِ، وَأَنَا خَيْرُكُمْ لِأَهْلِي»

(The best among you is he who is the best with his family. Verily, I am the best one among you with my family.) It was the practice of the Messenger of Allah to be kind, cheerful, playful with his wives, compassionate, spending on them and laughing with them. The Messenger used to race with `A'ishah, the Mother of the Faithful, as a means of kindness to her. `A'ishah said, "The Messenger of Allah raced with me and I won the race. This occurred before I gained weight, and afterwards I raced with him again, and he won that race. He said,

«هذِهِ بِتِلْكَ»

(This (victory) is for that (victory).)" When the Prophet was at the home of one of his wives, sometimes all of his wives would meet there and eat together, and they would then go back to their homes. He and his wife would sleep in the same bed, he would remove his upper garment, sleeping in only his lower garment. The Prophet used to talk to the wife whose night it was, after praying `Isha' and before he went to sleep. Allah said,

(Indeed in the Messenger of Allah you have a good example to follow) (33:21). Allah said,

(If you dislike them, it may be that you dislike a thing and Allah brings through it a great deal of good.) Allah says that your patience, which is demonstrated by keeping wives whom you dislike, carries good rewards for you in this life and the Hereafter. Ibn `Abbas commented on this Ayah, "That the husband may feel compassion towards his wife and Allah gives him a child with her, and this child carries tremendous goodness." An authentic Hadith states,

«لَا يَفْرَكْ مُؤْمِنٌ مُؤْمِنَةً، إِنْ سَخِطَ مِنْهَا خُلُقًا، رَضِيَ مِنْهَا آخَرَ»

(No believing man should hate his believing wife. If he dislikes a part of her conduct, he would surely like another.)

The Prohibition of Taking Back the Dowry

Allah said,

(But if you intend to replace a wife by another and you have given one of them a Qintar, take not the least bit of it back; would you take it wrongfully without a right and (with) a manifest sin) The Ayah commands: When one of you wants to divorce a wife and marry another one, he must not take any portion of the dowry he gave to the first wife, even if it were a Qintar of money. We mentioned the meaning of Qintar in the Tafsir of Surah Al `Imran. This Ayah is clear in its indication that the dowry could be substantial. `Umar bin Al-Khattab used to discourage giving a large dowry, but later on changed his view. Imam Ahmad recorded that Abu Al-`Ajfa' As-Sulami said that he heard `Umar bin Al-Khattab saying, "Do not exaggerate with the dowry of women, had this practice been an honor in this world or a part of Taqwa, then the Prophet would have had more right to practice it than you. The Messenger of Allah never gave any of his wives, nor did any of his daughters receive a dowry more than twelve Uwqiyah. A man used to pay a substantial dowry and thus conceal enmity towards his wife!" Ahmad and the collectors of Sunan collected this Hadith through various chains of narration, and At-Tirmidhi said, "Hasan Sahih". Al-Hafiz Abu Ya`la recorded that Masruq said, "`Umar bin Al-Khattab stood up on the Minbar of the Messenger of Allah and said, `O people! Why do you exaggerate concerning the dowry given to women The Messenger of Allah and his Companions used to pay up to four hundred Dirhams for a dowry, or less than that. Had paying more for a dowry been a part of Taqwa or an honor, you would not have led them in this practice. Therefore, I do not want to hear about a man who pays more than four hundred Dirhams for a dowry.' He then went down the Minbar, but a woman from Quraysh said to him, `O Leader of the Faithful! You prohibited people from paying more than four hundred Dirhams in a dowry for women' He said, `Yes.' She said, `Have you not heard what Allah sent down in the Qur'an' He said, `Which part of it' She said, `Have you not heard Allah's statement,

(And you have given one of them a Qintar)' He said, `O Allah! Forgive me...' He then went back and stood up on the Minbar saying, `I had prohibited you from paying more than four hundred Dirhams in a dowry for women. So, let everyone pay what he likes from his money.'" The chain of narration for this Hadith is strong.

(And how could you take it (back) while you have gone in unto each other) how can you take back the dowry from the woman with whom you had sexual relations and she had sexual relations with you Ibn `Abbas, Mujahid, As-Suddi and several others said that this means sexual intercourse. The Two Sahihs record that the Messenger of Allah said three times to the spouses who said the Mula`anah;

«اللهُ يَعْلَمُ أَنَّ أَحَدَكُمَا كَاذِبٌ، فَهَلْ مِنْكُمَا تَائِبٌ؟»

(Allah knows that one of you is a liar, so would any of you repent) The man said, "O Messenger of Allah! My money," referring to the dowry that he gave his wife. The Messenger said,

«لَا مَالَ لَكَ، إِنْ كُنْتَ صَدَقْتَ عَلَيْهَا فَهُوَ بِمَا اسْتَحْلَلْتَ مِنْ فَرْجِهَا، وَإِنْ كُنْتَ كَذَبْتَ عَلَيْهَا فَهُوَ أَبْعَدُ لَكَ مِنْهَا»

(You have no money. If you are the one who said the truth, the dowry is in return for the right to have sexual intercourse with her. If you are the one who uttered the lie, then this money is even farther from your reach.) Similarly Allah said;

(And how could you take it (back) while you have gone in unto each other and they have taken from you a firm and strong covenant) (Be kind with women, for you have taken them by Allah's covenant and earned the right to have sexual relations with them by Allah's Word.)

Marrying the Wife of the Father is Prohibited

Allah said,

(And marry not women whom your fathers married,) Allah prohibits marrying the women whom the father married, in honor and respect to the fathers, not allowing their children to have sexual relations with their wives after they die. A woman becomes ineligible for the son of her husband as soon as the marriage contract is conducted, and there is a consensus on this ruling. Ibn Jarir recorded that Ibn `Abbas said, "During the time of Jahiliyyah, the people used to prohibit what Allah prohibits (concerning marriage), except marrying the stepmother and taking two sisters as rival wives. Allah sent down,

(And marry not women whom your fathers married,) and,

(and two sisters in wedlock at the same time) (4:23)." Similar was reported from `Ata' and Qatadah. Therefore, the practice that the Ayah mentions is prohibited for this Ummah, being disgraced as an awful sin, r

(Indeed it was shameful and Maqtan, and an evil way.) Allah said in other Ayat,

(Come not near to Al-Fawahish (shameful acts) whether committed openly or secretly) (6:151), and,

(And come not near to unlawful sex. Verily, it is a Fahishah and an evil way.) (17:32) In this Ayah (4:22), Allah added,

(and Maqtan), meaning, offensive. It is a sin itself and causes the son to hate his father after he marries his wife. It is usual that whoever marries a woman dislikes those who married her before him. This is one reason why the Mothers of the Faithful were not allowed for anyone in marriage after the Messenger . They are indeed the Mothers of the Faithful since they married the Messenger , who is like the father to the believers. Rather, the Prophet's right is far greater than the right of a father, and his love comes before each person loving himself, may Allah's peace and blessings be on him. `Ata' bin Abi Rabah said that the Ayah, (and Maqtan), means, Allah will hate him,

(and an evil way), for those who take this way. Therefore, those who commit this practice will have committed an act of reversion from the religion and deserve capital punishment and confiscation of their property, which will be given to the Muslim Treasury. Imam Ahmad and the collectors of Sunan recorded that Al-Bara' bin `Azib said that his uncle Abu Burdah was sent by the Messenger of Allah to a man who married his stepmother to execute him and confiscate his money.

Surah: 4 Ayah: 23

﴿ حُرِّمَتْ عَلَيْكُمْ أُمَّهَٰتُكُمْ وَبَنَاتُكُمْ وَأَخَوَٰتُكُمْ وَعَمَّٰتُكُمْ وَخَٰلَٰتُكُمْ وَبَنَاتُ ٱلْأَخِ وَبَنَاتُ ٱلْأُخْتِ وَأُمَّهَٰتُكُمُ ٱلَّٰتِىٓ أَرْضَعْنَكُمْ وَأَخَوَٰتُكُم مِّنَ ٱلرَّضَٰعَةِ وَأُمَّهَٰتُ نِسَآئِكُمْ وَرَبَٰٓئِبُكُمُ ٱلَّٰتِى فِى حُجُورِكُم مِّن نِّسَآئِكُمُ ٱلَّٰتِى دَخَلْتُم بِهِنَّ فَإِن لَّمْ تَكُونُوا۟ دَخَلْتُم بِهِنَّ فَلَا جُنَاحَ عَلَيْكُمْ وَحَلَٰٓئِلُ أَبْنَآئِكُمُ ٱلَّذِينَ مِنْ أَصْلَٰبِكُمْ وَأَن تَجْمَعُوا۟ بَيْنَ ٱلْأُخْتَيْنِ إِلَّا مَا قَدْ سَلَفَ إِنَّ ٱللَّهَ كَانَ غَفُورًا رَّحِيمًا ﴾ ﴿٢٣﴾

23. Forbidden to you (for marriage) are: your mothers, your daughters, your sisters, your father's sisters, your mother's sisters, your brother's daughters, your sister's daughters, your foster mother who gave you suck, your foster milk suckling sisters, your wives' mothers, your step daughters under your guardianship, born of your wives to whom you have gone in - but there is no sin on you if you have not gone in them (to marry their daughters), - the wives of your sons who (spring) from your own loins, and two sisters in wedlock at the same time, except for what has already passed; verily, Allâh is Oft-Forgiving, Most Merciful.

Transliteration

23. Hurrimat AAalaykum ommahatukum wabanatukum waakhawatukum waAAammatukum wakhalatukum wabanatu al-akhi wabanatu al-okhti waommahatukumu allatee ardaAAnakum waakhawatukum mina alrradaAAati waommahatu nisa-ikum waraba-ibukumu allatee fee hujoorikum min nisa-ikumu allatee dakhaltum bihinna fa-in lam takoonoo dakhaltum bihinna fala junaha AAalaykum wahala-ilu abna-ikumu allatheena min aslabikum waan tajmaAAoo bayna al-okhtayni illa ma qad salafa inna Allaha kana ghafooran raheeman

Tafsir Ibn Kathir

Degrees of Women Never Eligible for One to Marry

This honorable Ayah is the Ayah that establishes the degrees of women relatives who are never eligible for one to marry, because of blood relations, relations established by suckling or marriage. Ibn Abi Hatim recorded that Ibn `Abbas said, "(Allah said) I have prohibited for you seven types of relatives by blood and seven by marriage." Ibn `Abbas then recited the Ayah,

(Forbidden to you (for marriage) are: your mothers, your daughters, your sisters...) At-Tabari recorded that Ibn `Abbas said, "Seven degrees of blood relation and seven degrees of marriage relation are prohibited (for marriage)." He then recited the Ayah,

(Forbidden to you (for marriage) are: your mothers, your daughters, your sisters, your father's sisters, your mother's sisters, your brother's daughters, your sister's daughters) and these are the types prohibited by blood relation." Allah's statement,

(Your foster mothers who suckled you, your foster milk suckling sisters) means, just as your mother who bore you is prohibited for you in marriage, so is your mother from suckling prohibited for you. Al-Bukhari and Muslim recorded that `A'ishah, the Mother of the Faithful, said that the Messenger of Allah said,

《إِنَّ الرَّضَاعَةَ تُحَرِّمُ مَا تُحَرِّمُ الْوِلَادَةَ》

(Suckling prohibits what birth prohibits.) In another narration reported by Muslim,

《يَحْرُمُ مِنَ الرَّضَاعَةِ مَا يَحْرُمُ مِنَ النَّسَبِ》

(Suckling establishes prohibited degrees just as blood does.)

`Suckling' that Establishes Prohibition for Marriage

Less than five incidents of suckling will not establish prohibition for marriage. In his Sahih, Muslim recorded that `A'ishah said, "Among the parts of the Qur'an that were revealed, is the statement, `Ten incidents of suckling establishes the prohibition (concerning marriage).' It was later abrogated with five, and the Messenger of Allah died while this statement was still recited as part of the Qur'an.'" A Hadith that Sahlah bint Suhayl narrated states that the Messenger of Allah ordered her to suckle Salim the freed slave of Abu Hudhayfah with five." We should assert that the suckling mentioned here must occur before the age of two, as we stated when we explained the Ayah in Surat Al-Baqarah,

((The mothers) should suckle their children for two whole years, (that is) for those (parents) who desire to complete the term of suckling) (2:233). The Mother-in-Law and Stepdaughter are Prohibited in Marriage Allah said next,

(Your wives' mothers, your stepdaughters under your guardianship, born of your wives unto whom you have gone in - but there is no sin on you if you have not gone in unto them,) As for the mother of the wife, she becomes prohibited for marriage for her son-in-law when the marriage is conducted, whether the son-in-law has sexual relations with her daughter or not. As for the wife's daughter, she becomes prohibited for her stepfather when he has sexual relations with her mother, after the marriage contract is ratified. If the man divorces the mother before having sexual relations with her, he is allowed to marry her daughter. So Allah said;

(Your stepdaughters under your guardianship, born of your wives unto whom you have gone in -- but there is no sin on you if you have not gone in unto them,) to marry the stepdaughter.

The Stepdaughter is Prohibited in Marriage Even if She Was Not Under the Guardianship of Her Stepfather

Allah said,

(...your stepdaughters under your guardianship,) The majority of scholars state that the stepdaughter is prohibited in marriage for her stepfather (who consummated his marriage to her mother) whether she was under his guardianship or not. The Two Sahih recorded that Umm Habibah said, "O Messenger of Allah! Marry my sister, the daughter of Abu Sufyan (and in one narration `Azzah bint Abu Sufyan)." He said,

«أَوَ تُحِبِّينَ ذٰلِكِ»

("Do you like that I do that" She said, "I would not give you up for anything, but the best of whom I like to share with me in that which is righteously good, is my sister." He said,

«فَإِنَّ ذٰلِكِ لَا يَحِلُّ لِي»

"That is not allowed for me." She said, "We were told that you want to marry the daughter of Abu Salamah." He asked,

«بِنْتَ أُمِّ سَلَمَةَ»

"The daughter of Umm Salamah" She said, "Yes." He said,

«إِنَّهَا لَوْ لَمْ تَكُنْ رَبِيبَتِي فِي حِجْرِي مَا حَلَّتْ لِي، إِنَّهَا لَبِنْتُ أَخِي مِنَ الرَّضَاعَةِ، أَرْضَعَتْنِي وَأَبَا سَلَمَةَ ثُوَيْبَةُ، فَلَا تَعْرِضْنَ عَلَيَّ بَنَاتِكُنَّ وَلَا أَخَوَاتِكُنَّ»

"Even if she was not my stepdaughter and under my guardianship, she is still not allowed for me because she is my niece from suckling, for Thuwaybah suckled me and Abu Salamah. Therefore, do not offer me to marry your daughters or sisters. ") In another narration from Al-Bukhari,

«إِنِّي لَوْ لَمْ أَتَزَوَّجْ أُمَّ سَلَمَةَ مَا حَلَّتْ لِي»

(Had I not married Umm Salamah, her daughter would not have been allowed for me anyway.) Consequently, the Messenger stated that his marriage to Umm Salamah was the real reason behind that prohibition.

Meaning of `gone in unto them

The Ayah continues,

(Your wives unto whom you have gone in), meaning, had sexual relations with them, according to Ibn `Abbas and several others.

Prohibiting the Daughter-in-Law for Marriage

Allah said,

(The wives of your sons who (spring) from your own loins,) Therefore, you are prohibited to marry the wives of your own sons, but not the wives of your adopted sons, as adoption was common practice in Jahiliyyah. Allah said,

(So when Zayd had accomplished his desire from her (i.e. divorced her), We gave her to you in marriage, so that (in future) there may be no difficulty to the believers in respect of (the marriage of) the wives of their adopted sons when the latter have no desire to keep them (i.e. they had divorced them).) (33:37) Ibn Jurayj said, "I asked `Ata' about Allah's statement,

(The wives of your sons who (spring) from your own loins,) He said, `We were told that when the Prophet married the ex-wife of Zayd (who was the Prophet's adopted son before Islam prohibited this practice), the idolators in Makkah criticized him. Allah sent down the Ayat:

(The wives of your sons who (spring) from your own loins),

(nor has He made your adopted sons your real sons.) (33:4), and,

(Muhammad is not the father of any of your men) (33:40).'" Ibn Abi Hatim recorded that Al-Hasan bin Muhammad said, "These Ayat are encompassing,

(the wives of your sons), and,

(your wives' mothers). This is also the explanation of Tawus, Ibrahim, Az-Zuhri and Makhul. It means that these two Ayat encompass these types of women, whether the marriage was consummated or not, and there is a consensus on this ruling.

A Doubt and Rebuttal

Why is the wife of one's son from suckling prohibited for him for marriage - that is, if she is no longer married to his son from suckling - as the majority of scholars state, although they are not related by blood The answer is the Prophet's statement,

$$\text{«يَحْرُمُ مِنَ الرَّضَاعِ مَا يَحْرُمُ مِنَ النَّسَبِ»}$$

(Suckling prohibits what blood relations prohibit.)

The Prohibition of Taking Two Sisters as Rival Wives

Allah said,

(...and two sisters in wedlock at the same time, except for what has already passed;) The Ayah commands: you are prohibited to take two sisters as rival wives, or rival female-servants, except for what had happened to you during the time of Jahiliyyah, which We have forgiven and erased. Therefore, no one is allowed to take or keep two sisters as rival wives, according to the consensus of the scholars of the Companions, their followers, and the Imams of old and present. They all stated that taking two sisters as rival wives is prohibited, and that whoever embraces Islam while married to two sisters at the same time is given the choice to keep one of them and divorce the other. Imam Ahmad recorded that Ad-Dahhak bin Fayruz said that his father said, "I embraced Islam while married to two sisters at the same time and the Prophet commanded me to divorce one of them."

www.ingramcontent.com/pod-product-compliance
Lightning Source LLC
Chambersburg PA
CBHW081110080526

44587CB00021B/3535